Management of Science-Intensive Organizations

Ellie Okada

Management of Science-Intensive Organizations

Catalyzing Urban Resilience

Ellie Okada
Boston Cancer Policy Institute
Somerville, MA, USA

ISBN 978-3-030-64041-5 ISBN 978-3-030-64042-2 (eBook)
https://doi.org/10.1007/978-3-030-64042-2

© The Editor(s) (if applicable) and The Author(s), under exclusive licence to Springer
Nature Switzerland AG, part of Springer Nature 2021
This work is subject to copyright. All rights are solely and exclusively licensed by the
Publisher, whether the whole or part of the material is concerned, specifically the rights
of translation, reprinting, reuse of illustrations, recitation, broadcasting, reproduction on
microfilms or in any other physical way, and transmission or information storage and
retrieval, electronic adaptation, computer software, or by similar or dissimilar methodology
now known or hereafter developed.
The use of general descriptive names, registered names, trademarks, service marks, etc.
in this publication does not imply, even in the absence of a specific statement, that such
names are exempt from the relevant protective laws and regulations and therefore free for
general use.
The publisher, the authors and the editors are safe to assume that the advice and information in this book are believed to be true and accurate at the date of publication. Neither
the publisher nor the authors or the editors give a warranty, expressed or implied, with
respect to the material contained herein or for any errors or omissions that may have been
made. The publisher remains neutral with regard to jurisdictional claims in published maps
and institutional affiliations.

This Palgrave Macmillan imprint is published by the registered company Springer Nature
Switzerland AG
The registered company address is: Gewerbestrasse 11, 6330 Cham, Switzerland

PREFACE

This study investigates managerial mechanisms in which science-intensive organizations contribute to urban resilience processes, broadening beneficiaries of the resilience. It defines science-intensive organizations as those whose major driving force of the product and service development is science. This book's study provides a novel approach for the socioeconomic construct of resilience by focusing on functional mechanisms of science-intensive organizations.

Urban resilience is the ability that embraces not only bouncing to the former states but discontinuously creating new dynamism of socioeconomic, ecological, and technological transformation (Coaffee & Lee, 2016; Gunderson & Holland, 2003; Meerow, Newell, & Stults, 2016; Yamagata & Maruyama, 2016).

While reviewing economic resilience literature, this study found two contradicting management theories underpinning resilience. One is Sutton (1998)'s escalation model of entrepreneurial firms. The other is the transaction-cost-based R&D model (Pisano, 1990; Williamson, 1979). OECD (2004) implicitly bases on the former, while Orr and Topa (2006), the latter. Despite their differing approaches, they point out the same phenomenon: specific populations remain outside of the resilience.

Further investigation reveals that they assume different industrial sciences that Niosi (2000) categorized. Meanwhile, the impacts of Particulate Matter size fraction 2.5 microns ($PM_{2.5}$) on indoor workers' productivity became an economic topic (see Chang, Zivin, Gross, &

Neidell, 2016). A short-and-mid-term resolution might be building materials' innovation that reduces the impacts. However, emerging environmental material sciences are outside of the industrial sciences category. These puzzles are the starting point of this study.

After all, focus on the linkage between evolutionary urban resilience and evolutionary (managerial) economics reconciled the theoretical conflict. However, there remains a missing link to science organizations, despite their critical functions. This research thus contributes to the literature by linking and adding management aspects of science-intensive organizations.

The personal origin of this research may be the experience of the historic 1995 Great urban Earthquake. It destroyed residential and commercial buildings, urban infrastructure, and massive small-to-midscale firms forcing them into bankruptcy. I accused myself of being a management scholar but unable to save such companies. Meanwhile, American companies' regional headquarters based in the city resumed operation in just three days while providing a supply chain for relief supplies. Fifteen years later, already away from the city, I read in the newspaper that the city, a city of fashion and foreign mansion, was reborn as a biotechnology center.

Now, despite the university facility closure for the COVID-19 pandemic, I have written this manuscript. If I had no experience of the earthquake disruption, I might not have been able to do such a thing.

This manuscript owes several suggestions and encouragement.

Professor Joseph L. Bower, emeritus of Harvard Business School, advised on differentiated aspects of entrepreneurial firms and established ones concerning emerging sciences. Professor Richard B. Freeman, Chair of Economics at Harvard, suggested reinforced economic inequity at the Science Economic Seminars jointly held with Science-based Business Initiative at Harvard. Dr. John Trumpbour, research director at the Labor and Worklife Program at Harvard Law School, suggested firms' barriers to overcome. Professor Susan Pharr and Dr. Shinju Fujihira at Weatherhead Center for International Affairs, Harvard University, presented marginalized populations' perspectives during my Harvard stay. Professor Hugh T. Patrick, emeritus of Columbia Business School, and Professor David Weinstein, Professor of Economics at Columbia University, suggested the directions of resilience during my stay at Columbia. Professor I. Glenn Cohen, Harvard Law School, and Professor Robert D. Truog, Legal Medicine at Harvard Medical School, suggested several ethical dilemmas and reconciliation involving entrepreneurial and established firms.

PREFACE vii

Furthermore, the opinions and suggestions offered by the peer-reviewer have been enormously helpful in improving the manuscript.

This book owes the arrangements, suggestions, and continuous encouragement from Mr. Marcus Burlenger, Commissioning Editor of Palgrave Macmillan, Ms. Hemapriya Eswanth, a project coordinator of Palgrave Macmillan, and the team. I have been working for Harvard University Libraries as a visiting researcher since 2013. This research owes a vast amount of literature to which Harvard provided access.

No one expected that the pandemic would happen when I proposed the manuscript last summer. I hope this pandemic will be the catalyst for the transformation of various issues.

Somerville, USA   Ellie Okada

References

Chang, T., Zivin, J., Gross, T., & Neidell, M. (2016). Particulate pollution and the productivity of pear packers. *American Economic Journal: Economic Policy, 8*(3), 141–169.

Coafee, J., & Lee, P. (2016). *Urban resilience: Planning risk, crisis and uncertainty.* London: Palgrave.

Gunderson, L. H., & Holling, C. S. (Eds.). (2002). *Panarchy: Understanding transformations in human and natural systems.* Washington: Island Press.

Meerow, S., Newell, J. P., & Stults, M. (2016). Defining urban resilience: A review. *Landscape and Urban Planning, 147*, 38–49.

Niosi, J. (2000). Science-based industries: New Schumpeterian taxonomy. *Technology in Society, 22*, 429–444.

OECD (Organization for Economic Cooperation and Development). (2004). *Entrepreneurship: Catalyst for urban regeneration.* Paris: OECD.

Orr, J., & Topa, G. (2006). Challenges facing the New York metropolitan area economy. *Current Issues in Economics and Finance, 12*(1). Retrieved from: https://www.newyorkfed.org/medialibrary/media/research/current_issues/ci12-1.pdf.

Pisano Pisano, G. P. (1990). The R&D boundaries of the firm: An empirical analysis. *Administrative Science Quarterly, 35*, 153–176.

Sutton, J. (1998). *Technology and market structure.* Cambridge, MA: The MIT Press.

Williamson, O. (1979). Transaction cost economics: The governance of contractual relations. *Journal of Law and Economics, 22*(2), 233–261.

Yamagata, Y., & Maruyama, H. (Eds.). (2016). *Urban resilience: Transformative approach.* Switzerland: Springer International.

CONTENTS

Part I   Theoretical Framework for Science-Intensive Organizations

1   Research Questions and Frameworks — 3
   1   Issues Present — 3
   2   Urban Resilience and Science-Intensive Organizations — 6
      2.1   Previous Literature and Positioning of the Study — 6
      2.2   Management Theories Coherent with Resilience Studies — 9
      2.3   Anchor Firms and Knowledge-Intensive Organizations — 16
      2.4   Environmental Exposure and Inequity — 17
      2.5   Anticipation and Citizen Scientists' Movement — 22
      2.6   The Missing Link with Science-Intensive Organizations — 23
   3   Categorization of Industrial Sciences — 24
      3.1   From Emerging Sciences to Technological Capabilities — 24
   4   Organizational Forms to Broaden Beneficiaries — 25
   References — 29

x CONTENTS

2 Urban Resilience and Opportunity Identification of Social Entrepreneurs 39
- *1 Why Urban Resilience Matters?* 39
- *2 Facilitators* 41
  - *2.1 Structural and Strategic Contexts of Anchor Corporations* 41
  - *2.2 External Disturbance and Corporate Entrepreneurship* 44
- *3 Constraints* 49
  - *3.1 Internal Structural and Strategic Contexts* 49
  - *3.2 Resource Allocation to Risky Investment* 49
- *4 Governance and Boundaries* 50
  - *4.1 Governance Structure as the Internal Structural Contexts* 50
  - *4.2 Loose Coupling* 51
- *Appendix* 53
- *References* 54

3 Emerging Technologies and Organizations for Urban Resilience 61
- *1 Emergence of New Technologies* 61
- *2 Academic Knowledge-Intensive Organizations* 62
  - *2.1 Motivation for Research Investment* 63
  - *2.2 Resource Allocation and Performance* 67
  - *2.3 Relations with Beneficiaries' Preferences* 69
- *3 Anchor Institutions* 70
  - *3.1 Motivation* 70
  - *3.2 Resource Allocation and Performance* 72
  - *3.3 Relations with Beneficiaries' Preferences* 74
- *4 Set Conditions* 74
- *References* 76

Part II Entrepreneurship in Urban Resilience

4 Addressing Environmental Inequity by New Sciences 83
- *1 When Anchor Institutions Are Absent* 83
- *2 Environmental Inequity* 84

| | | CONTENTS | xi |

	2.1	Environmental Inequity	84
	2.2	Consequences of Reinforced Environmental Inequity	87
3	Attracting Foreign Anchors		88
	3.1	Outline of the Case	88
	3.2	Seeking New Attributes of Industrial Sciences	96
4	Investment Toward Variety		96
References			101

5	**Emergence and Dynamism of New Material Sciences**		**105**
1	Schumpeterian Mark II Category		105
2	Variation and Capability Renewal		106
	2.1	Variation	106
	2.2	Definition of Variety	108
	2.3	Organization Forms that Manage a Given Outcome Variety	111
	2.4	Capability Renewal of Mark II Multinationals	112
3	Subsequent Competition in the Urban Contexts		115
	3.1	The Involvement of Other Industrial Science Categories	115
	3.2	Subsequent Competition in the Urban Context	122
4	New Science-Intensive Category		123
References			126

6	**Artificial Intelligence to Broaden Beneficiaries**		**131**
1	New and Established Science Categories		131
2	New Vehicle of Tier-II Translation		132
	2.1	New Image of Tier-II Translation	132
	2.2	Application to Urban Resilience Models and Practices	137
3	How Algorithms Affect Organizations		139
	3.1	Shift of Desired Skills of Humans	139
	3.2	Human Tasks in Measuring Environmental Exposure	140
	3.3	Impacts on Organizations	142
4	More Inclusive Organizations		146
References			147

xii CONTENTS

Part III Revolution of Beneficiaries

7 Scale-up of Social Enterprises 153
  1 Significance of Scale-up 153
  2 Replication to Other Settings 154
    2.1 Adaptation Costs to Firms 154
    2.2 Productive Assets 158
    2.3 Case Observations 160
  3 Governance to Support Scale-up 170
    3.1 Modification of Framework 170
    3.2 Social Entrepreneurial Organizations 173
  4 New Categorization 175
  References 178

8 Strategy and Governance 183
  1 Issues Present 183
  2 Voice of Silence 185
    2.1 Urban Resilience Through Entrepreneurship 185
    2.2 Necessary Component to Add to New Industrial
      Sciences 192
  3 Governance for Broadening Beneficiaries 197
    3.1 Urban Planning Viewpoints 197
  4 Vision of Heterogeneous Knowledge Variation 202
  References 202

Index 207

LIST OF TABLES

Chapter 1

Table 1	Management theories that have coherence with resilience theories	18
Table 2	Current categories of industrial sciences	25

Chapter 2

Table 1	Classification for administrative purposes (after the 1969 Private Foundation Act)	53

Chapter 3

Table 1	Elements of anchor organizations and academic knowledge-intensive organizations	75

Chapter 4

Table 1	Actions and events before and after the resilience initiative	97

Chapter 5

Table 1	Organization forms to optimize a variety	116

PART I

Theoretical Framework for Science-Intensive Organizations

CHAPTER 1

Research Questions and Frameworks

1 ISSUES PRESENT

The book's theme is the broadening of science beneficiaries by science in the course of urban resilience. This book addresses research questions on what mechanisms enable science-intensive organizations to contribute to broadening beneficiaries of science by science in urban resilience settings. This study focuses on managerial aspects of science-intensive organizations that engage in environmental sciences, particularly in environmental material sciences. It defines science-intensive organizations as those whose major driving force of the product and service development is science. This broadened definition encompasses not only academic knowledge-intensive organizations (KIOs), but also (R&D units of) multinational enterprises, and entrepreneurial firms that handle emerging sciences.

It pursues the research question by basing on the management and governance theories. It highlights a subject where the role of science is confused.

By following Meerow, Newell, and Stults (2016), this book comprehensively defines urban resilience as follows:

> The ability of urban *system*-and its constituting socio-economic, ecological, and technological *networks* to recover desired functions in the face of a disturbance, adapt to change, and to quickly transform systems that limit current or future adaptive capacity. (Meerow et al., 2016. See Coafee &

© The Author(s), under exclusive license to
Springer Nature Switzerland AG 2021
E. Okada, *Management of Science-Intensive Organizations*,
https://doi.org/10.1007/978-3-030-64042-2_1

Lee, 2016; Gunderson & Holling, 2002; Yamagata & Maruyama, 2016. Italic is by the author)

Thus, the concept of resilience is embracing not only bouncing to the former, stable condition, but also more positively and discontinuously creating new dynamic conditions (Coafee & Lee, 2016).

Given the above definition of urban resilience, this book provides a novel approach for the socioeconomic construct by focusing on functional mechanisms of science-intensive organizations.

The background of the issues is the presence of specific populations that are outside of the economic and environmental resilience.

Breakthrough sciences contributed to the U.S. and E.U. urban resilience in the 1990s by reversing the trend of the intergenerational inheritance of poverty (Giloth, 2004; Jargowski, 2003; OECD, 2004). Mainly, entrepreneurial endeavors converted discoveries in information communication technologies (hereafter, ICT) and life sciences to new technologies in the last half of the twentieth century.

However, specific inner-city residents remain outside of the dynamic economic cycle of resilience (OECD, 2004).

Several analyses associate such residents' isolation with the low skills, education levels, and failure of adaptation to new technologies. However, sets of socioeconomic drivers reinforce a vicious cycle of poverty for specific groups of people.

Recent years have witnessed the environmental factors that negatively affect workers' productivity (Chang, Zivin, Gross, & Neidell (2016). Environmental pollutants appear to spread equally. However, some groups of people are more exposed to environmental contaminants where they live or work (Anerson, Coulberson, & Phelps, 1993; Manisalidis, Stavropoulou, Stavropoulos, & Bezirtzoglou, 2020; U.S. Environmental Protection Agency website[1]). The problem is that they are more likely physically impaired than others when it is not affordable for them to protect themselves from contaminants' toxicity. Such physical disfunctioning has the potential to contribute to the loss of good opportunities that reinforce poverty.

For example, specific nanoparticles, such as Particulate Matter size fraction 2.5 microns ($PM_{2.5}$) (see, Buzea, Pacheco, & Robbie, 2007) linked to heat affect not only outdoor—but also indoor—workers' productivity (Chang et al., 2016). In a certain inner-city district, air pollution is often

---

[1] U.S. Environmental Protection Agency. Retrieved from http://epa.gov.

beyond the Federally permissible level. In a nearby city, the asthma-related emergency visit of children with a specific color is five times higher than children without color (Massachusetts Center for Health Information and Analysis, n.d.; Massachusetts Department of Public Health, 2017).

Some of them have more intellectual ability than the average citizen to the extent that they graduate from top global universities. They also are gifted with emotional intelligence. It is hard to ascribe the long-term job loss to the low skills and the lack of ability. It is loss for the whole society not to utilize the full capacity of these people.

Paths to reverse and even transform the condition (Coafee & Lee, 2016) are desired.

The urban planning theories approach the environmental risks by reducing exposure to threat (Yamagata & Maruyama, 2016). This method is often used in disaster resilience. Some cities, such as Adelaide, isolate heatwave by creating green spaces (Benger, Murakami, & Yamagata, 2016; Ziter, Pedersen, Kucharik, & Turner, 2019). However, living close to green areas depends on people's ability to pay (Benger et al., 2016). Thus, environmental inequity remains in the previous resilience approach. As the urban resident percentage will grow roughly to eighty-five percent by 2050, globally (Coafee & Lee, 2016; United Nations Department of Economic and Social Affairs (UN-DESA), 2018), the urban issues have significance for the survival and sustainability of human species.

Many people tend to ascribe economic and social divides to the progress of science. However, it is the sciences that reverse the vicious cycle.[2]

Therefore, this book pursues a research question on how science-intensive organizations can contribute to urban resilience by broadening beneficiaries of science by science in urban resilience. The engineered urban algae strands and bioinspired construction material are one of the examples.

The analysis of this book starts with seeking coherent attributes between theories of urban resilience and management.

Then, it seeks a proper industrial science category for environmental sciences by reviewing the theories of new industrial science categorization that goes beyond Schumpeterian Mark I (such as biotechnology) and Mark II (such as chemical and heavy industrial sciences) (Niosi, 2000. See, Arthur, 1994; Kaldor, 1972; Nelson & Winter, 1982).

---

[2] This book's study acknowledges peoples' preference regarding acceptability and adaptability of new science and technologies. This problem is outside of the focus of this book's study.

6   E. OKADA

Next, it maps academic institutions, established multinationals, and entrepreneur firms in each science category. Then, it will develop a scholarly management framework to invest and implement projects of new environmental material sciences. In other words, it seeks organization models to invest in material and related life sciences where users' willingness to pay (Sutton, 1998) does not affect R&D performance or is not affected by a quality upgrade by R&D.

As it focuses on management and organizations' roles, the national innovation system and the U.S. and U.K. politics of urban revitalization (such as Roberts & Sykes, 2000) are outside of the scope. The proposed inquiry understands that there is a research stream, such as Rappaport & Smith (2010), that defines "environment" as the body's internal chemical environment, and "exposures," as the amounts of biologically active chemicals in this internal environment. This book's study is not medical literature; it follows the traditional definition of the United States Environmental Protection Agency (EPA) regarding environment and exposure (see, Ziter et al., 2019).

This chapter starts with conceptual definitions of urban resilience and coherent theories of management. It then reviews the framework of new science categorization (Niosi, 2000) and maps behavioral R&D traits of science-intensive organizations by basing on Sutton (1998). Then, it outlines the structure of this book.

2   Urban Resilience and Science-Intensive Organizations

2.1   Previous Literature and Positioning of the Study

The desired goal of this book is the scholarly management contribution to urban resilience. Therefore, it first reviews the literature on urban resilience in urban planning disciplines. It reviews literature from the connectivity to the management theories, not from their superiority in their field.

Urban resilience and regeneration attract attention from several disciplines. It is because cities have been exposed to systemic threats and discontinuity mainly since the 1980s. Sources of threats and discontinuity are economic downturns, ecological and environmental changes, and disruptive technological development. Drastic changes also coincide in combination with the dramatic population growth in urban settings. The acknowledgment of this combination also makes urban issues an urgent problem for policymakers (Coafee & Lee, 2016; Meerow et al., 2016; Yamayaga & Maruyama, 2016).

The academics' interests are to address disaster resilience and risk reduction and the adaptation and regeneration. The approaches vary from science disciplines such as mathematics and biology through social science disciplines such as economics, psychology, and others (Coafee & Lee, 2016; Yamagata & Maruyama, 2016). The U.S. National Academies (NAS) (2019) also has arranged working groups to design sustainable regeneration of the ecological system and network by using big data.

As above stated, this book comprehensively defines urban resilience by following Meerow et al. (2016). Emphases are transforming systems that limit the current or future adaptive capacity (See, Coafee & Lee, 2016; Meerow et al., 2016; Roberts & Sykes, 2000; Yamagata & Maruyama, 2016). It is an integrated attempt that leads to the simultaneous achievement of reduced risks and sustainable resolution of urban problems ((Roberts & Sykes, 2000).

Being given the system and network perspectives of resilience (Meerow et al., 2016), the book's study will focus mainly on the system viewpoint that constitutes urban resilience attributes. In balancing the mechanisms and contexts (Coafee & Lee, 2016), this study investigates the contribution of academic knowledge-intensive organizations (KIOs), U.S. and foreign multinational enterprises, entrepreneur firms, and citizen science groups.

The scholars of resilience acknowledge that the concept of resilience originates from studies of systems ecology by Holling (1973, 1996, 2001) and Gunderson & Holling (2002) (See, Coafee & Lee, 2016). Before Holling (1973), scholars and policymakers appreciated the attributes of stability, conservation, and restoration to the former stable condition in the face of turbulence. Therefore, the concept of resilience used to be almost equivalent to the repair to the former state. Under this condition, Holling (1973) initiates a framework of dynamic processes of the adaptive cycle. The constructs of resilience are destruction, reorganization, and adaptation (see, Coafee & Lee, 2016).

Holling (1973) defines resilience as a system's ability to absorb change and disturbance and maintain the same relationships between populations or state variables. This cycle of system development constitutes of four phases: the exploitation, conservation, release, and reorganization of resources (Holling, 1973). The stage of the reorganization of resources implies what it means by the transformation in these days.

The approach of Holling differentiates itself from previous literature of ecological systems that emphasize a stable basis (Coafee & Lee, 2016). The adaptive cycle model embeds the dynamism in which collapse of stable equilibrium and the spontaneous reorganization leads to a new growth phase similar to the Schumpeterian creative destruction (Coafee & Lee, 2016; Walker & Cooper, 2011).

On the other hand, this conceptualization relies on a system's viewpoint, and does not necessarily incorporate network viewpoints (see, Meerow et al., 2016). According to Meerow et al. (2016), previous literature on resilience can comprise two streams: One that emphasizes the system's viewpoints and the other, the network viewpoints. Though these two viewpoints have a complementary relationship, the literature has relied on either of the two.

Also, Holling's adaptive system's emphasis still lies in "the coming back to a condition that is required to retain normal functioning" (Coafee & Lee, 2016; Folke, 2006). It is not autonomous to know what it means by "normal functioning." Given the systems approach in any field that mimics living organisms (see Chapter 5), it is impossible to regard that a condition with some disfunctioning is deviant from a "normal" state.

Therefore, the understanding of resilience gradually has incorporated an evolutionary approach that bears constantly changing nonequilibrium systems (Coafee & Lee, 2016. See Carpenter et al., 2005; Majoor, 2015).

The core concept of resilience is the adaptability in the evolutionary approach (Holling, 1996. Also see, Saviotti, 1996). In biological usage, adaptation is the process in which an organism fits itself to its environment (Holling, 1996). Experience guides changes in the organism's structure so as to make better use of its environment for its ends along with the passage of time (Holling, 1996). It captures the capacity of a system to learn, combine experience and knowledge, and adjust its responses to changing external drivers and internal processes (Coafee & Lee, 2016; Folke, Carpenter, Walker, Scheffer, Chapin III, & Rockstrom, 2010). This view of resilience embeds network viewpoints (see, Meerow et al., 2016) by incorporating the loosely coupled[3] linkages between internal and external variants. They enhance the system's responsiveness and evolutionary trajectories (Coafee & Lee, 2016; Pike, Dawley, & Tomaney, 2010).

---

[3] Note that a concept of loosely coupled system is widely used in the studies of innovation management. See, Heller (1999); Orton and Weick (1990); Sundbo and Gallouj (2000).

At the same time, the guiding concepts and practice of resilience invoked several criticisms. Among them, what is particularly relevant to the management theories is the decentralization of responsibility to the local scale that has occurred since around the 2000s (Coafee & Fussey, 2015; See also, Roberts, 2000). A fundamental guiding principle of decentralization is subsidiarity (see, U.K. Cabinet Office, 2013/2005, Sec. 1 Art. 7, Sec. 2 Art. 8; Coafee & Lee, 2016). It can extend the responsiveness to local needs that might otherwise be neglected in the scale economy. However, the principle of subsidiary also invites questions over the capacity and connectivity of resilience practices in a small regional community. Furthermore, commentators questioned the extent to which the national government translated its hierarchical orders to the local level by decentralizing responsibility at the time of crisis (Coafee & Lee, 2016). Further, the argument occurs that concerns about the resilience responsibility movement toward individual actors and local government operations.

Scholars label the redistribution of responsibility and governance from the national level to the local level as a form of neoliberal citizenship (Neocleous, 2013, p. 5). The governance of resilience, particularly the interactions between citizens and a state, has been progressively responsibilizing (Gerland, 1996. See also, Coafee & Lee, 2016).

On the other hand, this decentralization shapes the agenda back toward the nation-state through a constant release of national guidance documents (MacKinnon and Dirickson, 2013. See also, Coafee & Lee, 2016).

This resilience framework suggests that everybody now has a moral responsibility in the resilience practices with an implicit agenda of civil responsibilization. It also means passing on the implementation of risk management from states to citizens (Coafee & Lee, 2016).

This stream of resilience studies encompasses both the promise and critiques over the current resilience practices. At the same time, it has facilitated the emergence of the evolutionary view of resilience (Coafee & Lee, 2016; Saviotti, 1996) that has the coherence with management studies.

2.2   Management Theories Coherent with Resilience Studies

The evolutionary approach of resilience emerges by proposing a different view against the equilibrium model of resilience. Holling (1973) is the origin of this view (Coafee & Lee, 2016). Holling explored a resilience model with a complex adaptive system by observing and mimicking nature, such as the ecological system, immune system, and central nervous system (see Holling, 1996).

According to Saviotti (1996), the evolutionary approach in any discipline consists of the following phases: the generation of variety (variation), selection, reproduction and inheritance, and fitness and adaptation (see, Saviotti, 1996). The following attributes characterize this approach:

> "preparedness and persistence," "adaptability, responsiveness and resourcefulness," "redundancy and diversity," and "cycles and feedback. (Coafee & Lee, 2016)

These attributes provide the capacity to prepare, persist, and adapt to any variety in the system.

Among the above attributes, the one that most significantly differentiates from the equilibrium approach is "redundancy" (see, Coafee & Lee, 2016). The redundancy is an essential element in the evolutionary view since it absorbs shocks in the event of disruption and the loss of functionality (Coafee & Lee, 2016). The redundancy provides alternative resources, sub-systems, and back-up functions (Bruneau et al., 2003; Coafee & Lee, 2016). The most distinct aspect of the redundancy is that it has a role to reduce path dependencies through resource utilization to enhances the development of alternative pathways (Coafee & Lee, 2016). Thus, the evolutionary approach of resilience positively positions redundancy as a source of transformation (Coafee & Lee, 2016).

On the other hand, the equilibrium approach has long recognized the redundancy as a source of inefficiency (see, Coafee & Lee, 2016).

This conflict is the same as that between economic theories and management theories. Though behavioral economics has introduced various variables related to the bounded rationality of human cognition (Simon, 1957), it still regards redundancy as an inevitable inefficiency, not the source of reducing path dependencies.

In this sense, the redundancy in the evolutionary approach has coherence with management theories below mentioned.

2.2.1 Resource-Based View, Dynamic Capability, Corporate Entrepreneurship

Redundancy is consistent with the concept of "underused, or unused organizational resources" in management studies, particularly Penrose

(1959). Penrose (1959) focuses on resources that provide productive service to firms.[4]

According to Penrose (1960),

> growth is governed by a creative and dynamic interaction between a firm's productive resources and its market opportunities. Available resources limit expansion; unused resources (including technological and entrepreneurial) stimulate and largely determine the direction of expansion.

In this approach, underused resources are the source of related diversification that leads organizations to grow in the fields (Penrose, 1959). According to empirical evidence, related diversification creates value by leveraging redeployable resources beyond synergy (Sakhartov & Folta, 2014. See Anand & Singh, 1997; Bryce & Winter, 2009; Helfat & Eisenhardt, 2004). Resource redeployability is an option to withdraw resources from one product market and transfer them to another. If the diversification is a related one, the company has more potential to save opportunity costs to retain human resources and facilities (Sakhartov & Folta, 2014).

This notion has an inherent tension against governance economics that supports unrelated diversification (Eisenmann & Bower, 2005. Also, see Dundas & Richardson, 1980; Hill, 1988; Hill, Hitt, & Hoskisson, 1992; Hill & Hoskisson, 1987). Then, organizations that initiate a related diversification embed inherent redundancy.

Here is an overlap between management studies and resilience studies regarding redundancy. The next step is to consider how the overcoming of the path dependency occurs.

Translation of Penrose's (1959) "productive service" to "resource-based view" (Wernerfelt, 1984) and "capabilities" (Barney, 1991) reaches the framework of dynamic capability by Teece, Pisano, and Shuen (1997).

Dynamic capability is the firm's ability to integrate, build, and reconfigure internal and external competences to address rapidly changing environments (Teece et al., 1997. Also see, Amit & Schoemaker, 1993; Helfat et al., 2007). It is the process to reconfigure or transform the existing strategic assets through learning and building new investments. Thus, the ultimate motivation for dynamic capability is transformation

---

[4] The concept of productive service is similar to that of capabilities (Nair, Trendowski, & Judge, 2008).

12   E. OKADA

of existing capabilities through the interactive process of internal and external assets.

Then, the next to consider is what is the starting point of the process to grasp the opportunity through the interaction between internal and external assets.

The essential starting point of the process is the (change of) logic that (re)defines resource allocation patterns and their technological and economic elements (Bower, 1970; Bower & Gilbert, 2005). Without redefining the technological and economic factors, firms would fail to allocate the resources to areas of transformation. In this framework, a set of internal and external forces affects firms' (re)definition. The resource allocation process model defines such forces as the structural contexts (Bower, 1970; Bower & Gilbert, 2005).

Therefore, the structural contexts and (the change of) logic is critical in the framework.

Simultaneously, the interface between the internal and external organization needs to be a loosely recoupled one (Orton & Weick, 1990; Weick, 1976). Incorporating the concept of loose recoupling at the interface has the potential to create variation. Variation is a constituent of the evolutionary phases in the resilience theories. Thus, the management theories that focus on productive resources have coherence with resilience theories.

2.2.2   *Organization Behaviors, Evolution, and Strategic Reorientation*

There is another stream that directly focuses on organizational evolution. It is theories of organization behaviors that have formulated the evolution of organizations through the following constructs:

1. Processes of convergence to align the complex of sociopolitical and technical-economic activities that support a firm's overall strategic orientation[5];
2. periods of reorientation;
3. executive leadership (Tushman & Romanelli, 1985).[6]

---

[5] Strategic orientation denotes what business the firm is in and how it competes (Tushman & Romanelli, 1985).

[6] Strategic orientation consists of (1) core beliefs, (2) products, markets, technology, and competitive timing, (3) the distribution of power, (4) the organization's structure,

1 RESEARCH QUESTIONS AND FRAMEWORKS   13

Factors that affect organizational evolution are core values, strategy, distribution of powers, structure, and control. These constructs also have to be consistent with each other. Performance is a consequence of proper activities concerning political and economic requirements and of achieving consistencies in and among organizational activities. It, in turn, stimulates dynamism of escalated performance, but also, inertia.

In addition to performance, organization-environment and intra-organizational consistencies are associated with developing structural and socially anchored inertia (Hannan & Carrol, 1992; Lant, Miliken, & Batra, 1992; Gordon, Stewart, Sweo, & Luker, 2000).

Under this condition, the emergence of social and structural processes facilitates the convergence of a strategic orientation by enforcing rules and norms that constrain the premises of participants' behaviors (see, North, 1990). Convergence is a process of incremental and interdependent change activities and decisions that work to achieve greater consistency of internal activities with strategic orientation and operate to impede radical or discontinuous change (Tushman & Romanelli, 1985).

In other words, structural contexts disrupt internal consistency, which leads to the dynamics of the redefinition and subsequent strategic choice (see Bower, 1970; Bower & Gilbert, 2005; Burgelman, 1983). Under the situation that necessitates organization evolution, only executive leadership can mediate between forces for convergence and forces for change and initiate a strategic reorientation (Hambrick & Schechter, 1983). Direct executive intervention is required because inertial factors operate to maintain the status quo, often despite clear dysfunctional consequences (Bower, 1970; Eisenmann & Bower, 2000; Tushman & Romanelli, 1985).

2.2.3   Corporate Entrepreneurship
The organizational behavioral approach advances the understanding on the sources and strategic process of redefinition (Bower, 1970; Bower & Gilbert, 2005; Burgelman, 1983; Eisenmann & Bower, 2000) and organizational renewal (Zahra, Neubaum, & Hayton, 2016). It does not necessarily use concepts that overlap the resilience studies. On the other

and (4) the nature, type, and pervasiveness of control systems (Tushman & Romanelli, 1985).

14 E. OKADA

hand, the understanding of the organizational renewal leads to corporate entrepreneurship that motivates anchor's involvement in the resilience process. This framework is discussed in detail in Chapter 2.

2.2.4 Industrial Organizations and Market of Technology

The industrial organization approach is complementary to the population ecology approach. The basic unit of analysis in this discipline is the industries. The research paradigm focuses on contexts, such as entry and exit barriers, concentration ratios, demand elasticity, conduct, price, innovation, and vertical integration. They are to drive economic performance.

In this approach, firms in different markets and competitive structures develop different configurations of economic activities and decisions to achieve performance.

At the same time, this approach enables us to examine how entrepreneurial efforts lead to scale-up while outperforming existing products in the submarket (Sutton, 1998). Mainly, Sutton (1998) enables us to understand the entry mode and timing in which firms' intensified research investment in emerging sciences affects their ability to scale-up through breakthrough products.

The OECD (2004) implicitly bases on this approach in analyzing relations between entrepreneurial firms and urban resilience.

2.2.5 Ecological Approach

There are two viewpoints regarding the ecological approach. One is the sociologically oriented approach to organization (Amburgey, Kelly, & Barnett, 1993; Carrol & Hannan, 2015; Hannan & Carrol, 1992), and the other, economical approach (Nelson & Winter, 1982; Saviotti, 1996). The former involves studies on populations of organizations. The theoretical emphasis is on the process of selective replacement of relatively inert organizations. The research areas range from niche width, density dependence, and resource partitioning by developing and testing ecological theory (Carrol & Hannan, 2015).

On the other hand, the latter investigates how and why the economy changes (Meyerhoff, 2016). It consists of three main pillars:

a. the focus on economic dynamics,
b. the concept of irreversible, historical time, and

c. the emphasis on explaining innovation and diffusion (Meyerhoff, 2016; Witt, 1987).

It examines, at the micro-level, the growth and coordination of economically relevant knowledge (Meyerhoff, 2016). The economically relevant knowledge denotes routines or a combination of routines (Hermann-Piliath, 2002; Meyerhoff, 2016; Nelson & Winter, 1982). Routines represent acquired decision-making rules that define actors' common, acquired behaviors (Dopfer, 2007).

At the meso-level, this approach examines the adoption of routines in a population level (Meyerhoff, 2016).

As this study's objective is to seek the contribution of science-intensive organizations to the economic, technological, and environmental resilience, this study adopts the economic approach of evolution in explaining resilience.

The evolutionary view of resilience will be better used in full capacity by introducing the concept of "variety." Saviotti (1996) defines the variety as an addition to a system derived from innovation (Saviotti, 1996). Based on Saviotti (1996), this study defines variety as follows.

If an economic system is a set of elements, then the variety of this set will increase when the number of distinguishable elements of the set increases. (see, Saviotti, 1996)

A series of evolutionary economics studies introduce the concept of variety in evolutionary biology (see, Saviotti, 1996; Nelson & Winter, 1982, among others). This concept has several layers.

In general, organizations are more likely to survive or prosper when potentially valuable innovation occurs (Miner, 1994). This statement assumes that not all of the innovations are valuable, since, in the evolutionary viewpoint, innovations are equivalent to mutations. Mutations in biology often cause uncontrollable cell death: cancers (see, Miner, 1994).

Being given such evolution, organizations can affect the types of variation and innovation in several manners (Miner, 1994).

The first type of variation occurs through the interaction with organizations and the economy that surrounds organizations. It is a naturally occurred variation..

The second type of variation occurs in institutionalized experimentation (Freeman, 1982; Maidique, 1980; Miner, 1994) at the national and local levels (Armaniois & Eesley, 2018; Armanios, Lanahan, & Yu, 2020; Lanahan & Armanios, 2018). In this framework, the roles and functions of champion and entrepreneurship work as drivers of exploring variations inside of the organization. Please note that championing is also a frontline layer of forces in defining and selecting economic and technical elements of a project (Bower & Gilbert, 2005; Eisenmann & Bower, 2000; Miner, 1994).

The third type of variation occurs in direct and indirect incentives for individuals to produce useful variations (Miner, 1994; Williamson, 1979). Incentives for scientists in science-intensive organizations often take place through scientific resource allocation internal and external of organizations.

It is not autonomously determined which type of variation is better than others in producing useful variations. It partly depends on what attributes the emerging industrial sciences have in which organizations engage.

2.3 Anchor Firms and Knowledge-Intensive Organizations

Previous literature that addresses organizational contribution to urban resilience investigates academic knowledge-intensive organizations (KIOs), typically universities. Due to the Bayh-Dole's legacy, the public encourages universities to contribute to economic development through the technology transfer of science-based inventions. Since the financial crisis in the 2000s, economic articles began to introduce the concept of anchor organizations. However, many assume academic institutions and large-scale public organizations (such as hospitals) as anchors in a cluster.

Under this condition, Orr and Topa (2006) claim more positive industrial organizations' roles as the anchor of urban resilience. In their framework, anchor organizations are usually established firms such as multinational enterprises.

This book's study follows Orr and Topa (2006) and modifies the anchor organization's definition as below stated.

> Anchor organizations are established organizations that play an essential role in the area resilience or cluster building by assisting the emergence of new knowledge and technologies and providing product lines before the new technology revolution.

This definition can encompass foreign multinationals in the scope of anchors. Being given this broadened scope, anchor firms have the potential to contribute to urban resilience by adding a variety of technologies and productive services. Such variety will then be a part of the transformation of the areas and beyond by leveraging redundant resources toward productive service resources (Table 1).

2.4   Environmental Exposure and Inequity

Above stated are the evolutionary aspects of urban resilience and their coherence with management theories. This study will pursue the research question by mainly reconfiguring constructs of management theories. More specifically, it will contrast the market-structure-based entrepreneurial escalation model (Sutton, 1998) and transaction-cost-based governance model (Pisano, 1990), ameliorate the gap by the resource-based corporate entrepreneurship theories (Eisenmann & Bower, 2005; Zahra et al., 2016). Then it will connect to the managerial and organizational framework to the evolutionary resilience approach by focusing on the variety generation by Saviotti (1994).

Despite the theoretical development, unresolved phenomena remain regarding the inner-city residents.

The years of 1990s are characterized as the prosperous variety. The Variation-Intensive industrial sciences (Niosi, 2000) generated numerous startups by applying information communication technologies. Some of them outperformed established firms by intensifying R&D at a specific condition of fragmented submarket (see, Sutton, 1998).

Some of the new technologies upgrade productivity that liberates specific skills. However, the speed at which new products and technologies generate new demands was more rapid. Then, the increase of net variety generates economic growth by absorbing and converting redundant resources (Saviotti, 1996). These processes reversed the trend that appeared to have linked to the intergenerational inheritance of poverty (Giloth, 2004; Jargowski, 2003. See, OECD, 2004).

However, specific inner-city residents remain outside of the economic cycle (OECD, 2004).

Social enterprises found opportunities in addressing their need. However, they also began to sink with the isolated population (OECD, 2004). It is partly because their resilience practices lack the scale. As stated

Table 1 Management theories that have coherence with resilience theories

Management Theories		Resilience Theories			Representative Statements
Representative theories	Attributes	Representative theories	Coherent attributes	Representative statements	
Resource-based View Penrose (1957) Barney (1991); Wernerfelt (1984) *Resource deployability* Sakhartov ans Folta (2014). Also see, Anand & Singh, (1997); Bryce & Winter, (2009); Helfat & Eisenhardt, (2004). *Dynamic capability* Teece et al. (1997) Also, see Amit and Schoemaker, (1993); Helfat et al. (2007) *Adaptation cost theory* Wernerfelt (2016)	Resource redundancy; Unused resources (including technological and entrepreneurial) Productive service resources (Organizational capability) Diversification; Resource deployability Dynamic capabilities	Holling (1995); Bruneau et al. (2006); Coafee and Lee (2016) Coafee and Lee (2016); Folke et al. (2010) Gunderson and Holling (2002)	Resource redundancy Learn, Combine experience and knowledge, adjust its responses to external drivers and internal processes; Experience	Growth is governed by a creative and dynamic interaction between a firm's productive resources and its market opportunities. Available resources limit expansion; unused resources (including technological and entrepreneurial) stimulate and largely determine the direction of expansion (Penrose, 1957) Redundancy has a function to reduce path dependencies through the resource utilization in a way that it enhances the development of alternative pathways, thus transformation (Coafee & Lee, 2016) Dynamic capability is firm's ability to integrate, build, and reconfigure internal and external competences to address rapidly changing environments (Teece et al., 1997)	

Management Theories		Resilience Theories		Representative Statements
Representative theories	Attributes	Representative theories	Coherent attributes	Representative statements
Organization Behaviors	Adaptation to market	Evolutionary view of resilience Holling (1973, 1996, 2001)	Adaptability	Theory of organization behaviors that have formulated evolution of organizations through the following constructs:
Contingency theory Burns and Stalker (1961); Luthans and Stewart (1977)	Situational variables; Interaction with environment; Systems approach	Gunderson and Holling (2002); Coafee and Lee (2016); Folke et al. (2010)	Fitness to environment; Systems approach; System to adjust its responses to changing external drivers and internal processes	Processes of convergence to align the complex of socio-political and technical economic activities that support a firm's overall strategic orientation; periods of reorientation; executive leadership (Eisenmann & Bower, 2002; Tushman & Romanelli 1985)
Evolution of organizations Tushman and Romanelli (1985); Hambrick and Schechter (1983)	Formulated evolution; Convergence; Reorientation; Executive leadership; Structural and strategic contexts	Coafee and Lee (2016); Pike et al (2010) [Neocleous (2013); MacKinnon and Dirickson (2013)]	Loose recoupling; Network viewpoints; Decentralization of responsibility	An organization's long-term adaptation, spanning multiple generation of CEOs, critically depends on maintaining the strategic renewal capability of its internal ecology of strategy making (Bower, 2005)
Resource allocation process model Bower (1970); Bower and Gilbert (2005); Burgelman (1983); Bower (2005)	Dilemmas of organizational adaptation; Strategy making as long-term adaptive organizational capability; Loose recoupling; Retaining of separation and identity	Orr and Topa (2006); OECD (2004); Coafee and Lee (2016); Meerow et al. (2016); Yamagata and Maruyama (2016)	Anchor organization; Entrepreneurship as a catalyst of urban resilience; Variety is an addition to a system derived from innovation. Preparedness, persistence, adaptability, responsiveness,	This resilience view incorporates the loosely recoupled linkage between internal and external variants to enhance the system's responsiveness and evolutionary trajectories (Coafee & Lee, 2016; Pike et al. 2010) The presence of academic institutions is the necessary condition of urban resilience, while that of anchor organization, the sufficient condition (Orr & Topa, 2006) Entrepreneurship is a catalyst of urban resilience (OECD, 2004) These attributes (of evolutionary approach) provide the capacity to prepare, persist, and adapt to any variety in the system

(continued)

Table 1   (continued)

Management Theories		Resilience Theories			Representative Statements
Representative theories	Attributes	Representative theories	Coherent attributes	Representative statements	
Loose recoupling Weick (1976); Orton and Weick (1992) Heller (1999) Sundbo & Gallouj (2000). **_Adaptation_** Miner (1994) Farjoun (2010) **Corporate Entrepreneurship** **_Entrepreneurial M-Form_** Bower (1970); Burgelman and Doz (1997); Eisenmann and Bower (2000)	Stability and change Redefinition Renewal Strategic integration Redefinition Rejuvenation Renewal Transformation Scale-up of entrepreneurial firms Variety Routine Search activities The generation of variety, selection, reproduction and inheritance, and fitness and adaptation				

Management Theories		Resilience Theories			Representative Statements
Representative theories	*Attributes*	*Representative theories*	*Coherent attributes*	*Representative statements*	
Corporate entrepreneurship Covin and Miles (1999); Kuratko and Covin (2015) Dess et al. (2003) Zahra (1996) Zahra, Neubaum, and Hayton (2016) **Industrial Organization** Sutton (1998) **Ecological Approach (Economic viewpoints)** Saviotti (1996) Nelson and Winter (1982)	— preparedness, persistence, adaptability, responsiveness				

22   E. OKADA

in Coafee and Lee (2016), decentralization and redistribution have localized the resilience practice in several areas that cannot claim the scale economy.

Many of the Variation-Intensive firms rapidly grew into multinationals in the 2000s. However, they began to hire U.S.-and EU-university graduates who returned to less-developed home countries (Glaeser & Hausman, 2019). It is partly due to the information technologies' advancement that reduced the inflictions of ex-ante and ex-post monitoring.

Thus, the economic divide remained in a specific population. The vicious cycle began to reinforce not only poverty but also the environmental inequity. Notably, the air contaminants localize in locations of a traffic jam and heatwave that affect peoples' physical disfunctioning.

Under this condition, many people misunderstand that the promotion of science reinforces the economic and social gaps and segregation. However, it is scientific discoveries that can contribute to the broadening of beneficiaries.

For example, one of West Coast-based multinationals is applying academic discoveries of robotic science to warehouses operation. Since then, it has dramatically increased returns and the employment by complimenting humans' cognitive limits. Such an application also has contributed to improving the job for elderly and physically dis-functioned people who might otherwise constitute the isolated population.

At the same time, it requires necessary and sufficient conditions that the science promotion facilitates economic growth and broadens its beneficiaries (Saviotti, 1996). It is the speed in which added varieties create new demands that absorb and convert underused competencies (Saviotti, 1996).

The details of this condition will be discussed in Chapter 5.

2.5   *Anticipation and Citizen Scientists' Movement*

Along with the responsibilization of resilience, "anticipation" entered the field of resilience practices. "Anticipation" is a practice in the transition from adaptation toward evolution-based resilience (Coafee & Lee, 2016).

"Anticipation" is also a dimension that comprises responsible research and innovation (hereafter, RRI). It envisions and understands how the current dynamics affect or help to design the future (Stigloe, Owen, & Macnaghten, 2013. See, Barben, Fischer, Selin, & Guston, 2008). It constitutes a governance modality that bound those involved with collective norms (Barben et al., 2008; Marchant, Abbott, & Allenby, 2013. See, Lessig, 1999).

According to Coafee and Lee (2016), the networked structure of anticipation passed on the urban resilience's responsibility from states to citizens. It is tough to translate the broad, hierarchical order of states' resilience practices to a localized scale.

On the other hand, it has generated the citizen participation movement. The area of Particulate Matter (PM)2.5 became a representative case of the citizen science's contribution (see, Carvlin et al., 2019. See also, Guerrini, Majumber, Lewellyn, & McGuire, 2019). Their level of scientific integrity exceeds a specific level (Carvlin et al., 2019). The impacts on physical disfunctioning and anticipated future risks likely the major driver (see, Chapter 7).

The organizational management mitigates the conflicts between responsibilization and citizen-involved anticipation. As for the details of the underlying framework, see Chapter 7.

2.6 *The Missing Link with Science-Intensive Organizations*

In reviewing previous literatures, what are missing are the science organization's viewpoints. Also, the field of advanced material sciences has little attention both in the scholarly management and environmental aspects of resilience theories.

Examples include a U.S. large-scale chemical company that began to research nitrogen since around the mid-twentieth century. Nitrogen is a constituent element of amino acids, and therefore, of proteins and nucleic acids (RNA and DNA). It constitutes 78 percent by volume of the earth's atmosphere.[7] Being given its significance to the earth and life, the company researched and developed a nitrogen stabilizer and diversified into an "agribusiness." The diversification led to developing a material that captures nitrogen dioxide from nitrogen, and entered the "soil remediation service." This segment provided a foundation for creating a new company of "new energy solution service" by strategically integrating products of the firm's existing segments.

---

[7] Oxford Languages. Retrieved from: www.lexico.com, among others.

24   E. OKADA

Thus, Mark II firms can also contribute to urban resilience through science-based products and new business creation. However, their pathways of contribution are understudied.

3   CATEGORIZATION OF INDUSTRIAL SCIENCES

On the other hand, the processes in which emerging sciences grow into technologies and productive service resources are not uniform. Science itself is an abstract idea of how things work (Bush, 1945). It does not provide what Penrose (1959) calls "productive services" to organizations. Science should be converted to productive services, or technological capabilities, to be a foundation of new products and services.

3.1   *From Emerging Sciences to Technological Capabilities*

There are several patterns in which emerging sciences grow into new technologies. As the emergence of new sciences and technologies affects processes and structures of industrial and public organizations, several pieces of literature have investigated their attributes.

Among them, Niosi (2000)'s new typologies of emerging industrial sciences are comprehensive and have relevance to management studies. In focusing on the dimensions of initial condition (sources of innovation) and R&D's trend toward outcomes, Niosi categorizes new industrial sciences into a four-cell matrix. They are (1) Schumpeterian Mark II, (2) Dynamic Increasing Returns, (3) Variation-Intensiveness, and (4) Schumpeterian Mark I (see, Table 2).

Though it is one of the most comprehensive categorizations, it has not deliberated the environmental sciences. Details are discussed in Chapters 2 and 5.

In general, it is tough to address environmental material sciences. If new inventions are coming from new firms, Sutton (1998)'s scale-up model provides a good foundation. As stated earlier, Sutton (1998)'s theory demonstrates how a new firm that intensifies R&D at a specific point of the fragmented market has the potential to escalate its performance beyond incumbents. Key concepts in this theory building are " technological, trajectories" and their associated "submarkets." A technological trajectory denotes a trajectory that specifically associated with (a group of) products (Sutton, 1998). The parameter consists of two variants: (a) R&D elasticity that relates R&D to upgraded quality and (b)

1 RESEARCH QUESTIONS AND FRAMEWORKS   25

Table 2 Current categories of industrial sciences

Initial condition of R&D	Trends of R&D toward outcomes	Industrial science categories	Related industries
Concentration	Concentration	Mark II	Heavy industries, Chemical and material industries
Dispersion	Concentration	Dynamic increasing return	Supercomputing industry, Pharmaceutical industry
Concentration	Dispersion	Variation-intensive	Semiconductor industry, Information communication technology industries
Dispersion	Dispersion	Mark I	Biotechnology

Sources Created by referring to Niosi (2000). Also, see Arthur (1994), Kaldor (1972); Nelson & Winter (1982), Saviotti (1996)

the strengthened linkage between different submarkets (or technological trajectories).

However, Sutton (1998) also comments that his model does not necessarily fit the field in which consumers' willingness to pay does not reward upgraded quality. In this regard, many environment-relevant products hold to this type. Therefore, this field requires additional frameworks.

This book's study will focus on the emerging sciences and science-intensive organizations related to environmental material sciences, given this understudied condition. Details will be discussed in Chapter 5.

4   ORGANIZATIONAL FORMS TO BROADEN BENEFICIARIES

Environmental material science firms also have difficulty in investigate their organizational renewal process.

In general, established firms have a motivation to introduce entrepreneurs' discoveries and renew their technological capabilities (Abernathy & Clark, 1980; Zahra et al., 2016). However, it is tough to understand when and how they introduce variation in their R&D, given the R&D concentration in the initial condition and subsequent trend. In Dynamic Increasing Return firms, they internalize emerging sciences through several forms of internalization, such as merger and acquisition (hereafter, M&A), joint venture, joint research, and technology transfer. However, the pathways of renewal and transformation are unclear in Mark II's chemicals.

As stated in Chapter 5, a couple of organizations engage in environmental material sciences outside of the existing industrial science. The examples include architectural companies. Although their inventions have an abundance of potential to contribute to the ecological aspects of urban resilience, such an organization's very existence receives little awareness. Then, a question arises what categorization is appropriate for new material sciences: what attributes are proper to categorize them; what pathways they contribute to the environmental aspects of urban resilience.

This book aims to address organization models to broaden the science's beneficiaries by sciences in facing conceptual problems. It pays particular attention to material sciences and relevant sciences that mimic nature (such as bioinspired material) to address urban resilience. It investigates organizational forms and arrangements to broaden beneficiaries to overcome the inequity of environmental contaminant exposure.

Later chapters discuss the following issues

1. What factors facilitate or hinder the organizational resource allocation to this process (Chapters 2 and 3).
2. With what dimensions to map material sciences to new science categories (Chapters 4–6).
3. How to link the management of scale-up to integrating the disadvantaged community regarding the exposure to environmental contaminants (Chapter 7).

This book will seek to expand the organizational model of resource allocation and scale-up related to environment-related sciences.

Chapter 2 pursues the research question by focusing on the facilitators and constraints of science-intensive organizations. This chapter particularly highlights factors that encourage and discourages potential anchors from redefining their technological and economic elements of science-based projects. The main theoretical bases are the market structure of technologies (Sutton, 1998) and the resource allocation process model (Bower, 1970; Eisenmann & Bower, 2002). The particular attention is on the firms with Mark II sciences. Then, it points out the need for new attributes of industrial sciences, particularly for environmental materials.

The acceptance of the anchor roles mainly comes from the structural contexts and strategy of corporate renewal. On the other hand, the internal structural and strategic contexts often pose constraints to firms with multidivisional forms (M-Forms). They constrain the strategic integration that requires putting resources by crossing different units (Eisenmann & Bower, 2000; Leonard-Barton, 1992; Kuemmerle, 2005).

A question arises, while a significant part of knowledge comes from emerging sciences, how to incorporate their discoveries, the loosely coupled structure (Clark, 1983; Orton & Weick, 1990), or anything else.

Chapter 3 is to build a rough framework for further investigation of later chapters. The actors to examine are academic knowledge-intensive organizations (KIOs), established multinationals, and entrepreneur firms. Particular attention is paid to tensions between those related to Mark II sciences and new environmental material sciences.

This chapter proposes new attributes, "mimic of nature (environment)" and "integration into the design (sustainability)," to address material and environmental sciences.

Chapter 4 research questions through a representative case of environmental aspects of urban resilience. Research questions are on what factors motivate the established multinationals to play as anchor institutions in a market failure area; How can they use their resources to reduce environmental inequity prevalent in inner-city regions. A particular focus is on a condition in which potential anchors are absent in an urban area.

Research shows that a clean technology incubator plays the role of an intermediate organization that connects related parties, including entrepreneurs, foreign anchors, manufacturers that produce prototypes, third-sector funds, and city government. The incubator creates a multi-sided market to coordinate and align actors' incentives.

Chapter 5 pursues research further to investigates new attributes for material environmental sciences; what organization forms facilitate their emergence and contribution to a variety. The theoretical base is a variety by Saviotti (1996).

If an economic system is a set of elements, then the variety of this set will increase when the number of distinguishable elements of the set increases. The growth in variety is a necessary requirement for long-term development (Saviotti, 1996. See, Pasinetti, 1981, 1990).

Simultaneously, a system characterized by a variety of constituents is also a system that requires a more significant amount of information (see Galbraith, 1973). Organizations can reduce the process variety and increase output variety.

One way to achieve this optimization is to store and process less information by configuring the elements as ordered as possible (Saviotti, 1996). The other is the reconfiguration of routines (Saviotti, 1996. Also, see Caves, 2007/1982; Feldman, 2000; Nelson & Winter, 1982). The variety will partly destroy once established routines (Nelson & Winter, 1982). The reconfiguration of timely renewed routines will necessitate placing new and heterogeneous elements to reduce randomness (Saviotti, 1996).

The next issue is the more factual investigation regarding what science categories of emerging sciences affect the variation and technological alteration of Mark II firms. This study then investigates the emergence that comes from Mark II sciences and those from civil engineering sciences.

Chapter 6 pursues a research question on whether artificial intelligence technologies (AI) contribute to the broadening of environmental science beneficiaries. The AI has the potential to contribute to broadening beneficiaries of sciences by its nondiscriminatory way. This potential comes from removing human prejudice in its functioning. However, AI also has the potential to reinforce social prejudice. If the input variants do not adequately represent the set characteristics, AI calculation outcomes are deviant.

This chapter will analyze whether the AI use broadens beneficiaries through the impacts on science-intensive organizations. The theoretical starting points are frameworks by King and Roberts (2018: science viewpoints) and Raisch and Krakowski (2020: scholarly management viewpoints). Both contain the elements of automation and augmentation.

Policymakers acknowledge the cities' responsibility to address the rise of poverty, hunger, resource consumption, and a loss of biodiversity (NAS, 2016). Under this condition, the AI-based algorithm can make the anticipation easier by integrating satellite data, ground-based data, and other datasets. Second, retaining human responsibility is essential in data-driven resilience. Third, automation's efficiency will offset the negative aspects of variety that will lead to giving up the scale. The efficiency spares humans' time to intervene to rule the better quality of services to diversified people.

Then, the AI will support both the variety and scale in urban resilience used to conflict with each other. Thus, the adequate adoption of AI will broaden the science beneficiaries in the future urban transformation.

Chapter 7 addresses a research question on appropriate organization designs for new types of science-intensive organizations. This chapter pursues the research question through an inductive–deductive analysis while extending the adaptation cost theory by Wernerfelt (2016).

Firstly, the adaptation theory issue lies in comparing gains from service specialization in the market and business specialization in bilateral trade. Second, the exchange object does not fit the science-intensive social entrepreneurial firms that mobilize academics, students, and citizen scientists.

In this regard, an academic KIO develops a mechanism that optimizes production costs and search costs incur at sponsoring organizations, specializing faculties, and educational effects on diversified students' academic performances.

A social entrepreneurial firm creates a multisided space where the primary transaction object is a moral ownership[8] of people. It unconsciously roots in natural rights that are precepts of collaboration (Finnis, 1980). Anticipation motivates them to strengthen their commitment.

As evidence, this collective force led to reverse the withered land in Arizona State and broaden its geographic scope.

In both cases, the scale-up depends on the design of multi-sided space. In the design, the activation of anticipation and moral responsibilities is critical for the scale-up that corresponds to the evolutionary urban resilience.

Chapter 8 outlines the book's studies while proposing integrating heterogeneous knowledge toward resilience and transformation.

References

Abernathy, W. J., & Clark, K. B. (1980). Innovation: Mapping the winds of creative destruction. *Research Policy, 14*(1), 3–22.

---

[8] Regarding the concept of moral ownership, see Hannah, Avolio, & May (2011).

30 E. OKADA

Amburgey, T. L., Kelly, D., & Barnett, W. P. (1993). Resetting the clock: The dynamics of organizational change and failure. *Administrative Science Quarterly, 38*(1), 51–73.

Amit, P., & Schoemaker, P. H. (1993). Strategic assets and organizational rent. *Strategic Management Journal, 14*(1), 33–46.

Anand, J., & Singh, H. (1997). Asset redeployment, acquisition and corporate strategy in declining industries. *Strategic Management Journal, 18,* 99–118.

Anerson, Y. B., Coulberson, S. L., & Phelps, J. (1993). Overview of the Epa/Niehs/ Atsder Workshop–"Equity in environmental health: Research issues and needs". *Toxicology and Industrial Health, 9*(5), 679–683.

Armaniois, D. E., & Eesley, C. E. (2018). Scaffolds and intermediaries: How changing institutional infrastructure can alleviate normative and cultural-cognitive barriers to regulatory changes supporting entrepreneurship. *SSRN Working Paper.* Available at: https://papers.ssrn.com/so13/cfm?abstract_id=3006825, as cited by Amanios, D.E., Lanahan, L., & Yu, D. (2020). *op. cit.*

Armanios, D. E., Lanahan, L., & Yu, D. (2020). Varieties of local government experimentation: US.-state led technology-led economic development policies, 2000–2015. *Academy of Management Discoveries,* forthcoming.

Arthur, W. B. (1994). *Increasing returns and path dependency in the economy.* Ann Arbor: University of Michigan Press.

Barben, D., Fischer, E., Selin, C., & Guston, D. H. (2008). Anticipatory governance of nanotechnology: Foresight, engagement, and integration. In E. J. Hackett, O. Amsterdamska, M. Lynch, & J. Wajcman (Eds.), *The handbook of science and technology studies* (3rd ed., pp. 979–1000). Cambridge (US): MIT Press.

Barney, J. B. (1991). Firm resources and sustained competitive advantage. *Journal of Management, 17,* 99–120.

Benger, S., Murakami, D., & Yamagata, Y. (2016). Modeling urban heatwave risk in Adelaide, South Australia. In Y. Yamagata & H. Murayama (Eds.), *Urban resilience: Transformative approach* (pp. 45–62). Switzerland: Springer International.

Bower, J. L. (1970). *Managing the resource allocation process.* Boston: Harvard Business School Press.

Bower, J. L., & Gilbert, C. G. (Eds.). (2005). *From resource allocation to strategy.* New York: Oxford University Press.

Bower, J. L. (2005). Modeling the resource allocation process. In J. L. Bower & C. G. Gilbert (Eds.), *Ibid* (pp. 26–37).

Bruneau, M., Chang, S. E., Eguchi, R. T., Lee, G. C., O'Rourke, T. D., Reinhorn, A. M., ... & Von Winterfeldt, D. (2003). A framework to quantitatively assess and enhance the seismic resilience of communities. *Earthquake Spectra, 19*(4), 733–752.

Bryce, D. J., & Winter, S. G. (2009). A general industry relatedness index. *Management Science, 55*, 1570–1585.

Burgelman, R. (1983). A model of the interaction of strategic behavior, corporate context, and the concept of strategy. *Academy of Management Review, 3*(1), 61069.

Burgelman, R., & Doz, Y. (1997). *Complex strategic integration in the lean multi-business corporation* (INSEAD Working paper, 97/03.SM).

Burns, T., & Stalker, G. M. (1961). *Management of Innovation.* London: Tavistock.

Bush, V. (1945). *Science, the endless frontier.* A report to the President by Director of Office of Scientific Research and Development. Washington, DC: U.S. Government Printing Office.

Buzea, C., Pacheco, I. I., & Robbie, K. (2007). Nanomaterials and nanoparticules: Sources and toxicity. *Biointerphases, 2*(4), 17–71.

Carpenter, S. R., Turner, M. G., & Westley, S. (2005). Surrogates for resilience of social-ecological systems. *Ecosystems, 8*(8), 941–944.

Carrol, G. R., & Hannan, M. T. (2015). Organizational ecology. In *International encyclopedia of social and behavioral sciences*, 17. 2nd Ed. (pp. 358–363). Amsterdam: Elsevir.

Carvlin, G. N., Lugo, H., Olmedo, L., Bejarano, E., Wilkie, A., Meltzer, D., ... & Seto, E. (2019). Use of citizen science- derived data for special and temporal modeling of particulate matter near the US/Mexico border. *Atmosphere, 10*, 495. https://doi.org/10.3990/atmos10090495.

Caves, R. E. (2007/1982). *Multinational enterprise and economic analysis* (3rd ed.). Cambridge: Cambridge University Press.

Chang, T., Zivin, J., Gross, T., & Neidell, M. (2016). Particulate pollution and the productivity of pear packers. *American Economic Journal: Economic Policy, 8*(3), 141–169.

Clark, B. R. (1983). *The higher education system: Academic organization in cross-national perspective.* Berkeley: University of California Press.

Coafee, J., & Fussey, P. (2015). Constructing resilience through security and surveillance: The politics, practices and tnesions of security—driven resilience. *Security Dialogue, 46*(1). https://doi.org/10.1177/0967010614557884.

Coafee, J., & Lee, P. (2016). *Urban resilience: Planning risk, crisis and uncertainty.* London: Palgrave.

Covin, J. G., & Miles, M. P. (1999). Corporate entrepreneurship and the pursuit of competitive advantage. *Entrepreneurship Theory and Practice, 23*(3), 47–63.

Dandas, K., & Richardson, P. (1980). Corporate strategy and the concept of market failure. *Strategic Management Journal, 1*, 177–188.

Dess, G. G., Ireland, R. D., Zahra, S. A., Floyd, S. W., Janney, J. J., & Lane, P. J. (2003). Emerging issues in corporate entrepreneurship. *Journal of Management, 29*(3), 351–378.

Dopfer, K. (2007). Grundzüge der Evolutionsökonomie-Analytik, Ontologie und theoritische Schlüsselkonzepte. *Discussion Paper* 2007–10, Universität St. Gallen. Available at: http://ux-tauri.unisg.ch/RePEc/usg/dp2007/DP-10-Do.pdf.

Eisenmann, T., & Bower, J. (2000). The entrepreneurial M-Form: Strategic integration in global media firms. *Organization Science, 11,* 348–355.

Eisenmann, T. R., & Bower, J. L. (2005). The entrepreneurial M-Form: A case study of strategic integration in a global media company. In J. L. Bower & C. G. Gilbert (Eds.), *From resource allocation to strategy* (pp. 307–329). Oxford: Oxford University Press.

Farjoun, M. (2010). Beyond dualism: Stability and change as a duality. *Academy of Management Review, 35*(2), 202–225.

Feldman, M. S. (2000). Organizational routine as a source of continuous change. *Organization Science, 11*(6), 661–629.

Folke, C. (2006). Resilience: The emergence of a perspective for social-ecological systems analysis. *Global Environmental Change, 16,* 253–267.

Folke, C., Carpenter, S. R., Walker, B. H., Scheffer, M., Chapin III, F. S., & Rockstrom, J. (2010). Resilience thinking: Integrating resilience, adaptability and transformability. *Ecology and Society, 15*(4), 20. Available at: http://www.ecologyandsociety.org/vol15/iss4/art20/.

Freeman, C. (1982). *The economics of industrial innovation.* London: F Pinter.

Galbraith, J. R. (1973). *Designing complex organizations.* Reading: Addison-Wesley.

Gerland, D. (1996). The limits of the sovereign state: Strategies of crime control in contemporary society. *The British Journal of Criminology, 36*(4), 334–371.

Giloth, R. (2004). Social enterprise and urban rebuilding in the United States. *OECD, entrepreneurship: A catalyst for urban regeneration* (pp. 135–157). Paris: OECD.

Glaeser, E., & Hausman, N. (2019). *The spatial mismatch between innovation and joblessness* (National Bureau of Economic Research Working Paper No. 25913).

Gordon, S. S., Stewart, W. H., Sweo, R., & Luker, W. (2000). Convergence versus strategic reorientation: The antecedents of fast-paced organizational change. *Journal of Management, 26*(5), 911–945.

Guerrini, C. J., Majumber, M. A., Lewellyn, M. J., & McGuire, A. L. (2019). Citizen science, public polity. *Science, 361*(6398), 134–136.

Gunderson, L. H., & Holling, C. S. (2002). *Panarchy synopsis: Understanding transformations in human and natural systems.* Washington, DC: Island Press.

Hannah, S. T., Avolio, B. J., & May, D. R. (2011). Moral maturation and moral conation: A capacity approach to explaining moral thought and action. *Academy of Management Review, 36*(4), 663–685.

Hannan, M. T., & Carrol, G. R. (1992). *The dynamics of organizational populations*. New York: Oxford University Press.

Hambrick, D., & Schechter, S. (1983). Turnaround strategies for mature industrial product business units. *Academy of Management Journal, 26,* 231–248.

Helfat, C. E., & Eisenhardt, K. M. (2004). Intertemporal economies of scope, organizational modularity, and the dynamics of diversification. *Strategic Management Journal, 25,* 1217–1232.

Helfat, C. E., Teece, D., Peteraf, M., Winter, S. G., Finkelstein, S., Singh, H., & Mitchell, W. (2007). *Dynamic capabilities: Understanding strategic change in organizations*. Malden: Blackwell Publishing.

Heller, T. (1999). Loosely coupled systems in corporate entrepreneurship. Imagining and management the innovation project/host organization interface. *Entrepreneurship Theory and Practice,* 24(2), 25–31.

Hermann-Piliath, C. (2002). *Grundriß der Evoluionökonomik*. München: Wilhelm Fink Verlag.

Hill, C. (1988). Internal capital market controls and financial performance in multidivisional firms. *Journal of Industrial Economics,* 37(1), 67–83.

Hill, C., Hitt, M., & Hoskisson, R. (1992). Cooperative versus competitive structures in related and unrelated diversified firms. *Organization Science,* 3(4), 501–521.

Hill, C., & Hoskisson, R. (1987). Strategy and structure in the multipdoruct firm. *Academy of Management Review,* 12(2), 331–341.

Holling, C. S. (1973). Resilience and stability of ecological systems. *Annual Review of Ecology and Systematics, 4,* 1–23.

Holling, C. S. (1996). Engineering resilience versus ecological resilience. In P. C. Schultz (Ed.), *Engineering within ecological constraints* (pp. 31–44). Washington, DC: National Academy Press.

Jargowski, P. A. (2003, May 1). *Stunning progress, hidden problems: The dramatic decline of urban poverty in the 1990s*. Washington, DC: Brookings Institution Center on Urban and Metropolitan Policy Report.

Kaldor, N. (1972). The irrelevance of equilibrium economics. *Economic Journal, 82,* 1237–1255.

King, R. D., & Roberts, S. (2018). Artificial intelligence and machine learning in science. In OECD. *Science, technology and innovation outlook 2018: Adapting to technological and societal disruption*. Paris: OECD Publishing. Retrieved from https://doi.org/10.1787/sti_in_outlook-2018-10-en.

Kuemmerle, W. (2005). The process of international expansion: Comparing established firms and entrepreneurial start-ups. In J. L. Bower & C. G. Gilbert (Eds.), *From resource allocation to strategy* (pp. 176–204). Oxford: Oxford University Press.

Kuratjim, D. F., & Covin, J. G. (2015). Forms of corporate entrepreneurship. In C. L. Cooper (Ed.), *Wiley encyclopedia of management*. Chichester: Wiley. https://doi.org/10.1002/9781118785317.weom030016.

Lanahan, L., & Armanios, D. (2018). Does more certification always benefit a venture? *Organization Science, 29*(5), 931–947.

Lant, T. K., Miliken, F. J., & Batra, B. (1992). The role of managerial learning and interpretation in strategic persistence and reorientation: An empirical exploration. *Strategic Management Journal, 13,* 585–608.

Leonard-Barton, D. (1992). Core capabilities and core rigidities: A paradox in managing new product development. *Strategic Management Journal, 13,* 111–125.

Lessig, L. (1999). *Code and other laws of cyberspace*. New York: Basic Books.

Luthans, F., & Stewart, T. I. (1977). A general contingency theory of management. *Academy of Management Review, 2*(2), 181–195.

MacKinnon, D., & Dirickson, K. D. (2013). From resilience to resourcefulness: A critique of resilience policy and activism. *Progress in Human Geography, 13*(2). https://doi.org/10.1177/0309132512454775.

Maidique, M. A. (1980). Entrepreneurs, champions, and technological innovation. *Sloan Management Review,* pre-1986, 21(2), 59.

Majoor, S. (2015). Resilient practices: A paradox-oriented approach for large-scale development projects. *Town Planning Review, 86*(3), 257–277.

Manisalidis, I., Stavropoulou, E., Stavropoulos, A., & Bezirtzoglou, E. (2020). Environmental and health impacts of air pollution: A review. *Frontiers in Public Health,* 8: 14. https://doi.org/10.3389/fpubh.2020.00014.

Massachusetts Center for Health Information and Analysis (n.d.). *CY2008-2012 MA Department of Emergency Discharge Database*, as cited in Massachusets Department of Public Health. (2017). *The facts about pediatric asthma in Boston.*

Massachusetts Department of Public Health. (2017). *The facts about pediatric asthma in Boston.* Boston: MA Department of Public Health.

Marchant, G. E., Abbott, K. W., & Allenby, B. (Eds.). (2013). *Innovative governance models for emerging technologies*. Cheltenham: Edward Elgar.

Meerow, S., Newell, J. P., & Stults, M. (2016). Defining urban resilience: A review. *Landscape and Urban Planning, 147,* 38–49.

Meyerhoff, J. (2016). The perspectives of pluralism economics. *Exploring Economics.* Available at: https://www.exploring-economics.org/en/orientation/evolutionary-economics/.

Miner, A. S. (1994). Seeking adaptive advantage: Evolutionary theory and adaptive action. In J. A. Baum & J. V. Singh (Eds.), *Evolutionary dynamics of organizations* (pp. 76–89). New York: Oxford University Press.

Nair, A., Trendowski, J., & Judge, W. (2008). The theory of growth of the firm, by Edith T. Penrose, Oxford: Blackwell, 1959 (Book review). *Academy of Management Review*, 33(4), 1026–1028.

National Academies of Science, Engineering, and Medicine. (2016). *Pathways to urban sustainability: Challenges and opportunities for the United States*. Washington, DC: National Academies Press. https://doi.org/10.17226/23551.

National Academy of Science, Engineering, and Medicine. (2019). *Building and measuring community resilience: Actions for communities and the Gulf Research Program*. Washington, DC: National Academies Press. https://doi.org/10.17226/25383.

National Library of Medicine, Compound summary: Nitrogen. Retrieved from https://pubchem.ncbi.nlm.nih.gov/compound/Nitrogen.

Nelson, R. R., & Winter, S. G. (1982). *An evolutionary theory of economic change*. Cambridge: Harvard University Press.

Neocleous, M. (2013). Resisting resilience. *Radical Philosophy*, 178-2-8.

Niosi, J. (2000). Science-based industries: New Schumpeterian taxonomy. *Technology in Society*, 22, 429–444.

North, D. C. (1990). *Institutions, institutional change, and economic performance*. Cambridge, UK: Cambridge University Press.

OECD (Organization for Economic Cooperation and Development). (2004). *Entrepreneurship: Catalyst for urban regeneration*. Paris: OECD.

Orr, J., & Topa, G. (2006), Challenges facing the New York Metropolitan area economy. *Current Issues in Economics and Finance*, 12(1). Available at: https://www.newyorkfed.org/medialibrary/media/research/current_issues/ci12-1.pdf.

Orton, J. D., & Weick, K. E. (1990). Loosely coupled systems: A reconceptualization. *Academy of Management Review*, 15(2), 203–223.

Pasinetti, L. L. (1981). *Structural change and economic growth*. Cambridge: Cambridge University Press.

Pasinetti, L. L. (1990). Structural change and unemployment. *Structural Change and Economic Dynamics*, 1, 7–14.

Penrose, E. T. (1959). *The theory of the growth of a firm*. New York and Oxford: Blackwell.

Penrose, E. T. (1960). The growth of a firm—A case study: The Hercules Powder Company. *Business History Review*, 34(1), 1–23.

Pike, A., Dawley, S., & Tomaney, J. (2010). Resilience, adaptation, and adaptability. *Cambridge Journal of Regions Economy and Society*, 3(1), 59–70.

Pisano, G. P. (1990). The R&D boundaries of the firm: An empirical analysis. *Administrative Science Quarterly*, 35, 153–176.

36   E. OKADA

Raisch, S., & Krakowski, S. (2020). Artificial intelligence and management: The automation-augmentation paradox. *Academy of Management Review*, forthcoming. https://doi.org/10.5465/2018.0072.

Rappaport, S. M., & Smith, M. T. (2010). Environment and disease risks. *Science, 330*(6003), 460–461. https://doi.org/10.1126/science.1192603.

Roberts, P. (2000). The evolution, definition and purpose of urban regeneration. In P. Roberts & H. Sykes (Eds.), *Urban regeneration: A handbook* (pp. 9–36). New York: Sage.

Roberts, P., & Sykes, H. (2000). *Urban regeneration: A handbook*. New York: Sage.

Sakhartov, A. V., & Folta, T. B. (2014). Resource relatedness, redeployability, and firm value. *Strategic Management Journal, 35*, 1781–1797.

Saviotti, P. P. (1994). Variety, economic and technological development. In Y. Shionoya & M. Perlman (Eds.), *Technology, Industries and Institutions: Studies in Schumpeterian perspective*. Ann Arbor: University of Michigan Press.

Saviotti, P. P. (1996). *Technological evolution, variety and the economy*. Cheltenham: Edward Elgar.

Simon, H. A. (1957). *Models of man, social and rational*. New York: Wiley.

Stigloe, J., Owen, R., & Macnaghten, P. (2013). Developing a framework for responsible innovation. *Research Policy, 42*(9), 1568–1580.

Sundbo, J., & Gallouj, F. (2000). Innovation as a loosely coupled system in services. *International Journal of Services, Technology and Management, 1*(1), 15–36.

Sutton, J. (1998). *Technology and market structure*. Cambridge: The MIT Press.

Teece, D. J., Pisano, G., & Shuen, A. (1997). Dynamic capabilities and strategic management. *Strategic Management Journal, 18*(7), 509–533.

The U.K. Cabinet Office (2013/2005). *Responding to emergencies: The U.K. Central Government response. Concept of operations*. Retrieved from https://assets.publishing.service.uk.govCONOPs_incl_revised_chapter24_Apr-13.pdf.

Tushman, M. L., & Romanelli, E. (1985). Organizational evolution: A metamorphosis model of convergence and reorientation. In L. L. Cummings & B. M. Staw (Eds.), *Research in organizational behavior* (Vol. 7, pp. 171–222). JAI Press: Greenwich and London.

United Nations Department of Economic and Social Affairs. (2018). *2018 Revision of world urbanization prospects*. New York: United Nations.

Walker, J., & Cooper, M. (2011). Generalogies of resilience: From systems ecology to the political economy of crisis adaptation. *Security Dialogue, 42*(2). https://doi.org/10.1177/0967010611399616.

Weick, K. E. (1976). Educational organizations as loosely coupled systems. *Administrative Science Quarterly, 21*(1), 1–19.

Wernerfelt, B. (1984). A resource-based view of the firm. *Strategic Management Journal, 5*(2), 171–180.

Wernerfelt, B. (2016). *Adaptation, specialization, and the theory of the firm: Foundations of the resource-based view.* Cambridge: Cambridge University Press.

Williamson, O. (1979). Transaction cost economics: The governance of contractual relations. *Journal of Law and Economics, 22*(2), 233–261.

Witt, U. (1987). *Individualistische Grundlagen einer evolutorischen Öconomic,* Tübingen: Mohr Siebeck.

Yamagata, Y., & Maruyama, H. (Eds.). (2016). *Urban resilience: Transformative approach.* Switzerland: Springer International.

Zahra, S. A. (1996). Governance, ownership, and corporate entrepreneurship: The moderating impact of industry technological opportunities. *The Academy of Management Journal, 39*(6), 1713–1735.

Zahra, S. A., Neubaum, D. O., & Hayton, J. C. (2016). *Handbook of research on corporate entrepreneurship.* Cheltenham and Northampton: Edward Elgar.

Ziter, C. D., Pedersen, E. J., Kucharik, C. J., & Turner, M. G. (2019). Scale-dependent interactions between tree canopy cover and impervious surfaces reduce daytime urban heat during summer. *Proceedings of the National Academy of Sciences,* 201817561. https://doi.org/10.1073/pnas.181756 1116.

CHAPTER 2

Urban Resilience and Opportunity Identification of Social Entrepreneurs

1   WHY URBAN RESILIENCE MATTERS?

This chapter pursues the research question by focusing on the facilitators and constraints of science-intensive organizations for the purpose of this study. The research question of this study is to seek factors and mechanisms that enable science-intensive organizations to contribute to broadening beneficiaries of science by science in urban resilience settings. This chapter highlights factors that encourage and discourage potential anchors from redefining their technological and economic elements of science-based projects. The main theoretical bases are the market structure of technologies (Sutton, 1998) and the resource allocation process model (Bower, 1970; Eisenmann & Bower, 2000). The particular attention is on the firms with Mark II sciences. Then, it points out the need for new attributes of industrial sciences, particularly for environmental materials.

As previously stated, the urban revitalization in the1990s contributed to reversing the vicious cycle of reinforced poverty and disadvantage in the urban areas (Giloth, 2004; Jargowski, 2003). The Schumpeterian Mark I firms (biotechnology) and those in the new Variation-Intensive category (information communication technology) worked as drivers to this trend.

Meanwhile, social enterprises (Carter, 2004) found opportunities to support isolated groups with a well-defined business model (Carter, 2004;

© The Author(s), under exclusive license to
Springer Nature Switzerland AG 2021
E. Okada, *Management of Science-Intensive Organizations*,
https://doi.org/10.1007/978-3-030-64042-2_2

40 E. OKADA

Giloth, 2004). However, setting aside from exceptional cases (Carter, 2004; Kanter, 1999), the isolation remained.

This isolation is partly because of the mutual misunderstanding between social enterprises and large corporations (Kanter, 1999), whose collaboration is vital to resolving inclusive resilience issues. The source of misunderstanding is the lack of connectivity between potential anchor corporations, rapidly growing entrepreneur firms, and social enterprises. Even when corporations have the potential to become anchors, social enterprises often avoid them. Then, many less-resourced social enterprises have missed opportunities to scale-up. Without the scale-up, they will not be able to encompass broader beneficiaries in their scope.

There are good reasons why the connectivity lacks among them. Potential anchors belong to either Schumpeterian Mark II or Dynamic Increasing Return (hereafter, DIR) categories by Niosi (2000). Their industrial sciences necessitate intensified R&D towards outcomes, requring firms, requring firms to have the standard of doing the business. However, their size and contents rarely match the target of social enterprises.

Second, when it comes to issues on the social enterprise size, the umbrella term of "social" tends to invite misunderstanding (Carter, 2004; Kanter, 1999). Social enterprises have a well-defined business model. This point differentiates them from charity organizations (Carter, 2004). Despite this difference, what makes things complicated is that some governmental agencies classify many social enterprises as a public charity just for administrative reasons (see Appendix). However, those who are not familiar with administrative procedures tend to regard that all social enterprises are a charity mistakenly. This situation impedes den Hertog (2000)'s ideal of knowledge circulation among heterogeneous institutions.

Issues of cities are essential since cities' agglomeration provides opportunities and cultural exchange spaces. However, cities' physical connectivity and density that characterize their advantage also place challenges. According to the 2018 Report of the United Nations (UN) Department of Economic and Social Affairs (DESA), two out of three in the global population are likely to be living in urban areas by the year 2050. As the swelling populations will place extra demands on both resources and services in urban areas, many countries will face challenges meeting their growing urban needs (UN, 2018). The Report is sending more alert to resourceless countries. However, resource-rich countries that have long faced common problems will continue to face if they leave things undone.

Remarkably, recent economic and societal disparity forges people to live in locations where environmental pollutants exacerbate the gap in many advanced economic countries. This condition reinforces the disparity by affecting physical functioning. Social mobility has stagnated in OECD countries [Organization for Economic Cooperation and Development (OECD), 2018], so the disparity persists, causing a lack of sustainability.[1]

This chapter will understand facilitators and constraints to include specific populations to the dynamic trends of resilience. Theoretical bases are the escalation model of new firms (Sutton, 1998) and the resource allocation process model (Bower & Gilbert, 2005). Then, it will map social companies in the new science categorization. It will then suggest enhancing theoretical bases to frame academic institutions, established organizations, and entrepreneur firms.

2   Facilitators

2.1   Structural and Strategic Contexts of Anchor Corporations

Urban resilience necessitates the anchor organizations as a sufficient condition (Orr & Topa, 2006). However, the anchors roles do not occur automatically. The anchor roles require them to reduce resources that have led them to the current stable conditions. Particularly, firms with Mark II sciences necessitate concentrated R&D to remain in the market (Sutton, 1998. Also see, Arthur, 1994; Kaldor,1972; Niosi, 2000).

Other things being equal, the acceptance of anchor roles has risks to conflict with existing intangibles that provide organizations productive services. Customers' preferences are the one of examples (Christensen & Bower, 1996). Emerging science itself is not a productive service. Science has to be converted to technological capabilities through organizational processes of discovery and application. What provides firms with technological capabilities are the unalienable resources accumulated around routines (Choi & Millar, 2005; von Krogh, Ichijo, & Nonaka, 2000; Nelson & Winter, 1982; Pisano, 1990). R&D units of the firms form

---

[1] A notable example is the air-related infection such as the COVID-19 that affected vulnerable populations who handled essential supply.

these resources through several sources, including interaction with manufacturing units and core customers. However, the responsiveness to the existing core customers often screens out the external opportunities from emerging sciences (Christensen & Bower, 1996).

Also, introduction of new products that contain emerging sciences usually forges them to give up the scale economies, at least in the initial stage (see Saviotti, 1996). The adjustment will require organizational restructuring that affects established coordination pathways and routines (Caves, 2007/1982).

Despite these conflicts, there are forces to urge established companies to allocate resources to emerging sciences: they are the structural and strategic contexts (Bower, 1970; Bower & Gilbert, 2005; Christensen & Bower, 1996; Eisenmann & Bower, 2000). Notably, the acceptance of the anchor roles mainly come from the strategic corporate renewal (Covin & Miles, 1999; Kuratko & Covin, 2015; Zahra, Neubaum, & Heiton, 2016) associated with their capabilities.

Potential anchors usually have a complex organization form, typically, M-Form. The project decision processes of M-Forms construct of the (re)definition and selection spectrums (Bower & Gilbert, 2005). What is critical for contemporary M-Forms is the definition spectrum. It contains components such as awareness, logic, and behaviors (Bower, 1970). Among them, logic is a critical element (see, Prahalad & Bettis, 1986), especially for redefining technological and economic factors.

The process of definition originates from a gap between the current business position and where its leadership believes it needs to be (Bower & Gilbert, 2005; Cyert & March, 1963). The desired position emerges from the awareness of emerging technologies' potential superior quality (Sutton, 1998) and internal and external critiques (Bower & Gilbert, 2005). The then initiated processes will result in a strategic response of top management that accompanies the commitment to the project and change of resource allocation patterns (Bower & Gilbert, 2005).

Then, Schumpeterian Mark I and Variation-Intensive firms not only were a driving force of the 1990s' urban resilience. They also are the external structural contexts that affect the resource allocation processes of established firms.

2.1.1 An Example of Structural Contexts: Monoclonal Antibodies

Examples include monoclonal antibodies, immune system proteins created in the laboratories (National Cancer Institute, 2019). They have generated a wide variety of applications to autoimmune diseases and cancers in the Mark I industrial science category. The critical discovery for the application comes from Kohler and Milstein (1975). Their origin dates back to the 1890s when two immunologists discovered the immune system. They found its character of protective antitoxins in the animals' blood exposed to diphtheria (Rajewsky, 2019). Despite their crucial role in adaptive immunity, the inability to produce molecularly defined, homogeneous antibodies with predetermined specificity was a significant hurdle for broader applications to overcome. Kohler and Milstein (1975) overcame this major hurdle (Rajewsky, 2019).

The monoclonal antibody achieved the first milestone in 1997. It is the FDA approval of monoclonal antibody-based blood cancer treatment (Smithsonian Institution). This achievement is by a biotechnology company founded in the mid-1970s.

Meanwhile, numerous entrepreneurial firms have been involved in the process, or created several supportive services (see, Pisano, 2006), such as the antibody development services, antibody production services, and cell-line development services. Simultaneously, the monoclonal-antibody-based research tools explored a new logic of pharmacology (see, Pisano, 1990), which obliged established firms to allocate more resources to new sciences.

On the other hand, with a few exceptions, entrepreneur firms usually lack resources to produce and market therapeutic products (see, Ryan, Freeman, & Hybel, 1995). Such resource constraints on both sides lead to form several arrangements of internalization, such as M&A (Mock & Yueng, 1991; Pisano, 1990; Williamson, 1991a), joint venture, and other noncontractual alliances (Abernathy & Clark, 1980; Buckley & Casson, 1976; Caves, 2007/1982; Pisano, 1990, 2006; Teece, 1986). The contractual schema also determines overseas technology transfer styles to differentiate technological performance (Caves, 2007/1982; Davidson & MacFetridge, 1984; Horstmann & Markusen, 1987; Katz & Shapiro, 1985; Teece, 1986; Telesio, 1979).

These organizational forms provide opportunities for taking anchor roles to established corporations.

2.2 External Disturbance and Corporate Entrepreneurship

2.2.1 Corporate Entrepreneurship

As examined in Chapter 4, corporate entrepreneurship is the process whereby an individual or a group of individuals, in association with an existing organization, create a new organization or redefine, rejuvenate, renew, and transform capabilities within that organization (Bower, 1970; Covin & Miles, 1999; Kuratko & Covin, 2015; Sharma & Chrisman, 1999; Zahra et al., 2016). Entrepreneurial activity of established firms encompasses two categories of phenomena: corporate venturing and strategic renewal (Kuratko & Covin, 2015). The former consists of the entrepreneurial phenomena in which existing organizations create, add, or invest in new businesses. The latter encompasses the process, contents, and outcomes of rejuvenation or substitution of an organization's attributes that can significantly affect its long-term prospects (Agawal & Helfat, 2009). Its processes involve the domain redefinition, organizational rejuvenation, regeneration, renewal, business model reconstruction, and transformation (Covin & Miles, 1999; Kuratko & Covin, 2015; Zahra et al., 2016) associated with their organizational capabilities.

The critical starting point of the process is the redefinition. This construct overlaps the resource allocation process model.

2.2.2 Corporate Entrepreneurship by Crossing Borders

Corporate entrepreneurship also occurs by crossing borders. This form incredibly fit the acceptance of anchors' roles since partnering with domestic competitors often invokes complication of rivalry (Caves, 2007/1982).

Firms can enhance their values through the international market expansion of (a group of) products (Alcacer, Cantwell, & Piscitello, 2016; Caves, 2007/1982; Cockburn, Henderson & Stern, 2000; Dunning, 1979; Eisenmann & Bower, 2005). This tendency is multiplied when the (group of) products necessitate a significant investment and low commercial probability. Without market expansion, the products that apply for a small segment of customers or low-income populations will drain up companies' resources. As the environmental material sciences belong to market failure areas, it is worthwhile to examine the corporate entrepreneurship process that accompanies overseas expansion.

A global multimedia industry provides a representative case for the investigation (Eisenmann, 2000; Eisenmann & Bower, 2000). Below, while reviewing Eisenmann and Bower (2000, 2005), this study will consider the process including overseas expansion. Companies that produce and distribute theatrical films and television programming (hereafter, content) tend to be linked in a vertical structure and compete globally. Content production requires a large amount of risky investment while only their small shares are commercially successful (Eisenmann & Bower, 2005). To spread fixed production costs, content studios must secure global distribution through distributors. However, technologies and regulatory landscape evolved rapidly in the 1980s and 1990s. There emerged several types of delivery channels enabled by Variation-Intensive technologies. Meanwhile, established distributors periodically faced the threat of substitution (Eisenmann & Bower, 2005).

Such a threat constitutes the primary factor that forms the external structural contexts for M-form firms to further expand the market globally.

Firms' growth process consists of contractual relations of heterogeneous assets that determine boundaries of control (Caves, 2007/1982). They avoid the market incompleteness for firm-specific assets by vertically internalizing the market (Buckley & Casson, 1976; Caves, 2007/1982; Chandler, 1992; Coase, 1937; Dunning, 1979; Rugman, 1981; Williamson, 1979). Elements that affect the boundaries are codability of intangibles, ex-ante and ex-post monitoring, and haggling costs (Coase, 1937; Buckley & Casson, 1976; Kogut & Zander, 1993; Riordan & Williamson, 1985; Rugman, 1981). Well-defined proprietary assets provide firms with a condition also for horizontal cross-border expansion because (i) intangibles' marginal usage cost is minimal, and (ii) their quasi-universal contents are not bound to a specific location (Caves, 2007/1982; Dunning, 1979). Thus, the structure of multinational companies[2] emerges (Caves, 2007/1982; Teece, 1985).

From a knowledge-flow perspective, motivation differs between established and new firms. The former conduct cross-border R&D to exploit their home-country-based capabilities and expand the market.[3] The latter augments firms' home-based capacity through foreign spillovers

---

[2] In following Teece (1985) and Caves (2007/1982), this study adopts the definition of a multinational enterprise as a firm that controls and manages production establishments in at least two countries.

[3] The product life cycle model (Vernon, 1966) is a classic form of home-based exploitation.

46 E. OKADA

(Kummerle, 1999, 2005. Also see, Alcacer & Chang, 2007; Anand & Kogut, 1997; Porter, 2000). Thus, motivation depends on their size and experiences (Kuemmerle, 1996, 1999).

2.2.3 Subsequent Competition that Affects Types of Entrepreneurship

In any case, firms encounter replication dynamics (Saviotti, 1996) from competitors at the location.

In global media companies, the content distributor usually must build infrastructure in advance of demand, even using unproven technologies (Eisenmann & Bower, 2005). Content production and distribution companies then limit an operating risk by vertical integration. This form results in facilitating the entrepreneur firms' access to new distribution channels. Then, the integration provides proprietary assets for the content distributor, which results in foreclosed competition (Eisenmann & Bower, 2005). This competition has the potential to limit the replication dynamics from competitors at the location.

At the same time, this mode can also facilitate the entrepreneurs' innovative content production under a fragmented technology market. Such behaviors may lead them to outperform incumbents (Sutton, 1998).

The above two globalization types represent theoretical conflict: The former's theoretical underpinning is the governance efficiency based on transaction cost economics (Caves, 2007/1982; Williamson, 1979). That of the latter is the market structure of technology by Sutton (1998) in which, under a certain condition, entrepreneurial firms have the potential to outperform established firms through innovative products.

Note that, in Orr and Topa (2006)'s analysis, the former is the facilitator of anchors that is the sufficient condition of urban resilience. From OECD (2004)'s perspective, the latter is the facilitator of entrepreneur firms that is a driving force of urban resilience. What is different is the starting point of theorizing and focused industrial sciences.

In the latter, the technological performance escalation occurs as a function of R&D elasticity (β) and economies of scope (σ). The former (β) relates R&D expenditures to product quality. In other words, it represents consumers' willingness to pay to the upgraded technical performance R&D brings. The latter (σ) measures the strength of the links between different R&D trajectories or submarkets that reflect the values of scope economy (Sutton, 1998).

In other words,

$\alpha\ (\beta, \sigma)$.

α: escalation parameter

β: R&D elasticity

σ: scope economies

More specifically, R&D elasticity, β, constitutes of (a) the impacts of R&D on technical performances, and (b) consumers' willingness to pay for a rise in technical performance. However, consumers' willingness to pay does not necessarily reward improved technological performances in market failure areas, such as environmental material sciences. Also, the organizational arrangement may differ depending on emerging sciences' types. Therefore, it again needs to investigate emerging sciences categorization by Niosi (2000).

2.2.4 Again, Categorization of Industrial Sciences

Scientific breakthroughs generate new science categories by recombining similar or distant disciplines (see Whitley, 2000). They impact several dimensions of technology development. In reviewing previous literature, Niosi (2000) explores a new typology of science-based industries beyond the Schumpeterian Mark I and II categorization. Firms' strategic responses to breakthroughs created new categories and the industrial dynamics (Niosi, 2000. Also, see Arthur, 1994; Kaldor, 1972; Nelson & Winter, 1982; Saviotti, 1996). One is "Dynamic Increasing Return" (DIR) category, and the other, the "Variation-Intensive" category.

When new technologies combine with facilitated access (Hilgartner & Randt-Rauf, 1994; Hilgartner, 1995), they introduce a new level of uncertainty to the innovation processes (Kuemmerle, 2005). Firstly, they alter the desired composition of products (Anderson & Tushman, 1990; Nelson & Winter, 1982; O'Reilly & Tushman, 2008). Secondly, they induce a variation in the product market.

Such an evolving structure (Newman, 1978) necessitates multidivisional firms to redefine their domain, integrate common resources across units, and restructure the coordination processes and governance (Caves, 2007/1982, pp. 93–94, 100–102; Eisenmann & Bower, 2005).

Theoretically, such alteration affects the input factors' construct to produce firms' proprietary knowledge (Dunning, 1979). It subsequently invokes the long-term change of organizational capabilities (Teece, Pisano, & Shuen, 1997), particularly for established multinationals.

When established firms face disturbance, the existing coordination patterns differentiate the ways of adaptation and degree of persistence (Caves, 2007/1982; Eisenmann & Bower, 2000; see, Feldman, 2000; Nelson & Winter, 1982). One way to adapt to the market variation is strategic integration[4] (Burgelman & Doz, 1997; Eisenmann & Bower, 2005). This arrangement usually necessitates a corporate center to play an active role in opportunity identification, redefinition, cross-unit resource integration, and stretch into new spaces (Eisenmann & Bower, 2005).

Meanwhile, despite the scientific evolution, pharmaceutical, chemical, and supercomputer industries appear to have reinforced their concentration.

This concentration derives from their market characteristics that require a high intensity of R&D and specialized marketing activities (Niosi, 2000; Scherer, 1984; Sutton, 1998). Only companies that can tolerate that intensity can continue to play in the market with unknown risks (Arthur, 1994; Kaldor, 1972; Niosi, 2000; Sutton, 1998).

In the pharmaceutical industry, new inventions in new technological regimes (Dosi, 1982; Melarba & Orsenigo, 1996; Niosi, 2000) created variety to the pharmacology (Niosi, 2000; Pisano, 2006) in combining with academic discoveries and governments' supportive infrastructures (Niosi, 2000; Ryan et al. 1995; Teece, 1986). Under this condition, established pharmaceuticals concern over the appropriability of intangibles and a small-number-bargaining-hazard. These concerns led them to procure Mark I's discoveries through internalization (Pisano, 1990).

Therefore, DIR pharmaceutical multinationals have a reason to be anchors of Mark I biotech firms.

On the other hand, organizational behaviors in Mark II sciences have not thoroughly been investigated. Therefore, in starting from the mapped R&D behaviors of firms, the following chapters will examine foreign multinationals that invested in emerging environmental material sciences.

---

[4] Strategic integration involves the combination of resources from different unit to create new businesses and operational integration. On the other hand, operational integration involves routinely interdependent activities such as joint procurement. See Burgelman and Doz (1997), Eisenmann and Bower (2005).

3 Constraints

3.1 Internal Structural and Strategic Contexts

Setting aside from external constraints such as regulatory limits, internal structural, and strategic contexts often pose constraints to M-Forms.

The organizational growth provides multinationals not only with the scale and scope economies and R&D intensity, but also the organizational complexity. Once established governance and coordination patterns persist (Bower, 2017; Caves, 2007/1982). Organizational routines that construct organizational capabilities (Nelson & Winter, 1982; Feldman, 2000) also form internal forces at unit manager levels. When too much decision-making powers are delegated to unit or subunit level managers, the dynamics of defensive behaviors tend to mitigate necessary, risky investment (Eisenmann & Bower, 2000; Leonard-Barton, 1992).

3.2 Resource Allocation to Risky Investment

Significantly, they constrain strategic integration that requires putting resources by crossing different units (Eisenmann & Bower, 2000; Eisenmann, 2000; Leonard-Barton, 1992; Kuemmerle, 2005). These constraints moderate potential anchors' investment, particularly in the market failure areas.

In general, the corporate planning office also is reluctant to support risky projects that require strategic integration. It is because risky plans have a higher probability of failure that can negatively affect their career (Eisenmann & Bower, 2005).

Unit managers may be more sensitive to a threat since they are closer to the frontline. However, strategic integration is nonroutine activity. It conflicts with the unit managers' job description to design standard operation procedures. Also, division managers may not monitor remote markets where opportunities that require strategic integration emerge. It is particularly so when such options are in an emerging field (Eisenmann & Bower, 2005; Hamel & Prahalad, 1993).

These internal contexts constrain established multinationals' behaviors to accept anchors' roles that involve emerging sciences, particularly in foreign countries.

4   Governance and Boundaries

4.1   Governance Structure as the Internal Structural Contexts

The internal structural contexts encompass governance structure as a part.

Then, one way to overcome the constraints is to introduce anticipation to the governance mechanisms.

From managerial economics viewpoints, governance has the following dimensions (Filatochev, Poulsen, & Bell, 2018) (a) The choice of an organizational boundary that divides internal and external control (Buckley & Casson, 1976; Macher, 2006; Pisano, 1990; Riordan & Williamson, 1985; Teece, 1986; Williamson, 1979, 1991), (b) board composition (Berle & Means, 1932; Chandler, 1977, 1992; Freeland, 1996) and (c) the ownership structure (Alcacer et al., 2016; Eisenmann, 2002). Among them, the integration of anticipation or Responsible Research and Innovation (RRI) has a relevance to the choice of the organizational boundary since the inclusive anticipation requires the considerations on the organizational boundary.

Previous literature (Abernathy & Clark, 1980; Kuemmerle, 1996; Pisano, 1990, 2006; Teece, 1986) has explored boundary decisions of science-intensive firms by basing on the theories of internalization, transaction cost economics, and contractual schema (Caves, 2007/1982; Chandler, 1992; Coase, 1937; Riordan & Williamson, 1985; Williamson, 1985, 1991a, 2005). One of the most significant attributes that determine a firm's boundary is asset specificity (Williamson, 1979. Also see, Buckley & Casson, 1976; Caves, 2007/1982).

More specifically, established firms' concerns in deciding boundaries are a small-number-bargaining-hazard and appropriability problems (Pisano, 1990). Small-number-bargaining-hazard emerges from the lack of the market in the field. Appropriability is the capacity of the firm to retain the added value it creates for its benefit (Kay, 1995; Pisano, 1990). Who benefits from the added value depends on the firm's decisions, the market structure, and the added values' sources (Kay, 1995).

In emerging industrial sciences, the scope of protection of property rights is an essential constituent of the structural contexts (see, Teece, 1986; Williamson, 1991a, 1991b). A problem for Mark IIs is that they traditionally have protected intellectual property by know-how and process.

As the protection by know-how suppresses the disclosure of inventions, the integration of anticipation may be more useful for the governance of environmental material sciences.

The second is to abstract new attributes. A couple of Mark II cases have emerged that alliance with Mark I and Variant-Intensive entrepreneurs (Chapter 5). The observation will lead to new attributes that also support the environmental material sciences.

Third, it is necessary to investigate constraints in translating discoveries into applications in environmental material sciences. Science-stage discoveries are not necessarily the firms' productive service resources. R&D units usually conduct follow-on discoveries to translate them to applications. However, there may be constraints outside of their organizations (see Chapters 3 and 5).

Forth, related to the above, it is necessary to examine organization forms that will facilitate the translation process. The organizational forms include the adoption of intermediate institutions and joint research with academic knowledge-intensive organizations (KIOs). The common aspect is to create loosely coupled interfaces between external constituents.

4.2   Loose Coupling

The evolutionary urban resilience theory also uses the loose coupling's concept (Chapter 1. See Coafee & Lee, 2016). It is a linkage between internal and external variants to enhance the system's responsiveness and, ultimately, the evolutionary trajectories of organisms (Coaffee & Lee, 2016; Heller, 1999; Orton & Weick, 1990; Pike et al., 2010; Sundbo & Gallouj, 2000). In management studies (Orton and Weick, 1990), loose recoupling allows any system to act on a technical level, which is closed to outside forces and an institutional level, which is open to external forces. The system can then produce stability at a technical level and flexibility at an institutional level (Orton & Weick, 1990).

Such a system enables an organism to fit itself into the environment, that is, adaptation (Holling, 1996). It is to adjust its responses to changing external structural contexts and internal processes. The adaptation process encompasses learning and the recombination of the internal capacity and the internal and external knowledge (see, Coaffee & Lee, 2016; Folke et al., 2010; Folke et al., 2011; Teece et al., 1997).

For science-intensive organizations, a significant part of knowledge derives from emerging sciences. Organizations that work on scientific knowledge have become more specialized in the autonomy of science (Clark, 1983; Orton & Weick, 1990). Therefore, the loosely coupled structure is an inevitable consequence of scientific knowledge-intensive organizations (Clark, 1983; Orton & Weick, 1990).

The ambiguity and external and internal fragmentation (Anderson & Tushman, 1990; Orton & Weick, 1990) also cause organizations to adopt the recoupling structure (Orton & Weick, 1990).

Among these causations, the external fragmentation that takes the form of dispersed stimuli (Orton & Weick, 1990) does not fit the traditional chemical industrial science. However, external fragmentation that takes incompatible expectations (Orton & Weick, 1990) are confronting Mark II chemicals. Such expectations can oblige the Mark IIs to sense dispersed stimuli (see, Chapter 5). Then, they have gradually come to incorporate the loose coupling into their innovation systems.

The following chapters will further examine managerial and governance aspects of science-intensive organizations that are contributing to urban resilience.

Appendix

See Table 1.

Table 1 Classification for administrative purposes (after the 1969 Private Foundation Act)

Legal classification by Internal Revenue Service	Outline of definition by the U.S. Internal Revenue Service	Primary constituents
For-profit firms		Firms
Charitable organizations	Charitable organizations organized and operate exclusively for religious, charitable, scientific, testing for public safety, literary, education, and other specific purposes and meet the requirements of Internal Revenue Code Section 503c3	Church University Medical institution Research Institute Public health-related research institute Literary collection School Museum
Private foundation	Charitable organizations, unless it falls into one of the categories specifically excluded from the definition of that term (referred to in section 509(a))	Same as the above, excluding institutions that have broad public support or actively function in a supporting relationship to such organizations; Certain charitable trusts
Political organizations under the Internal Revenue Code Section 527	Political organizations	A party, committee, association, fund, or other organization organized and operated primarily for the purpose of accepting contributions or making expenditures for an exempt function
Other Nonprofits	Social welfare organizations Civic leagues Social clubs Labor organizations Business leagues	An organization that operates an airport that serves the general public in the area where there is no other airport; An organization that tries to encourage the industrial development and relieve unemployment in the area by making loans to businesses so they will relocate to the area, among others

Source The U.S. Internal Revenue Service with modification

References

Abernathy, W. J., & Clark, K. B. (1980). Innovation: Mapping the winds of creative destruction. *Research Policy, 14*(1), 3–22.

Agawal, R., & Helfat, C. E. (2009). Strategic renewal of organizations. *Organization Science, 20*(2), 281–293.

Alcacer, J., Cantwell, J., & Piscitello, L. (2016). Internationalization in the information age: A new era for places, firms, and international business networks? *Journal of International Business Studies, 47*, 499–512.

Alcacer, J., & Chang, W. (2007). Location strategies and knowledge spillovers. *Management Science, 53*(5), 760–776.

Anand, J., & Kogut, B. (1997). Technological capabilities of countries, firm rivalry and foreign direct investment. *Journal of International Business Studies, 28*(3), 445–465.

Anderson, P., & Tushman, M. L. (1990). Technological discontinuities and dominant designs: A cyclical model of technological change. *Administrative Science Quarterly, 35*(4), 604–633.

Arthur, W. B. (1994). *Increasing returns and path dependency in the economy.* Ann Arbor: University of Michigan Press.

Berle, A., & Means, G. (1932). *The modern corporation and private property.* New Jersey: Transaction Publishers.

Bower, J. L. (1970). *Managing the resource allocation process.* Boston: Division of Research, Graduate School of Business Administration, Harvard University.

Bower, J. L. (2017). Managing resource allocation: Personal reflections from a managerial perspective. *Journal of Management, 43*(8). https://doi.org/10.1177/0149206316675929.

Bower, J. L., & Gilbert, C. G. (2005). *From resource allocation to strategy.* New York and Oxford: Oxford University Press.

Buckley, F. J., & Casson, M. (1976). *The future of the multinational enterprises.* London: Macmillan.

Burgelman, B. A., & Doz, Y. (1997). Complex strategic integration in the lean multibusiness corporation. *INSEAD Working Paper, 97/03/SM*, as cited by Eisemnann, T. R., & Bower, L. J. (2005).

Carter, A. (2004). Social enterprises and urban rebuilding in Europe. In OECD (Organization for Economic Cooperation and Development) *Entrepreneurship: A catalyst of urban regeneration* (pp. 150–199). Paris: OECD.

Caves. (2007/1982). *Multinational enterprise and economic analysis,* (3rd Ed.) Cambridge: Cambridge University Press.

Chandler, A. (1977). *The visible hand: The managerial revolution in American business.* Cambridge: Belknap Press.

Chandler, A. (1992). What is a firm? A Historical Perspective. *European Economic Review., 36*, 483–492.

Choi, C., & Millar, C. (2005). *Knowledge entanglement*. Hampshire and New York: Palgrave Macmillan.

Christensen, C. M., & Bower, J. L. (1996). Customer power, strategic investment, and the failure of leading firms. *Strategic Management Journal, 17*(3), 197–218.

Clark, B. R. (1983). *The higher education system: Academic organization in cross-national perspective*. Berkeley: University of California Press.

Coaffee, J., & Lee, P. (2016). *Urban resilience: Planning risk, crisis and uncertainty*. London: Palgrave.

Coase, R. H. (1937). The nature of the firm. *Economica, 4*(16), 386–405.

Cockburn, I. M., Henderson, R. M., & Stern, S. (2000). Untangling the origins of competitive advantage. *Strategic Management Journal, 21*, 1123–1145.

Covin, J. G., & Miles, M. P. (1999). Corporate entrepreneurship and the pursuit of competitive advantage. *Entrepreneurship Theory and Practice, 23*(3), 47–63.

Cyert, R. M., & March, J. G. (1963). *Behavioral theory of the firm*. New Jersey: Prentice Hall.

Davidson, W. H., & MacFetridge, D. G. (1984). International technology transactions and the theory of the firm. *Journal of Industrial Economics* (March), 253–264.

den Hertog, P. (2000). Knowledge intensive business services as co-producers of innovation. *International Journal of Innovation Management, 4*(4), 491–528.

Dosi, G. (1982). Technological paradigms and technological trajectories: A suggested interpretation of determinants and directions of technological change. *Research Policy, 11*, 147–162.

Dunning, J. H. (1979). Trade, location of economic activity and the MNE: A search for an eclectic approach. In B. Ohlin, P. Hesselborn, & P. M. Wijkman (Eds.), *The international allocation of economic activity*. London and Basingstoke: Macmillan.

Eisenmann, T. R. (2000). The U.S. cable television industry, 1948–1995: Managerial capitalism in eclipse. *Business History Review, 74*(1): 1–40.

Eisenmann, T. R., & Bower, J. L. (2000). The entrepreneurial M-Form: Strategic integration in global media firms. *Organization Science, 11*(3), 348–355.

Eisenmann, T. R., & Bower, J. L. (2005). The entrepreneurial M-Form: A case study of strategic integration in a global media company. In J. L. Bower & C. G. Gilbert (Eds.), *From resource allocation to strategy* (pp. 307–329). Oxford: Oxford University Press.

Feldman, M. S. (2000). Organizational routine as a source of continuous change. *Organization Science, 11*(6), 629–661.

Filatochev, I., Poulsen, A., & Bell, R. (2018). Corporate governance of a multinational enterprise: Firm, industry and institutional perspectives. *Journal of Corporate Finance, 3*(3). https://doi.org/10.1016/jjcorpfin.2018.02.004.

Folke, C., Carpenter, S. R., Walker, B., Scheffer, M., Chapin, T., & Rockstrom, J. (2010). Resilience thinking: Integrating resilience, adaptability and transformativity. *Ecology and Society, 15*(4), 20. Retrieved from http://www.eco logyandsociety.org/vol15/iss4/art20/.

Folke, C., Jansson, A., Rockström, J., Olsson, P., Carpenter, S.R., Chapin III, F.S., ... Wesley, F. (2011). Reconnecting to the biosphere. *Ambio, 26,* 719–738.

Freeland, R. F. (1996). The myth of the M-Form? Governance, consent, and organizational change. *American Journal of Sociology, 102*(2), 483–526.

Giloth, R. (2004). Social enterprise and urban rebuilding in the United States. *OECD, Entrepreneurship: A catalyst for urban regeneration* (pp. 135–157). Paris: OECD Publishing.

Hamel, G., & Prahalad, C. (1993). Strategy as stretch and leverage. *Harvard Business Review, 71*(2), 75–84.

Heller, T. (1999). Loosely coupled systems in corporate entrepreneurship. Imagining and management the innovation project/host organization interface. *Entrepreneurship Theory and Practice, 24*(2), 25–31.

Hilgartner, S. (1995). The human genome project. In S. Jasanoff, G. Markle, T. Pinch, & J. Petersen (Eds.), *Handbook of science, technology and society* (pp. 302–315). Newbury Park: Sage.

Hilgartner, S., & Randt-Rauf, S. J. (1994). Data access, ownership, and control. *Knowledge: Creation, Diffusion, Utilization, 15,* 355–372.

Holling, C. S. (1996), Engineering resilience versus ecological resilience. In P. C. Schultz (Ed.), *Engineering within ecological constraints* (pp. 31–44). Washington, DC: National Academy Press.

Horstmann, I., & Marcusen, J. (1987). Strategic investments and the development of multinationals. *International Economic Review, 28*(1), 109–121.

Kaldor, N. (1972). The irrelevance of equilibrium economics. *Economic Journal, 82,* 1237–1255.

Kanter, R. M. (1999). From spare change to real change: The social sector as beta site for business innovation. *Harvard Business School in Innovation* (pp. 153–177). Boston: Harvard Business School Press.

Katz, M. L., & Shapiro, C. (1985). Network externalities, competition, and compatibility. *The American Economic Review, 75*(3), 424–440.

Kay, J. (1995). *Foundation of corporate success: How business strategies add values.* Oxford: Oxford University Press.

Kogut, B., & Zander, U. (1993). Knowledge of the firm and the evolutionary theory of the multinational corporation. *Journal of International Business Studies,* 24(Fourth Quarter), 625–645.

Kohler, G., & Milstein, C. (1975). Continuous cultures of fused cells secreting antibody of predefined specificity. *Nature, 256,* 495–497.

Kuemmerle, W. (1996). *Home base and foreign direct investment in research and development: An investigation into the international allocation of research activity by multinational enterprises.* Doctoral dissertation, Harvard Business School, Cambridge, MA.

Kuemmerle, W. (2005). The process of international expansion: Comparing established firms and entrepreneurial start-ups. In J. L. Bower & C. G. Gilbert (Eds.), *From resource allocation to strategy* (pp. 176–204). Oxford: Oxford University Press.

Kummerle, W. (1999). The drivers of foreign direct investment into research and development: An empirical investigation. *Journal of International Business Studies, 30*(1), 1–24.

Kuratko, D. F., & Covin, D. G. (2015). Forms of corporate entrepreneurship. In C. L. Cooper (Ed.), *Wiley Encyclopedia of management.* Chichester: Wiley. https://doi.org/10.1002/9781118785317.weom030016.

Leonard-Barton, D. (1992). Core capabilities and core rigidities: A paradox in managing new product development. *Strategic Management Journal, 13,* 111–125.

Macher, J. (2006). Technological development and the boundaries of the firm: A knowledge-based examination in semiconductor manufacturing. *Management Science, 52*(6), 826–843.

Malerba, F., & Orsenigo, M. (1996). The dynamics and evolutions of industries. *Industrial and Corporate Change, 5*(1), 51–87.

Mock, R., & Yueng, B. (1991). Why investors value multinationality. *Journal of Business, 64,* 165–187.

National Cancer Institute. (2019). *Monochronal antibodies.* Retrieved from https://www.cancer.gov/about-cancer/treatment/types/immunotherapy/monoclonal-antibodies.

Nelson, R. R., & Winter, S. (1982). *An evolutionary theory of economic change.* Cambridge: Belknap Press.

Newman, H. H. (1978). Strategic groups and the structure-performance relationship. *The Review of Economics and Statistics, 60*(3), 417–427.

Niosi, J. (2000). Science-based industries: New Schumpeterian taxonomy. *Technology in Society, 22,* 429–444.

O'Reilly, C. A., III, & Tushman, M. L. (2008). Ambidexterity as a dynamic capability: Resolving the innovator's dilemma. *Research in Organizational Behavior, 28,* 185–206.

Organization for Economic Cooperation and Development (OECD). (2018). *A broken social elevator? How to promote social nobility.* Paris: OECD.

Orr, J., & Topa, G. (2006). Challenges facing the New York Metropolitan area economy. *Current Issues in Economics and Finance, 12*(1). Retrieved from https://www.newyorkfed.org/medialibrary/media/research/current_issues/ci12-1.pdf.

Orton, J. D., & Weick, K. E. (1990). Loosely coupled systems: A reconceptualization. *Academy of Management Review, 15*(2), 203–223.

Pike, A., Dawley, S., & Tomaney, J. (2010). Resilience, adaptation, and adaptability. *Cambridge Journal of Regions Economy and Society, 3*(1), 59–70.

Pisano, G. P. (1990). The R&D boundaries of the firm: An empirical analysis. *Administrative Science Quarterly, 35*, 153–176.

Pisano, (2006). *Science Business: The Promise, the Reality, and the Future of Biotech.* Boston: Harvard Business School Press.

Porter, M. E. (2000). Location, competition, and economic development: Local clusters in a global economy. *Economic Development Quarterly, 14*(1), 15–34.

Prahalad, C. K., & Bettis, R. A. (1986). The dominant logic: A new linkage between diversity and performance. *Strategic Management Journal, 7*, 485–501.

Rajewsky, K. (2019, November 4). The advent and rise of monoclonal antibodies. Nature.

Riordan, M., & Williamson, O. (1985). Asset specificity and economic organization. *International Journal of Industrial Organization, 3*, 365–378.

Rugman, A. M. (1981). *Inside the multinationals: The economics of internal markets.* London: Croom Helm.

Ryan, A., Freeman, J., & Hybels, R. (1995). Biotechnology firms. In G. R. Caroll & M. T. Hannan (Eds.), *Organizations in industry* (pp. 332–358). New York: Oxford University Press.

Santos, F. M., & Eisenhardt, K. M. (2005). Organizational boundaries and theories of organization. *Organization Science, 16*, 491–508.

Saviotti, P. P. (1996). *Technological evolution, variety and the economy.* Cheltenham: Edward Elgar.

Scherer, F. (1984). *Innovation and growth. Schumpeterian perspectives.* Cambridge: MIT Press.

Schumpeter, J. (1937). *Capitalism, socialism and democracy.* London: Allen & Unwin.

Sharma, P., & Chrisman, J. J. (1999). Toward a reconciliation of the definitional issues in the field of corporate entrepreneurship. *Entrepreneurship Theory and Practice, 23*(3), 11–27.

Smithsonian Institution, Monoclonal antibodies. Retrieved from https://www.si.edu/spotlight/antibody-initiative/monoclonal#ogmt-edan-search-results.

Sundbo, J., & Gallouj, F. (2000). Innovation as a loosely coupled system in services. *International Journal of Services, Technology and Management, 1*(1), 15–36.

Sutton, J. (1998). *Technology and market structure.* Cambridge: The MIT Press.

Teece, D. J. (1985). Multinational enterprise, internal governance, and industrial organization. *The American Economic Review, 75*, 233–238.

Teece, D. J. (1986). Transaction cost economics and the multinational enterprise. *Journal of Economic Behavior & Organization, 7*, 21–45.

Teece, D. J., Pisano, G., & Shuen, A. (1997). Dynamic capabilities and strategic management. *Strategic Management Journal, 18*(7), 509–533.

Telesio, P. (1979). *Technology licensing and multinational enterprises.* New York: Praeger.

United Nations Department of Economic and Social Affairs. (2018). *2018 revision of world urbanization prospects.* New York: United Nations.

Vernon, R. (1966). International investment and international trade in the product cycle. *The Quarterly Journal of Economics, 80*(2), 190–207.

von Krogh, G., Ichijo, K., & Nonaka, I. (2000). *Enabling knowledge creation: How to unlock the mystery of tacit knowledge and release the power of innovation.* Oxford: Oxford University Press.

Whitley, R. (2000). *The intellectual and social organization of science* (2nd ed.). Oxford: Oxford University Press.

Williamson, O. E. (1979). Transaction-cost economics: The governance of contractual relations. *Journal of Law and Economics, 22*, 233–261.

Williamson, O. E. (1991a). Comparative economic organization: The analysis of discrete structural alternatives. *Administrative Science Quarterly, 36*, 269–296.

Williamson, O. E. (1991b). Strategizing, economizing, and economic organization. *Strategic Management Journal, 12*, 75–94.

Williamson, O. E. (1985). *The economic institution of capitalism: Firms, markets and relational contracting.* New York: Free Press.

Williamson, O. E. (2005). Why law, economics, and organization?. *Annual Review of Law and Social Science, 1*(1), 369–396.

Zahra, S. A., Neubaum, D. O., & Heiton, J. C. (2016). Introduction. In S. A. Zahra, D. O. Neubaum, & J. C. Hayton (Eds.), *Handbook of research on corporate entrepreneurship* (pp. 1–9). Cheltenham: Edward Elgar.

CHAPTER 3

Emerging Technologies and Organizations for Urban Resilience

1 EMERGENCE OF NEW TECHNOLOGIES

This chapter investigates the research question from the perspectives of organizational models framed in the previous section. Its objective is to build a rough framework for the further investigation of later chapters. The actors to examine are academic knowledge-intensive organizations (KIOs), established multinationals, and entrepreneur firms. Particular attention is on tensions between those related to Mark II sciences and new environmental material sciences.

This chapter introduces the attributes of "mimic of nature (environment)" and "integration into the design (sustainability)" to address material and environmental sciences. These attributes will shift the tensions related to the Mark II industrial sciences. Later chapters will examine the plausibility of these attributes through the case method.

This study starts with the two conflicting theories that underlie the description of urban resilience by Orr and Topa (2006). They are the escalation model of entrepreneur firms (Sutton, 1998) and transaction-cost-based governance economies (Pisano, 1990; Williamson, 1979). The former model explains why new firms escalate their (group of) products' performance under a specific condition, particularly Variation-Intensive firms. The latter explains whether, why, and how established pharmaceuticals internalize dispersed sources of entrepreneurial discoveries (Pisano,

© The Author(s), under exclusive license to
Springer Nature Switzerland AG 2021
E. Okada, *Management of Science-Intensive Organizations*,
https://doi.org/10.1007/978-3-030-64042-2_3

61

1990; Williamson, 1979). While conflicting each other, both contribute to urban economic resilience when they add a variety to the market.

Variety is the concept that consists of the emergence of new technologies in an economic system. The elements that construct this emergence are actors, activities, organizations that create it, institutions, the types of knowledge, the process, and products (Saviotti, 1996).

Examining these elements will lead to understanding why, by what, and how a set of components characterize a given economic system and what transforms it into another system. In other words, the analysis is to understand the impact of technological change (see, Saviotti, 1996) on systems and their constructs. In following Saviotti (1996) and Solow (1956), this study defines technological change as anything that shifts the production function (Saviotti, 1996; Solow, 1956). A specific condition is necessary for technological changes to add a variety to the economy and contributes to economic growth (Saviotti, 1996).

This chapter's study will investigate how the anchor institutions and academic KIOs relate to emerging and Mark II sciences with the variety in mind. It examines the following dimensions: (a) motivation to invest in emerging sciences, (b) R&D allocation to emerging sciences and performance, and (c) relations with beneficiaries' preferences and economies of scope (Sutton, 1998; Teece, 1986). It will refer to Niosi (2000)'s new typologies for industrial science categories.

This chapter organizes the analysis as follows. The next section investigates the function and pathways of academic KIOs to contribute to urban resilience. The third section examines anchor institutions along with the above-stated elements. Finally, this study frames set conditions for urban resilience by leveraging emerging environmental technologies.

2   ACADEMIC KNOWLEDGE-INTENSIVE ORGANIZATIONS

Knowledge-intensive organizations (KIOs) are defined as entities in which knowledge is the primary production factor and goods offered (European Commission (EC), 2012, p. 6). This comprehensive definition encompasses academic organizations, such as universities and noncommercial research institutes, in the scope. The institutional underpinning that connected academic KIOs to resilience practices is the Bayh-Dole Act (Public Law 86-517 December 12, 1980). Its institutional intentions (35 USC Part II, Chapter 18, Section 200) implicitly encompass the Academic KIOs' contribution to economic resilience. However, this contribution has not been straightforward, as below stated.

2.1 Motivation for Research Investment

Academic KIOs' primary motivation towards research investment is to pursue scientific truth (Whitley, 2000). The product brought from this investment is knowledge.

The knowledge type produced has been basic science and epistemological knowledge performed without practical ends. This activity results in generalizable knowledge production and an understanding of nature and its laws (Bush, 1945, p. 13; Rubio et al., 2010). However, public institutional reforms started in Australia later became the global trends (Christensen, 2011), accompanying the renegotiated social contract with the public (Gibbons, 1999). The public began to expect academic KIOs to produce knowledge more applicable to practical ends. The Bayh-Dole Act of 1980 backed this direction.

The Bayh-Dole Act implicitly encompasses the aids of area resilience in its institutional intention. As evidence, the Act includes small businesses and entrepreneurial firms in its scope.

Also, the legal intention includes standardizing rules for the technology transfer process. In general, the rule standardization embeds fairness in a transaction. The expectation is to broaden beneficiaries of academic knowledge through unbiased partnering. As Wernerfelt (2016) points out, frequent transactions reduce the infliction in the bilateral agreements. Then, without regulatory intervention, it is less likely that a new firm becomes a joint research partner with academic KIOs due to concerns over potential inflictions. The rule standardization, in general, reduces the potential inflictions that involve in the contractual process. Then, the standardized processes facilitate academic knowledge transfer also to newcomers.

Further, explicit rules can enhance the entities' search activities regarding partners. The enhanced search activity is one of conditions for the evolutionary innovation process (Nelson & Winter, 1982).

The Bayh-Dole's underlying assumption is the small firms' capacity to produce follow-on discoveries and original discoveries that can add variety to the economy. The added demands will convert underused resources to productive service resources if the added variety generates new markets for the innovation.

2.1.1 Remained Problems

Overcoming of Constraints

Such institutional intention has manifested in several cluster buildings generated by entrepreneurs in Mark I and Variation-Intensive categories.

64   E. OKADA

These categories' common attribute is reduced entry barriers (Niosi, 2000; Ryan et al., 1996), including access to scientific resources and regulatory knowledge. The decreasing barriers facilitate translating academic sciences to applications, primarily due to entrepreneurs' follow-on discoveries. Thus, their activities enhance the academic sciences' potential for contributing to cluster building and area resilience.

There is a slightly different profile between the Variation-Intensive sciences and Mark I sciences regarding the initial R&D condition. For example, computing and semiconductor technologies have a strict road map. Firms must keep the pace of the road map in their R&D investment while differentiating products. This condition requires an intensified R&D and specialized marketing investment (see, Arthur, 1994; Kaldor, 1972; Niosi, 2000; Sutton, 1998).

Under this condition, entrepreneurial firms have changed product development logic by championing the platform (Henderson & Clark, 2000; Chesbrough, 2003; Gawer & Cusumano, 2002). They also formed a de-juri standard by creating international forums with academic KIOs.

Further, they have advanced the field through the recombination with Mark I sciences. It includes the recombination between machine learning and biological breakthroughs that emerged in the 1990s.

For example, the foundation of so-called big-data-based precision medicine (diagnostics) lies in the serial analysis gene expression (SAGE) (Adams et al., 1991; Nielsen, 2008; Velculescu, Zhang, Vogelstein, & Kinzler, 1995). This methodology allows the quantitative and simultaneous analysis of a large number of transcripts that organisms present (Velculescu et al., 1995). This recombination led to big-data-based biomarkers that distinguish humans' health-related characteristics (Disis, Tarczy-Hornoch, & Ramsey, 2013; Institute of Medicine, 2012).[1] The federal and private open access initiatives[2] have supported this research direction. These institutional and organizational activities created a variety to research tools, medical and diagnostics products and technologies in an unprecedented speed.

---

[1] This description is cited from Okada (2019, p. 7).

[2] The exception of open-access policy is the privacy considerations on identifiable data and biosecurity issues. See, Contreas (1992).

Remaining Problems

On the other hand, too much reliance on the Mark I, Dynamic Increasing Return and Variation-Intensive categories left a problem for urban resilience. It concerns the isolated populations from urban resilience.

The policymakers, therefore, shifted their focus from the private sector involvement to a more outstanding balance between public, private, and voluntary funding (Roberts, 2000. Also, see Lichfield, 1992; Stohr, 1989).

However, it is questionable whether the balanced view has spread enough to attain a stable position in the practice of urban regeneration.

Suppose the specific populations' isolation is mainly due to physical disfunctioning. Biomedical innovation (from public-and private partnerships) will ameliorate it with social enterprises. The once-disabled people can come back to regular works in the mainstream economy after their recovery. However, several empirical economic studies reveal that, once they suffer from physical disfunctioning, some external forces stigmatize them and almost force them to get out of the regular works that lead them to involve in a vicious cycle of financial deficit. Thus, there must be another cause for isolation.

One manifestation is what Radder (2010) is concerned about the biased selection of research agendas derived from biased values in the institution of science. His study scope is not an academic role in the urban regeneration. However, what overlaps concerns for an overemphasis on the partnership approach, particularly on the private–public partnerships (Radder, 2010; Roberts, 2000). Overemphasis, particularly on managerial effectiveness, limited universities' ability (Whitley & Gläser, 2014), leaving market failure areas with scientific significance understudied (Radder, 2010). The environmental technologies and equal resilience belong to the market failure areas. Then, the private sector's perspective might have affected the urban regeneration practices in a biased manner.

The mitigation of this effect will be discussed in Chapter 4.

Another possible explanation is the impacts of an internet-based sharing economy. The Variation-Intensive industrial sciences enabled the business model of the shared economy. It provides an excellent opportunity for consumers to spend spared time and money on other alternatives, thus adding variety to the markets. On the other hand, empirical researches also reveal some biases. For example, people with disabilities are categorically excluded from the pre-approval of the lodging

66 E. OKADA

offered in the private platforms despite the rules of the 1990 Americans with Disabilities Act (Ameri, Rogers, Schur, & Kruse, 2020).

Thus, people with certain disabilities are categorically excluded from employment and mobility opportunities that might lead to their reinforced isolation from resilience.

Confusion Over the Concept of Sustainability

What happened for urban scientists is that they have claimed the "introduction of the broader idea of environmental sustainability" in the realm of urban regeneration (Roberts, 2000. See, Lichfield, 1992; Stohr, 1989). Sustainability is a concept that constructs the system's approach. However, the system's approach and network approach were confused in the field (Coafee & Lee, 2016; Meerow, Newell, & Stults, 2016).

The scholarly management also had confused about the concept of sustainability. In management studies, the confusion occurred with the responsibility conceptualization (Bansal & Song, 2016). It may be because management literature has long discussed environmental issues as a part of corporate social responsibility. As Bansal and Song indicate, a sharp distinction is necessary. Responsibility research historically takes a normative position to alert the amorality of businesses. In contrast, sustainability takes a systems perspective, sending an alert to business-driven failures in natural systems (see, Bansal & Song, 2016). Thus, the systems perspective is critical in the field.

The resilience practice creates a more dynamic system's conditions by integrating underused capacities (Coafee & Lee, 2016. See, Penrose, 1959). However, in the real-world, economic inequality has been exacerbated at the expense of middle-wage occupations, leading to a hollowing of the middle class (Alabdulkareem et al., 2018). The economic disparities proportionate the environmental inequalities where citizens live and work (as examined in Chapter 4. See, Coafee & Lee, 2016; U.S. Environment Protection Agency: EPA).

Under this condition, this condition necessitates a knowledge circulation system that aligns private, public, and academic knowledge with a catalyst organization (den Hertog, 2000, p. 522). This image also fits the system's aspects of urban resilience.

2.1.2 The Need of Systems Approach

The systems approach is also necessary for academic sciences to address the remaining sustainability issues, through challenging in resource allocation, as below mentioned. The later chapters examine a system that involves a catalyst or intermediate organization in the framework of multi-sided space (Chapters 4, 5). It is to translate academic and entrepreneurial discoveries to environmental applications. This study will then apply the integrative vision of translational science to the practice of urban resilience with a focus on material and environmental sciences.

2.2 Resource Allocation and Performance

If future events are perfectly predictable, resource allocation would be simple. Academic KIOs will invest in the disciplines by referring to scientific and epistemological values, the potential impacts, and educational needs.

On the other hand, the future prediction encompasses more complex factors. For example, in the early 2010s, several universities closed the zoology programs and reallocated research budgets to the fields of increased needs. However, as stated in Chapter 5, zoology will resolve the barriers to translational science in the bioinspired construction material field. Thus, if academic KIOs allocate too much resource to the immediate societal knowledge demand, they miss scientific, epistemological, and future societal opportunities in facing further internal and external change.

The resource allocation process model (RAP model) thus holds also to academic KIOs. A critical concept is internal and external structural contexts (Bower, 1970, 2017; Bower & Gilbert, 2006). Internal structural contexts include bounded rationality (Cyert & March, 1963; Simon, 1957) of division managers and corporate offices' defensive behaviors of. The external structural contexts encompass several forces that can affect organizaitons' decision and behaviors, such as societal demands, funding agencies' policies, and other stakeholders' considerations.

Then, a problem is what the resource allocation should look like at academic KIOs. The concrete details would depend on long-term missions and short- and medium-term visions of academic KIOs. However, what is essential would be the core of what the academic KIO is.

2.2.1 The Potential of Academic-Specific Contributions

Academic KIOs have a unique organizational structure. It has a character that does not accept the control of outside and commercially motivated owners (von Nordenflycht, 2010). Under this condition, behavioral norms and internal codes ensure the trusteeship behaviors of the constituents (von Nordenflycht, 2010). The communication style is also different from commercial organizations. The attributes of scholarly communication are characterized by the components of academic norms, that is, openness in sharing academic results, disinterestedness, organized skepticism, and universalism (Anderson, Ronning, De Vries, & Martinson, 2010; Merton, 1942). They are necessary components to pursue truth.

Their governance has long been characterized as the self-regulation of sciences (or epistemological knowledge). The underlying assumption is that science is a social institution with autonomy regarding activities and agenda selection of science (Radder, 2010; Resnik, 2008; Ziman, 2000).

If an academic institution identifies itself as a research organization, it would will allocate more time and resources to create more universal knowledge with scientific methodologies. Journals are academics' knowledge-creation-and diffusion system in which scholars help others' knowledge generation through citation and a peer-review (see, Whitley, 2000). On the other hand, if an academic institution identifies itself as a community educational organization, it will allocate more resources to social welfare improvement, community-based empowerment, and community self-help in their research and educational agendas (see, Roberts, 2000; Stohr, 1989).

If academics produce abstract knowledge without any coercive power, such knowledge can be applied to break a bottleneck of conventional ways with a broader impact.

However, academic KIOs discarded several essential components during the renegotiated social contract. In the renegotiated social contract, the public obliged academic KIOs to involve in more practical needs (Gibbons, 1999; Nowotny, Scott, & Gibbons, 2001). Ironically, the discarded knowledge often conceives a clue to break barriers to societal demands in later years.

Under this condition, it is more productive for academic KIOs to reconstruct and transform scientific and epistemological knowledge-creation systems, rather than punish those who are responsible. Also, if academic KIOs desire to contribute to the urban regeneration, the direction is to allocate resources to the interface between science and humanistic disciplines (see, Radder, 2010; Kunemann, 2010).

2.3 Relations with Beneficiaries' Preferences

The academic sciences themselves do not always influence technical performance of industrial sciences directly. However, they have the potential to indirectly but significantly affect it. The mechanism is the alteration of the internal technological structure (Saviotti, 1996). The channels are technology transfer, joint research, and the public education.

For example, as stated in Chapter 5, university research has advanced an understanding of biofilm formation mechanisms. This understanding contributed to the invention and prototype formation of a more efficient and effective reactor at a Mark II chemical multinational. The company also plans to commercialize a biofilm-based reactor (see Donlan, 2002; Javis, 2020). If the new reactor diffuses in the market, it suggests the academic KIO's indirect contribution to generating a variety by altering the internal technological structure.

This case suggests the potential that the academic sciences positively affects the industrial R&D trajectory of Mark II sciences associated with a specific reactor submarket (a group of products).

The academic contributions to the environmental material science come from reconfiguring several disciplines even outside of the current industrial sciences' classification. Academic KIOs need to reconstruct and transform the existing knowledge generation and transmission systems that once diluted in the renegotiated social contract.

2.3.1 Contribution to a Variety

The above case also is adding a variety to the reactor submarket.

The growth of variety is a necessary condition for the long-term continuation of economic growth. The underlying assumption is that technological change introduces new goods that add new demands in the market (Pasinetti, 1981, 1990; Saviotti, 1996). The growing variety that accompanies new demands will offset the underemployment and under-utilization of capacity that may temporarily occur due to the technological change (Pasinetti, 1981; Saviotti, 1996).

The alteration of internal technological structure is significant to the upgraded quality of Mark II firms' products. However, the end beneficiaries do not necessarily pay for the upgraded quality brought by environmental material science. Therefore, the presence of academic KIOs is critical for research investment in such market failure areas.

70   E. OKADA

The academic and scientific knowledge on how things occur will promote the changes in the process and structure of the industrial sciences. On the other hand, academic KIOs do not produce products. Therefore, as Orr and Topa (2006) state, there is a need for the presence of anchor institutions as a sufficient condition of urban resilience.

3   ANCHOR INSTITUTIONS

The book's study expects anchors' activities to assist the emergence of new knowledge and technologies and provide product lines before the new technology revolution. However, anchors are not a philanthropy organization. There needs an incentive to contribute to taking such a role.

3.1   Motivation

Established organizations and multinationals wouldn't be anchor institutions if they had no intention to redefine technological and economic elements of their projects. What motivates them to take anchors' roles is their urgent need of corporate renewal (see, Pisano, 1990; Zahra et al., 2016) in facing turbulent market environment. The comparison with DIR pharmaceuticals will help to analyze the anchor institutions' motivation.

The relations between DIR pharmaceuticals, Mark I biomedical entrepreneurs, and the academic KIOs are almost established in the literature (Abernathy & Clark, 1980; Pisano, 1990, 2006). The scientific evolution and the technological regime change have almost forced established pharmaceuticals to internalize dispersed R&D sources in these decades (Dosi, 1982; Niosi, 2000; Pisano, 1990; Schumpeter, 1937; Sutton, 1998; Saviotti, 1996; Scherer, 1984). They then intensify the R&D investment in the subsequent phases (Niosi, 2000), since only companies that tolerate the R&D intensity (Arthur, 1994; Kaldor, 1972; Scherer, 1984; Sutton, 1998), specialized marketing (Schuhmacher, Kuester, & Hultink, 2018; Sutton, 1998), and high uncertainty of commercial success can continue to play in the market.

On the other hand, Mark II category is characterized by the attributes of R&D concentration, both in the initial condition and subsequent trends.

Notably, in the chemical industry, the continuous evolution of routines has been significant for the advancement of technological trajectories. The routines evolve by integrating new technological trajectories in the same or different submarket.

Then, questions arise:

- How emergence of discontinuous sciences occur in such a field where a continuous evolution of routines is significant;
- What motivates Mark II firms to relate to discontinuous emerging sciences;
- What organization forms they use.

In this regard, the introduction of the concept of search activities (Nelson & Winter, 1982; Saviotti, 1996) is useful in addition to the routines. Saviotti (1996) combines theories of economic development and innovation with a behavioral approach. According to Saviotti (1996), the evolutionary economics found it fruitful to introduce concepts of "organization routines" and "search activities" initiated by Nelson and Winter (1982). Since the evolutionary economics provides a platform for urban resilience studies, the current research will analyze Mark II firms' motivation by referring to the research stream of Nelson and Winter (1982) and Saviotti (1996).

3.1.1 Mark II Industrial Science Category and Variety

The traditional strength of Mark II firms has relied more on their unalienable knowledge accumulated around the routines and processes. Unalienable knowledge constructs the essence of why an organization exists (Coase, 1937; Nelson & Winter, 1989). It provides a rich source of innovation (Choi & Millar, 2005; Doz, 2005; Feldman, 2000; von Krogh, Ichijo & Nonaka, 2000). Its significance is more distinct in Mark II firms than those with other industrial sciences.

At the same time, new science-intensive categories are emerging in research trajectories that have not been traditionally in Mark II trajectories.

That means, if the Mark II firms are going to integrate emerging sciences in their processes, they need to conduct a distant search while evolving tacit knowledge around routines. It is because the emergence of breakthroughs does not necessarily come from Mark II's industrial sciences. The representative cases include engineered algae-inspired material and bioinspired construction materials (Chapter 5). These phenomena are not necessarily unusual regarding the evolutionary development of technological trajectories. The research strategies of scientists in the above fields are "the mimic of nature" and "integrating into the design process" in designing innovative and sustainable buildings (Imani, Donn, & Balador, 2018). These attributes are new to many of Mark IIs.

Thus, the external structural contexts urge Mark II firms to search and integrate distant scientific knowledge. Here is a critical factor that motivates the Mark II firms to take anchor roles.

3.1.2 The Need for Systems Approach

As for material sciences, more than eighty percent of the material is used in the construction material. Therefore, the economic and societal impacts of innovation will be larger in the field of construction material than those of other areas (Imani et al. 2018). Nonetheless, this direction of the application is not necessarily advancing.

The construction field requires a much higher level of safety criteria, such as stability, robustness, and reliability, due to the potential harm to humans' physical bodies. When Mark IIs are to procure discoveries in dispersed sources, they need to map the emerging sciences, construct the workflow, and put them in their research design, keeping an eye on the safety attributes.

Such processes require a systems approach. Due to the scale of concentration and required properties, their workflows and organizational forms will be more complex than other industrial sciences. The organizational arrangements play a significant role in advancing the Mark II's motivation.

3.2 Resource Allocation and Performance

3.2.1 Technological Discontinuity and Strategic Integration

According to Saviotti (1996), the M-form is an adequate structure for managing variety. However, from the organizational behavior perspective, the M-form is not always satisfactory. A challenging part is to motivate all the management levels and constituents to introduce variety(see, Bower, 1970, 2017; Burgelman & Doz, 1997; Eisenmann & Bower, 2000).

Here is a dilemma specific to Mark II sciences. Suppose technologies that derive from Mark II sciences require the properties of stability, robustness, and reliability. In that case, a large-scale strategic integration has the potential to put these properties at risk. It is because once established routines and coordination processes are tough to reconfigure. Firms will encounter the challenge of disturbing larger scopes of operations. Meanwhile, the redefinition of technological and economic elements that follow technological renewal is necessary.

One of the plausible methods in this space is to internalize entrepreneur firms and manage them in a portfolio. It is to purchase new firms and manage them independently from the existing processes. If they integrate the entrepreneur organization into existing processes, it will dilute the novel property of the entrepreneurial products. Mark II chemical and DIR supercomputer multinationals adopted this method in the 1990s while selling some of existing segments. However, this method is not always suitable.

The 1990s' restructuring target is to increase the specialty chemicals' ratio in their business and R&D portfolios while selling bulk chemicals. The specialty chemicals already had a stable revenue stream and high return on equity, though it was still a downsizing for Mark II chemicals. On the other hand, many of the new environmental materials are in the science stage. It is quite uncertain which technological trajectories survive and form a mainstream technology. Therefore, there need other organizational forms.

Other conventional organizational arrangements include the research investment in new science-intensive firms, joint research with academic KIOs, the introduction of academic discoveries, and the exploration of in-house research.

Among these forms, the first three are the forms DIR pharmaceuticals actively adopt. After developing core patents, they in-license commercial rights from academic KIOs and entrepreneurial organizations. On the other hand, the pharmaceuticals rely more on patents in product development than Mark II firms. Therefore, it needs an investigation of whether this organization form is feasible for Mark II firms.

New scientific attributes can also require more mixed organizational arrangements. The new attributes have the potential to bring Mark II industrial sciences closer to Mark I biotechnology, algorithms in Variation-Intensive category, and DIR supercomputer sciences.

Then, Mark II's CEOs will need to allocate more resources to search activities and designing organizations regarding emerging sciences.

3.3 Relations with Beneficiaries' Preferences

A factor that differentiates environmental material sciences from other industrial sciences is the relationship with beneficiaries' preferences. The beneficiaries of bioinspired construction material sciences are the public. They will benefit from the upgraded environmental quality. However, as already mentioned, beneficiaries do not necessarily pay for the upgraded quality.

In this sense, the advanced material sciences belong to the market failure area. A new organizational approach is necessary to provide market-based solutions to the market failure area (Table 1).

4   Set Conditions

This chapter investigated the organization models and actors that involve urban resilience. Particular attentions are on academic KIOs and anchor candidates. Its objective is to build a rough framework for the later chapters.

Previous literature has examined academic KIOs, entrepreneur firms, and social enterprises as actors of urban resilience. However, there is little attention to large-scale multinationals, except Orr and Topa (2006). The context of Orr and Topa (2006) is the urban resilience of the New York Metropolitan Area in the 2000s.

What should be added to the anchors' role in Orr and Topa (2006) is assisting the emergence of new knowledge and technology. This function is critical for cluster building in the context of area resilience. On the other hand, the anchors roles do not occur automatically. What motivates established firms to take anchors' functions is the urgency of redefining technological and economic elements followed by the corporate entrepreneurship process. However, there are several barriers for established firms to redefining their domain. First, M-Forms must overcome internal structural contexts to allocate resources for addressing emerging technologies (Bower, 1970; Bower & Gilbert, 2006). Though the M-Form is appropriate to manage a variety (Saviotti, 1996), this form also embeds constraints if the introduction of emerging technologies requires strategic integration (Eisenmann & Bower, 2000; Burgelman & Doz, 1997).

Table 1 Elements of anchor organizations and academic knowledge-intensive organizations

	Academic Knowledge-Intensive Organizations (KIOs)	Anchor organizations	Bridging factors or mechanisms
The motivation for research investment Remaining issues	The pursuit of truth; Contribution to the theories The need for a systems approach	Redefine technological and economic elements of projects that follow the corporate renewal Compatibility between the distant search for emerging sciences while evolving tacit knowledge around routines The need of additional attributes of industrial sciences The need for a systems approach	Follow-on discoveries of entrepreneurial firms Potential attributes of "mimic of nature (environment)" and "integration into the design process (sustainability)"
Resource allocation and performance Remaining issues	Depends on specific missions, such as research or education orientation Reconstruction and transformation of systems of scientific and epistemological knowledge creation that are altered during the renegotiated social contract	The management of a variety; Resolving issues in M-Forms Resolve the conflict between the distant search for emerging sciences and the essential properties of stability and reliability for safety purposes	Organizational forms (Chapter 5) Escalation of entrepreneur firms (Chapters 5, 7) New arrangements with scientists and non-scientists (Chapter 7)
Relations with beneficiaries' preferences Remaining issues	Contribute to altering internal technological structure in the market failure areas Contribute to the end beneficiaries' willingness to pay, indirectly The need for transforming systems approach that once corrupted	Beneficiaries do not necessarily pay for the upgraded quality brought by R&D investment Design new organizational arrangements	New organizational arrangements (Chapter 5)

(continued)

76 E. OKADA

Table 1 (continued)

	Academic Knowledge-Intensive Organizations (KIOs)	Anchor organizations	Bridging factors or mechanisms
Relations with creating a variety	Contribute to the alteration of internal technological structure	Contribute to the product development processes	New organizational arrangements (Chapter 5)

Second, a more systematic approach is necessary for both academic KIOs and anchor organizations. If Mark II firms must procure discoveries that emerge in a more dispersed manner, they will need to map the emerging sciences, construct the workflow, and put them in their research design. It requires more distant search activities of emerging sciences before and during the process. During this translation, the construction of workflow requires the disciplinary knowledge of zoology. However, several academic KIOs closed or reduced the resource allocation to the zoology programs. The filling of this gap is critical for the further development.

Third, this chapter introduced the attributes of "mimic of nature (environment)" and "integration into the design (sustainability)" to address material and environmental sciences. Later chapters will pursue more details related to the new categorization of industrial sciences. This examination will lead to more appropriate organizational forms for urban resilience.

Therefore, the following chapters will investigate the points below stated: (a) organizational arrangements related to anchors, (b) set conditions for anchors' investment, and (c) details of additional attributes of the industrial science categorization for material and environmental sciences.

REFERENCES

Abernathy, W. J., & Clark, K. B. (1980). Innovation: Mapping the winds of creative destruction. *Research Policy, 14*(1), 3–22.

Adams, M. D., Kelley, J. M., Govayne, J. D., Dubnick, M., Polymeropoulos, M. H., Xiao, H., … & Venter, C. (1991). Complementary DNA sequencing: Expressed sequence tags and human genome project. *Science, 252*(5123), 1651–1656.

Alabdulkareem, A., Frank, M. R., Sun, L., AlShebli, B., Hidalgo, C., & Rahwan, I. (2018). Unpacking the polarization of workplace skills, *Science Advances, 4*(7). https://doi.org/10.1126/sciadv.aao6030.

Ameri, M., Rogers, S. E., Schur, L., & Kruse, D. (2020). No room at the inn? Disability access in the new sharing economy. *Academy of Management Discoveries, 6*(2). https://doi.org/10.5465/amd.2018.0054.

Anderson, M. S., Ronning, E. A., De Vries, R., & Martinson, B. C. (2010). Extending the mertonian norms: Scientists' subscription to norms of research. *The Journal of Higher Education, 81*(3), 366–393.

Arthur, B. (1994). *Increasing returns and path dependency in the economy.* Ann Arbor: University of Michigan Press.

Bansal, P., & Song, H. (2016). Similar but not the same: Differentiating corporate sustainability from corporate responsibility. *Academy of Management Annals, 11*(1). https://doi.org/10.5465/annals.2015.0095.

Bower, J. L. (1970). *Managing the resource allocation process.* Boston: Division of Research, Graduate School of Business Administration, Harvard University.

Bower, J. L. (2017). Managing resource allocation: Personal reflections from a managerial perspective. *Journal of Management, 43*(8). https://doi.org/10.1177/0149206316675929.

Bower, J. L., & Gilbert, C. G. (2006). *From resource allocation to strategy.* New York and Oxford: Oxford University Press.

Burgelman, B. A., & Doz, Y. (1997). Complex strategic integration in the lean multibusiness corporation. *INSEAD Working Paper, 97/03/SM,* as cited by Eisemnann, T. R., & Bower, L. J. (2005).

Bush, V. (1945). *Science, the endless frontier.* A report to the President by Director of Office of Scientific Research and Development. Washington, DC: U.S. Government Printing Office.

Chesbrough, H. W. (2003). *Open innovation: The new imperative for creating and profiting from technology.* Boston: Harvard Business School Press.

Choi, C., & Miller, C. (2005). *Knowledge entanglement.* Hampshire and New York: Palgrave Macmillan.

Christensen, T. (2011). University governance reforms: Potential problems of more autonomy? *Higher Education, 62,* 503–517.

Coafee, J., & Lee, P. (2016). *Urban resilience: Planning risk, crisis and uncertainty.* London: Palgrave.

Coase, R. H. (1937). The nature of the firm. *Economica, 4*(16), 386–405.

Cyert, R. M., & March, J. G. (1963). *Behavioral theory of the firm.* New Jersey: Prentice Hall & March.

den Hertog, P. (2000). Knowledge intensive business services as co-producers of innovation. *International Journal of Innovation Management, 4*(4), 491–528.

Disis, M. L., Tarczy-Hornoch, P., & Ramsey, B. W. (2013). Increasing the efficiency and quality of clinical research with innovative services and informatics tools. In B. Alving, K. Dai, & S. H. H. Chan (Eds.), *Translational research in biomedicine* (Vol. 3, pp. 89–97). Basel: S. KARGER AG.

Donlan, R. M. (2002). Biofilms: Microbial life on surfaces. *Emerging Infectious Diseases, 8*(9), 881–890.

Dosi, G. (1982). Technological paradigms and technological trajectories: A suggested interpretation of determinants and directions of technological change. *Research Policy, 11,* 147–162.

Doz, Y. (2005). Resource allocation processes in multidimensional organizations: MNCs and alliances. In J. L. Bower & C. G. Gilbert (Eds.), *From resource allocation to strategy* (pp. 365–392). Oxford: Oxford University Press.

Eisenmann, T., & Bower, J. (2000). The entrepreneurial M-Form: Strategic integration in global media firms. *Organization Science, 11,* 348–355.

Feldman, M. S. (2000). Organizational routine as a source of continuous change. *Organization Science, 11*(6), 629–661.

European Commission (EC). (2012). *Knowledge-intensive (business) service in Europe.* Luxembourg: Publication Office of the European Union.

Gawer, A., & Cusumano, M. A. (2002). *Platform leadership: How Intel, Microsoft and Cisco drive industry innovation.* Boston: Harvard University Press.

Gibbons, M. (1999). Science's new social contract with society. *Nature, 402,* C81–C84.

Henderson, R. M., & Clark, K. B. (2000). Architectural innovation: Reconfiguration of existing product technologies and the failure of established firms. *Administrative Science Quarterly, 35*(1), 9–30.

Imani, M., Donn, M., & Badalar, Z. (2018). Bio-inspired materials: Contribution of biology to energy efficiency of buildings. In L. Martinez, O. Kharissova (Eds.), Handbook of ecomaterials (pp. 2213–2236). Cham: Springer. https://doi.org/10.1007/2F978-3-319-68255-6_136.

Institute of Medicine. (2012). *Evolution of translational omics. Lessons learned and the path forward.* Washington, DC: National Academies Press.

Javis, L. M. (2020). Exploiting biofilms. Chemical and Engineering News, *American Chemical Society.* https://cen.acs.org/articles/86/i23/Exploiting-Biocilms.htnl.

Kaldor, N. (1972). The irrelevance of equilibrium economics. *Economic Journal, 82,* 1237–1255.

Kunemann, H. (2010). Viable alternatives for commercialized science: The case of humanistics. In H. Radder (Ed.), *The commodification of academic research: Science and the modern university* (pp. 307–336). Pittsburgh: University of Pittsburgh Press.

Lichfield, D. (1992). *Urban regeneration for the 1990's.* London: London Planning Advisory Committee.

Meerow, S., Newell, J. P., & Stults, M. (2016). Defining urban resilience: A review. *Landscape and Urban Planning, 147,* 38–49.

Merton, R. K. (1942). A note on science and democracy. *Journal of Legal and Political Sociology, 1*, 115–126.

Nelson, R. R., & Winter, S. G. (1982). *An evolutionary theory of economic change.* Cambridge: Harvard University Press.

Nielsen, K. L. (Ed.). (2008). *Serial analysis of gene expression (SAGE): Methods and protocols.* Totowa: Humana Press.

Niosi, J. (2000). Science-based industries: New Schumpeterian taxonomy. *Technology in Society, 22*, 429–444.

Nowotny, H., Scott, P., & Gibbons, M. (2001). *Re-thinking science: Knowledge and the public in an age of uncertainty.* Oxford: Polity Press.

Okada, E. (2019). *Management of knowledge-intensive organizations: Governance models for transformative discovery.* New York: Palgrave Macmillan.

Orr, J., & Topa, G. (2006). Challenges facing the New York Metropolitan area economy. *Current Issues in Economics and Finance, 12*(1). Retrieved from https://www.newyorkfed.org/medialibrary/media/research/current_issues/ci12-1.pdf.

Pasinetti, L. L. (1981). *Structural change and economic growth.* Cambridge: Cambridge University Press.

Pasinetti, L. L. (1990). Structural change and unemployment. *Structural Change and Economic Dynamics, 1*(1), 7–13.

Penrose, E. T. (1959). *The theory of the growth of a firm.* New York and Oxford: Blackwell.

Pisano, G. P. (1990). The R&D boundaries of the firm: An empirical analysis. *Administrative Science Quarterly, 35*, 153–176.

Pisano, G. P. (2006). *Science business: The promise, the reality, and the future of biotech.* Boston: Harvard Business School Press.

Radder, H. (2010). *The commodification of academic research: Science and the modern university.* Pittsburgh: University of Pittsburgh Press.

Resnik, D. B. (2008). Scientific autonomy and public oversight. *Philosophy of Science, 5*(2), 220–238. https://doi.org/10.3366/c1742360000800336.

Roberts, P. (2000). The evolution, definition and purpose of urban regeneration. In P. Roberts & H. Sykes (Eds.), *Urban regeneration: A handbook* (pp. 9–36). New York: Sage.

Rubio, D. M., Schoenbaum, E. E., Lee, L. S., Schteingart, D. E., Marantz, P. R., Anderson, K. E., … & Esposito, K. (2010). Defining translational research. *Academic Medicine, 85*(3), 470–475.

Saviotti, P. P. (1996). *Technological evolution, variety and the economy.* Cheltenham: Edward Elgar.

Scherer, F. (1984). *Innovation and growth. Schumpeterian perspectives.* Cambridge: MIT Press.

Schuhmacher, M. C., Kuester, S., & Hultink, E. J. (2018). Appetizer or main course: Early market vs. majority market go-to-market strategies for radical innovation. *The Journal of Product Market Innovation, 35*(1), 106–124.

Schumpeter, J. (1937). *Capitalism, socialism and democracy.* London: Allen & Unwin.

Simon, H. A. (1957). *Models of man, social and rational.* New York: Wiley.

Solow, R. M. (1956). A contribution to the theory of economic growth. *The Quarterly Journal of Economics, 70*(1), 65–94.

Stohr, W. (1989). Regional policy at the crossroad: A overview. In L. Albrechts, F. Moulaerts, P. Roberts, & E. Swyngedlouw (Eds.), *Regional policy at the crossroads: European perspectives.* London: Jessica Kingsley.

Sutton J. (1998). *Technology and market structure.* Cambridge: The MIT Press.

Teece, D. J. (1986). Transaction cost economics and the multinational enterprise. *Journal of Economic Behavior & Organization, 7,* 21–45.

Velculescu, V. E., Zhang, L., Vogelstein, B., & Kinzler, K. W. (1995). Serial analysis of gene expression. *Science, 270*(5235), 484–487.

von Nordenflycht, A. (2010). What is a professional service firm? Toward a theory and taxonomy of knowledge intensive firms. *Academy of Management Review, 35*(1), 155–174.

Von Krogh, G., Ichijo, K., & Nonaka, I. (2000). *Enabling knowledge creation: How to unlock the mystery of tacit knowledge and release the power of innovation.* Oxford: Oxford University Press.

Whitley, R. (2000). *The intellectual and social organization of science* (2nd ed.). Oxford: Oxford University Press.

Whitley, R., & Gläser, J. (2014). The impact of institutional reforms on the nature of universities as organizations. *Research in the Sociology of Organizations, 42,* 19–49.

Wernerfelt, B. (2016). *Adaptation, specialization, and the theory of the firm: Foundations of the resource-based view.* Cambridge: Cambridge University Press.

Williamson, O. (1979). Transaction cost economics: The governance of contractual relations. *Journal of Law and Economics, 22*(2), 233–261.

Zahra, S. A., Neubaum, D. O., & Hayton, J. C. (2016). *Handbook of research on corporate entrepreneurship.* Cheltenhamand Northampton: Edward Elgar.

Ziman, J. (2000). *Real science.* Cambridge: Cambridge University Press.

PART II

Entrepreneurship in Urban Resilience

CHAPTER 4

Addressing Environmental Inequity by New Sciences

1 WHEN ANCHOR INSTITUTIONS ARE ABSENT

Part II examines cases in which new industrial science attributes contribute to the broadening of beneficiaries in urban resilience.

This Chapter examines sub-research questions through a representative case of environmental aspects of urban resilience. Sub-research questions are as follows: what factors motivate the established multinationals to play as anchor institutions in a market failure area; How can they use their resources to help to reduce environmental inequity prevalent in inner-city regions. A particular focus is on a condition in which potential anchors are absent in an urban area.

Orr and Topa (2006)'s body of investigation is the economic resilient of New York City. The global dynamic increasing return (DIR) firms and financial institutions absorbed the unprecedented external disturbance while helping to create variety in product and service markets. However, many cities do no necessarily possess such an initial condition. Then, questions arise who can do for what when anchor institutions are absent in the area.

Previous literature mainly examines behaviors of established and new firms by focusing on Dynamic Increasing Return (DIR), Mark I, and Variation-Intensive industrial science categories by Niosi (2000). However, environment-related sciences have been outside of the scope.

© The Author(s), under exclusive license to
Springer Nature Switzerland AG 2021
E. Okada, *Management of Science-Intensive Organizations,*
https://doi.org/10.1007/978-3-030-64042-2_4

83

This study will then examine a case in which foreign Mark II multinationals conduct research investment in a new incubator of environmental sciences in the area where potential anchors are absent. This study will examine the U.S. case regarding the following elements Saviotti (1996) raises: actors, activities, organizations that create it, institutions, the type of knowledge, the process, and products (see Saviotti, 1996).

More specifically, it investigates a process in which loosely coupled organizations created a world-largest environmental incubator with a global Mark II multinationals. The theoretical bases of anchors' behaviors are the resource process allocation model (Bower, 1970; Bower & Gilbert, 2006; Eisenmann & Bower, 2000) and corporate entrepreneurship (Zahra, Neubaum, & Hayton, 2016). It combines the factors of urban resilience frameworks explored by Coafee and Lee (2016) and Roberts (2000).

The organization of this chapter is as follows. First, it outlines the factors that affect environmental inequity by reviewing literature of urban regeneration (Coafee & Lee, 2016; Roberts, 2000). It then describes a representative case in the U.S. city where potential anchors are absent. Second, it examines management and organization aspects of anchors that contribute to urban resilience since it is usually challenging for possible anchors to alter once created routines (Bower, 1970; Caves, 2007/1982; Leonard-Barton, 1992).

It is not always due to inertia and defensive actions but also attentional processes that prohibit them from making changes (Cyert & March, 1963). Therefore, this study focuses on what institutional and organizational factors facilitate corporate entrepreneurship of Mark II multinationals while overcoming barriers.

2   Environmental Inequity

2.1   Environmental Inequity

Previous chapters outline environmental inequity as a part of the residuals of urban resilience. This chapter more specifies details of the environmental inequity to make them operationalized.

Urban regeneration planners analyze environmental issues as an independent input factor along with the social and economic factors (Roberts, 2000). The planners put these factors with the internal and external change drivers. The internal drivers include preferences of residents, external drivers, transnational and national policies and strategies of competing cities. The inter-city competition is a significant driver, particularly since the early 2000s. It is because federal and national governments delegated resilience responsibilities to local governments (Coafee & Lee, 2016). The assumption (Coafee & Lee, 2016) is that the economic, social, and environmental welfare of residents and organizations depend on the area's resilience and transformation.

Outcomes of the above process are environmental actions and economic development designs, among others.
Environmental actions encompass:

- Company-based actions,
- Urban greening.

The economic development includes:

- The support for existing and new firms,
- Innovation, and
- Economic diversification (Roberts, 2000).

These factors interact with each other (Roberts, 2000). Further, the recognition of the location-specific issues has to coincide with the understanding of broader circumstances (Roberts, 2000).

For example, poverty began to occur in a broader, cross-county, inner-city area of the U.S. because of deindustrialization. The workers in the manufacturing industries lost jobs due to the withdrawal of factories. Also, the required skills shifted. Then, several workers began to search and detect new skill demands and acquired new skills. However, in some cities, they had no opportunities to obtain new skills and college-level knowledge.

The city-specific condition in such cities was that the workers were very busy and received relatively higher and fair wages in involving manufacturing works. Therefore, they felt no necessity to seek new skills (Glaeser & Hausman, 2019). What made things worse is that, after the job loss, their children had no chances to see what the workplace cultures should look like (Boudreau & Marx, 2019). This condition detracted organizations that might otherwise enter and operate in the geographic area.

86   E. OKADA

Then, the location's economic and social isolation began to occur (see, Glaeser & Hausman, 2019).

In this manner, it is necessary to have the second-and third-layers of understanding of area-specific events to reduce social isolation of the location. This understanding leads to enhancing the economic and social reintegration of isolated disadvantaged (McGregor & McConnarchie, 1995. See, Roberts, 2000).

A question arises what processes are necessary to integrate isolated inner-city residents. The economic studies concentrate on the impacts of skill shifts, education, and wage subsidies and have not thoroughly investigated the roles of management and organizations.

Therefore, this study will first examine how resilience occurred in the 1990s from the perspective of management studies. It will then observe the representative case in which the isolated population in the 1990s began to be integrated in the mid-2010s.

2.1.1   Resilience in the 1990s

Industrial sciences contributed to the 1990s' resilience are Mark I sciences and Variation-intensive sciences (see OECD, 2004; Orr & Topa, 2006). Corporate entrepreneurship of established DIR industrial firms and the escalation of Variation-Intensive firms supported the resilience.

The academic discoveries, such as Cohen and Boyer's recombinant DNA and Milstein and Kohler's monoclonal antibody, opened up bottlenecks of application (see Pisano, 2006; Ryan, Freeman, & Hybels, 1995). Then, a variety of applications followed. The 1980 Bayh-Dole Act and facilitated access to resources worked as their institutional support.

These breakthroughs did not necessarily substitute existing organizations, particularly in pharmaceutical industries (Abernathy & Clark, 1980; Henderson & Cockburn, 1996; Pisano, 1990; Sutton, 1998). Instead, established firms introduced entrepreneurs' discoveries in their processes. The observation reveals that they developed and manufactured products by introducing commercial rights of entrepreneurs' discoveries and distributed them in the global market. These activities accompanied corporate entrepreneurial processes that increased new pharmacology's ratio in R&D portfolio, followed by the market and industry capacities' renewal (see Covin & Miles, 1999; Dess et al., 2003; Kuratko & Covin, 2015; Ryan et al., 1995; Zahra et al., 2016).

Here is a need to understand corporate entrepreneurship in the context of urban resilience.

Meanwhile, several U.S. university graduates began to return to their home countries, since their home countries became relatively wealthy, enabling them to live a higher quality of life when they went back (Freeman, 2007). Such graduates came to provide a reliable workforce to foreign multinationals in their home countries (Acemogulu, Gallego, & Robinson, 2009). Then, established multinationals and new firms that later became multinationals began to hire such U.S. trained workforce with relatively reasonable wages. The measures vary from locating their facilities, creating joint ventures, and partnering with local entities (Wadhua, Rissing, Gereffi, Trumpbour, & Engardio, 2008). This trend distracted the U.S. firms to hire specific U.S. populations, which further reinforced the specific inner-city isolation (Glaeser & Hausman, 2019).

2.2   *Consequences of Reinforced Environmental Inequity*

Such residents have a higher possibility of suffering from environmental inequity, since the residential place depends on the income level. As social mobility is stagnated for decades, socioeconomic status more likely affects the place where people live. Then, low-income people more likely live around pollutant areas.

According to the U.S. Center for Disease Control and Prevention (CDC), people with asthma may have severe reactions to toxic substances. Further, immune-compromised people and people with chronic lung disease may get an infection in their lungs from the mold.[1] The low-income populations are more likely reside in houses with toxic molds. Immune-compromised people also can join this population with a high probability due to their limited ability to work. Then, the specific population more likely increases disease severity.

The more notable pollutants are a particle in the air pollutants, such as PM2.5. The primary sources of PM2.5 include emissions. According to a well-controlled public health statistics, seniors who are more exposed to PM2.5 are more likely to suffer from serious illness defined by the U.S. Food and Drug Administration (FDA). As already stated, PM2.5 affect indoor workers' productivity by inducing significant fatigue. Its toxicity is activated by the heatwave and penetrates windows. People who

---

[1] Retrieved from: www.cdc.gov. Last updated in December 2019.

88   E. OKADA

belong to the specific population more likely live in households where heat, dampness, and mold are not well controlled.

Thus, the socioeconomic divide related to environmental contaminants will affect people's physical ability to work. It can then reinforce the unsatisfactory conditions by reducing resources to manage these conditions. Further, it has the potential to disturb the urban system and its sustainability by allowing and normalizing such deviant.

3   ATTRACTING FOREIGN ANCHORS

If there are no organizations that can be anchors in urban areas, cities can attract anchor candidates outside of states. This section examines a representative case in which loosely coupled organizations attracted several multinational corporations.

3.1   Outline of the Case

City A once prospered as a suburban area of a U.S. multinational enterprise's Assembly. The Assembly was a corporate anchor from 1926 to 1958. However, due to the deindustrialization, it closed its plant in 1958. Its nearby retail center also closed the operation in 1976. Each laid off more than a thousand workers. During 1958–1976, most factories in the City closed. The area of the Assembly became a ghost town by 1976 (Shelton, 2005/2006).

After the Assembly's withdrawal, the employment and the population itself steeply declined. Based on the Census, the City's population in the 1950s was 102351 while in the 1990s, 76231. Empty office spaces with mold and damp became pervasive (Shelton, 2005/2006). The affected area spanned to the whole City, since the central part of the City's economy depended on the Assembly and its complementing industries.

The two closest counties to the Assembly suffered from the worst social issues and the economic impacts. It is an increase in the crime rate that had never happened before. Federally notable gang groups also emerged in the 1970s.

This urban area originally represented one of the America's earliest settlements in the mid-1600. The people are calm and hard workers. It is the loss of works that drove them to either negative or criminal behaviors. It was not for their fault but for the cause that was beyond their responsibility. It is established in the humanities disciplines that the work provides meaning to individuals. If people lose meaning in their life, they have the potential to make bad decisions that might otherwise be avoided (Beauchamp & Childress, 2013).

The residents' political contexts further complicate the social divide. There were four privileged, political categories in terms of the people's national origin. This condition divided the residents into the major who belong to one of the four national bases, and minor, the rest of them. Though the City's political leaders understood this historical divide, they had no measures to mitigate it.

The political divide brought residents' unproductive behaviors. For example, the minor group felt uncomfortable when privileged background people were going to intervene their ways of living, even if the intervention would bring positive results. If someone in the minor group showed socially obedient behavior, (s)he became a target of harassment by unknown groups. The minor groups likely communicated with each other through some kinds of devices. The police could do nothing unless someone were physically injured or impaired through the attack.

The City's revitalization efforts began in the 1990s when a subway infrastructure extended its line from a nearby city to the City's Western part (Shelton, 2005/2006). Transportation is one factor that catalyzes urban resilience by invoking people's mobility (Roberts, 2000). Transportation by itself does not always stimulate mobility (Glaeser & Hausman, 2019). However, in City A, the subway system facilitated the newcomers' entry.

There are a couple of universities in the nearby city that continuously have attracted international students and faculties. Historically, they lived in the surrounding areas of the universities. Meanwhile, the nearby city removed the upper limit of building rents due to the land price deregulation, invoking the increased residential lease fee (Shelton, 2005/2006). International students from very wealthy backgrounds contributed to this tendency. This condition unintentionally benefitted City A. Many students and young faculties of the universities moved to the City's Western part because of the rent affordability. The good thing is that most international students and young faculties are indifferent to the City's political conditions.

City A also has a high-level university in the Western area. However, according to the literature on the City's political condition, the residents historically were not interested in sending their children to the Western area's university. Therefore, the major part of students came from outside of the City. Since the City's transportation became organized, these students began to scatter in the broader areas of the City.

The City has a conservative atmosphere relative to the nearby city. However, the prevalence of young students and faculties began to attract the so-called young professionals in the City's vacant, low brick buildings. This movement began to occur twenty years after the City's revitalization initiative.

At first, despite the City's efforts to provide office spaces for the young professional, little was willing to enter because of the lack of supporting infrastructure. The businesses entered the office buildings in the earlier revitalization period did not add a variety to technologies nor applications. Therefore, economic growth did not occur.

However, along with the young students and faculties' prevalence, a supportive infrastructure began to spread, such as broadband and wireless hotspots, office support services, private deliveries, and takeaway restaurants. Notably, the City's middle part attracted entrepreneurs by providing abundant vacant spaces in low brick buildings. The young professionals began to enter the low, brick buildings one by one. Supportive professional also began to move to space, such as lawyers, accountants, and tax consultants.

Thus, a good cycle began to occur around the mid-2010s. The population recovered to 81360 in 2017.

3.1.1 The difference from the Resilience of New York City

In the early 2000s, there were still many vacant office spaces in the City. It is partly because the City's relatively wealthy residents went for work to the nearby cities and came back at night. They have little time to spend money in the City in the daytime. Young professionals' new businesses did not necessarily invite funds to pay to others: they had not enough funds to hire residents. The attention of the federal and private funds concentrated on the nearby city where numerous life science businesses flourished. Further, the City's two primary industries were unwilling to enhance the employment: They are the construction industry and the construction material manufacturing industry. The major employer of the City was the university in the Western area.

The City's economy lacks variety even in the late 2010s. The City's highest paying industries between 2016 and 2017 are mining, quarrying, and gas and oil extraction ($210,380), followed by manufacturing ($70,496), and professional, scientific, and technical services ($68.775).

The new businesses' percentage is small relative to major groups (Data USA, accessed in 2019).

Thus, the City lacked variety in the industry composition. This point is a significant difference from New York City that had the industry mix variety.

Another difference is that in the New York Metropolitan Area the excluded populations were those that did not adapt to the skill shift. According to Orr and Topa (2006), they were unwilling to participate in the formal education that was desired in the resilience pathways.

In City A, the excluded populations are not necessarily because of their ignorance of the skill shifts. In addition to the political complication, the industry mix lacked variety.

3.1.2   Trajectories to Focus on the Environment Startups

The City did not necessarily neglect the agglomeration development: As the nearby city is famous for the concentration of Mark I life science businesses and dynamic increasing return (DIR) pharmaceuticals, the City was going to attract these industries. The Mayor signed a mutual agreement with the nearby city to jointly invite biotechnology industries in the early 2010s. However, the agglomeration did not extend the geographic scope beyond the nearby city's border.

One of the global top biomedical companies once relocated its R&D unit to the low brick building in the City's middle part. A couple of law firms followed it. However, the migrated biomedical did not settle in this area: it soon moved away. It is potentially due to the residents' mindsets that want to differentiate themselves from the nearby city.

Meanwhile, the City began to pay attention to cultural heritage. There remain several historic sites established in the mid-and late 1600s. Then, the City created several monuments to explain each historical heritage. Also, many citizens likely had interests in arts and crafts rather than in biotechnology. With the help of foundation funds, many artists began to create crafts for their lives. Also, many poets began to work together and teach residents. Further, a European hospice founded a branch with a green courtyard.

For some time, the City began to create open gardens. The City also built a park to commemorate a famous American athlete who graduated from the City's public high school. It planted dark red maple trees in the park imported from Canada. The City further pulled out dead trees along the main street and planted new ones.

Afforestation went further. The City created an open kitchen garden. This garden is available not only to residents but also to those of other cities. People welcomed the kitchen garden because residents seldom had a large garden to plant fruits and vegetables: the City is one of the most populated urban areas in the U.S.

The City also began youth development. Students of the City's high school started to announce plays and other events in the open garden when visitors were gardening on weekends. A nonprofit organization was making arrangements for these events that may have contributed to mitigating the youth delinquency.

Another nonprofit also began to publish a town magazine that introduced the City's cultural events and restaurants. They distributed the magazine free of charge to residents. This publication has helped to encourage residents and business owners, regardless of their age or country origin. With a large-scale shopping and restaurant mall created in the former Assembly area, urban resilience began to integrate several layers of people, including troubling former youths in the surrounding counties.

Meanwhile, the City government was playing an active role not only in stimulating arts and businesses but also controlling the hygiene of residents. Examples include a waste handling initiative and soil remediation. In the mid-2010s, waste handling was still on the way. Then, the city government distributed large, standardized garbage barrels to families with the instruction of waste handling protocols. The City charged landowners whose lessees violated the protocol. At first, unknown groups tried to criminalize obedient newcomers. However, such activities have stopped for some time.

The City government also began to hold open town meetings regarding public parks' soil remediation. A public investigation revealed that the soil of some parks contaminated with toxic metals beyond the federal regulation's criteria. Public parks have significance for residents in the densely populated City. Therefore, the City government invited all the residents' participation to explain and discuss the plan.

3.1.3 Incubating Environmental Startups

Despite the afforestation efforts, there remain challenges related to health equity. One is air pollution near highways that induce several disorders. The pollution still impacts residents in older housing close to a highway intersection, many of whom are low-income, minority, or disadvantaged (Galvin, 2018; Shelton, 2005/2006).

Meanwhile, an environment-related incubator entered a brick building in the early 2010s. The incubator began the operation in 2011 to incubate startups that were to invent and apply clean technologies. The incubator rapidly increased members. The City's attention began to shift to support the environmental startups around the mid-and late 2010s.

At this time, the unknown troubling groups no more committed hate crimes to newcomers from privileged backgrounds. Also, the residents did not bother the so-called young professionals, despite the potential that the clean technologies they invent provide alternatives to construction material industries that dominate in the City. A question arises of what is different for the environmental startups in early 2010s.

Although this study is on management aspects of urban resilience, Robert(2000)'s framework partly answers the question. First, the City's actions ground comprehensive understanding on "area-specific events" that diluted the residents' political divide. Also, the City's focus on environmental startups differentiates its positioning from the nearby city's biomedical agglomeration.

Second, the City also has considered "broader circumstances" that require residents to provide inputs to resilience practices. Air pollutants and public parks' contaminants are externalities that affect all the residents. Therefore, the City has invited all the residents to provide inputs regardless of their age and national origin. These factors implicitly expect to reduce social exclusion (McGregor & McConnarchie, 1995. See, Roberts, 2000). Then, the mutually supportive system began to emerge regarding the resilience practices.[2]

3.1.4   The Anchors' Investment

As the clean technology incubator increased the member, it began to receive funding from the City and third sectors. The incubator expanded the intermediate organization's role: it began to attract the private investment from U.S. corporations of foreign multinationals. The foreign multinationals are located one of their newest machines and devices along with their technical staffs. The member entrepreneurs can receive

---

[2] The City also launched an aggressive action plan in 2018 for over the next 5–10 years toward the 2050 Carbon Neutrality Goal.

technical advice from dispatched personnel while using the incubator facility.

The critical factor that differentiates the clean technology incubator from other incubators is the arrangement to connect startups to manufacturing companies. The necessity of capital-intensive manufacturing is a factor that differentiates environmental startups from those in the Variant-Intensive categories.

Clean technology companies are more capital-intensive than other new industries. Their industrial science category is complicated, as discussed in Chapter 5. Though they need a manufacturing function to produce prototypes, it is impossible for less-resource startups to invest in manufacturing facilities.

Average chemical and construction companies are likely aware of the need to start the corporate entrepreneurial process. Some of them have the capacity to explore internal discoveries. However, it takes adaptation costs (Wernerfelt, 2016. See, Chapter 7) that vary depending on the frequency and contents of the change. Therefore, they have a motivation to find out entrepreneur firms that will provide R&D functions with fewer search costs.

Some manufacturing firms still have outdated production lines. As being outdated, they may be redundant resources from the efficiency viewpoints. However, they can be drivers to the related diversification to explore new services and resilience from the resource-based management perspective. They are stable to produce prototypes of startups' discoveries. Further, the firms expect to introduce new efficient and effective processes to produce competitive products upon the completion of the prototype testing. Therefore, the conventional manufactures also have a motivation to find out entrepreneurs.

On the other hand, what differentiates Mark IIs from pharmaceuticals is the invention protection method: they traditionally protected inventions through know-how. This method makes it more challenging to detect infringement that can clear the law enforcement requirements.[3] This difficulty places a barrier to develop alliances and partnerships. Therefore, parties must bear more inflictions than other industrial science firms to partner with each other.

---

[3] Though more types of patents have become applicable to the field, there has been no patent application in the City (last updated in 2019).

Here is a mutual need for an intermediate organization for established and new firms. They need intermediate organizations with a multi-sided market to help them to exchange tangible and intangible resources.

The incubator rapidly expanded its supporters to open a Global Center in May 2018. The new Center provides additional prototyping lab space, together with hydrogen fuel cell vehicle charging stations (News Release in 2018). A European ceramics multinational is one of the founding sponsors involved in building the Prototyping Lab. This sponsor expects the incubator's employees to work with member startups to evaluate new building materials, technology, and assemblies (News Release in 2018). Then, one of the motivations of the anchor investment is to test the new materials at the world-class facility.

A European chemical multinational is another founding sponsor that played a critical role in launching the Global Center. It provided the Wet Lab with startups to develop innovations in water, materials, and green chemistry (News Release, 2018). As discussed in Chapter 5, innovations in water, materials, and green chemistry have different attributes that are tough to categorize in the current new industrial science categories. Under this condition, the Wet Lab facilitates the entrepreneurs' opportunity identification and domain definition to explore new projects.

The Wet Lab also meets government agencies' demands, since the Federal government has delegated the primary responsibility of managing the quality of water, materials, and green chemistry to regional governments in many countries (Coafee & Lee, 2016).

For example, recent hazards related to water toxicity include the bloom of blue-green algae with unknown toxic mechanisms. The U.S. Center for Disease Control and Prevention (CDC) and Environment Protection Agency (EPA) warn about the hazardous and fatal effects of the blue-green algae to humans and animals. Nutrient (nitrogen and phosphorous) release from human activities increases the severity and frequency of the bloom (EPA). Its toxicity will ultimately hurt industries that depend on clean water.

However, regional governments are operating in fewer resource settings (Coafee & Lee, 2016). They require a partnership with academic KIOs, private companies, and third sectors. However, they have the potential of conflicts of interests if they directly partner with large corporations. Here is a need for an intermediate organization for them. They can invest in clean technologies through incubators.

The City A incubator has 76 alumni (on June 10, 2019) that overcame the bottlenecks of startups. They are already providing clean technology solutions to the region where they began to operate and beyond.

3.2   *Seeking New Attributes of Industrial Sciences*

Table 1 shows the City's resilience process. It complies with Robert (2000)'s framework. This study further extends the framework by adding the direction of attracting foreign anchors.

Further extension is necessary regarding the environmental aspect of resilience. The direction is to seek additional industrial sciences' attributes that involve in the environmental material sciences (Chapter 5). The potential attributes are the conceptualization of the "mimic of living organisms" (environment) and "integration into the design"(systems approach of sustainability). It is necessary to examine the conceptualization in the subsequent chapter further.

4   Investment Toward Variety

This chapter examines sub-research questions on (a) what factors motivate the established multinationals to play as anchor institutions in a market failure area; (b) How can they use their resources to help to reduce environmental inequity prevalent in inner-city regions. This study pursues these questions by analyzing a representative case of environmental aspects of urban resilience. A particular focus is on a condition in which potential anchors are absent in an urban area.

Scholarly management began to pay attention to traditional companies that enhance their operation to socially desired innovations. They provide market-based solutions in the public policy issue areas through partnerships and corporate entrepreneurship (Mahoney, McGahan, & Petleis, 2009; Zahra et al., 2016). This chapter addresses factors and organizational mechanisms of market-based solutions in which corporate anchors are involved by focusing on environmental aspects of urban resilience.

Research shows that a clean technology incubator plays an intermediate organization's role by creating a multi-sided market to coordinate and align actors' incentives.

Factors that motivate Mark II multinationals' research investment are the external structural contexts that forge them to redefine the technological and economic elements of projects. The corporate entrepreneurship

Table 1 Actions and events before and after the resilience initiative

Year	Actors	Actions	Institutions	Consequences; Types of knowledge or products created
1958	A former anchor organization	Withdrew the facility	The movement of deindustrialization	Withdrawal of traditional manufacturing; Skill demand shifts
1976	A retail nearby the former anchor; Factories of the city	Closed the operation		Withdrawal of traditional manufacturing and retails
Start of the Revitalization				
The 1990s	City government	Extended the subway line from a nearby city to the Western part of the City	Deregulation of land prices in the nearby city	The entry of newcomers became distinct, such as international students and faculties associated with the universities in the nearby city
	City government	Prepare office spaces by using vacant buildings		The entry of businesses that do not add a variety
The early 2010s	City government	Joint efforts to attract Mark I life science businesses	A mutual agreement with the nearby cities	
	City government	Support the cultural heritage of residents and the City; Support the art and crafts by residents		Cultural knowledge The cultural products, arts, poets, cultural food restaurants The entry of a foreign hospice with a green courtyard

(continued)

Table 1 (continued)

Year	Actors	Actions	Institutions	Consequences; Types of knowledge or products created
	City government	Creation of open spaces; Greening of the public space		Knowledge of environmental aspects of urban resilience planning An open playground and a park that commemorate a renowned federal athlete who graduated from the City's high school; Planting of trees at the park and the public streets; open kitchen gardens
	City government; Nonprofit organization	Youth development		Knowledge to upgrade education effectiveness High school students' performances at the open gatherings
	City government; a nonprofit organization	Publication and free distribution of a town magazine		Publication and free distribution of a town magazine that introduces local cultural events for youth, local cultural restaurants, and voices of residents
	City government	Upgrade the quality of hygiene; waste management; Recycling		Hygiene consciousness Consciousness to the circulating economy Standardized procedures for recycling and waste management for businesses and residents

Year	Actors	Actions	Institutions	Consequences; Types of knowledge or products created
	Private actors	Provide supportive infrastructure, such as broadband, wireless hotspot, office support services, private deliveries, takeaway restaurants		Digitization; Process knowledge The entry of young professionals
	Professional service firms	Provide supportive professional services, such as those of lawyers, accountants, and tax consultants		Professional service knowledge The entry of young professionals
2011	Entrepreneurs	Foundation of a clean energy incubator		Entrepreneurship; A multi-sided market (an intermediate organization). Foundation of a clean energy incubator in a vacant brick building. Connect entrepreneurial ideas to manufacturers that produce prototypes. Alumni of the incubator that provide clean technology solutions in the region and beyond (Seventy-six alumni until 2019)

(continued)

Table 1 (continued)

Year	Actors	Actions	Institutions	Consequences; Types of knowledge or products created
	City government	Invitation of all the residents to town meetings related to environmental resilience		Mutually supportive system Public meetings on soil remediation in public spaces, among others
2016	State government	Designate the City to the Green Initiative City		Authoritative support
2018	The clean technology incubator; Foreign anchor multinationals; Anchor firms; Third-sector funding agency (social enterprise); Professional service firms; City government.	Launched a Global Center that is closely located at the clean technology incubator		Scientific knowledge of emerging environmental sciences; Applications and validation of emerging environmental material sciences. Additional prototyping labs that evaluate new building materials, technology, and assembly; Wet labs that facilitate entrepreneurial innovation in water, materials, and green chemistry
2018	City government	Launched the action plan for the next 5–10 years toward the 2050 Carbon Neutrality Goal	The Action Plan for the next 5–10 years toward the 2050 Carbon Neutrality Goal	A set of prescriptions for constituents of the City toward a specific goal

process will follow the redefinition. However, problems are (a) the technological compatibilities between emerging sciences that requires distant search and the Mark IIs' process advantages that evolve tacit knowledge around routines. (b) Beneficiaries do not necessarily pay for the upgraded quality brought by R&D in the environmental material sciences. (c) If the condition necessitates the strategic integration, there is the potential conflict regarding the technological properties of stability, reliability, and safety. (d) Further, it is too much uncertain to determine which science-stage trajectories will survive as the mainstream trajectories (see, Chapter 3, Table 3.1).

In this regard, the intermediate organization absorbs the risk of disturbance that might otherwise broaden the inflictions between anchors and scattered sources of entrepreneurs. The anchors then can provide new research directions in environmental sciences and opportunities for prototyping by developing labs. These functions will help the emergence of new scientific knowledge and applications.

The study is contributing to theories by extracting managerial and organizational factors that induce anchors' research investment. Though environmental sciences require governmental investment, anchors' market-based solutions still have potentials.

This chapter also adds the precondition to attract anchors' investment. The representative case suggests that the use of redundant resources in a full capacity (Coafee & Lee, 2016; Penrose, 1959) is one of the essential components to remove barriers to anchors' activities. As the use of redundant resources adds a variety to the economy (Saviotti, 1996), a reversed cycle emerges that will lead to economic growth and inclusive resilience.

Further investigation is necessary on the additional attributes of new environmental material sciences and the corresponding organizational arrangements. The proposed attributes are the conceptualization of the mimic of living organisms and systematic design architecture (Chapter 3). Further study needs to validate and operationalize these attributes to analyze organization forms to manage the new environmental, material, and construction sciences.

REFERENCES

Abernathy, W. J., & Clark, K. B. (1980). Innovation: Mapping the winds of creative destruction. *Research Policy, 14*(1), 3–22.

Acemogulu, D., Gallego, F. A., & Robinson, J. A. (2009). *Institutions, human capital and development*. (National Bureau of Economic Research Working Paper 19933).

Beauchamp, T. L., & Childress, J. E. (2013). *Principles of biomedical ethics* (7th ed.). New York: Oxford University Press.

Boudreau, K. J., & Marx, M. (2019). From theory to practice: Field experimental evidence on early exposure of engineering majors to professional work. *National Bureau of Economic Research Working Paper*, 20163.

Bower, J. L. (1970). *Managing the resource allocation process*. Boston: Division of Research, Graduate School of Business Administration, Harvard University.

Bower, J. L., & Gilbert, C. G. (2006). *From resource allocation to strategy*. New York and Oxford: Oxford University Press.

Caves, R. E. (2007/1982). *Multinational enterprise and economic analysis*, 3rd Ed. Cambridge: Cambridge University Press.

Coafee, J., & Lee, P. (2016). *Urban resilience: Planning risk, crisis and uncertainty*. London: Palgrave.

Contreas, J. L. (2011). Bermuda's legacy: Policy, patents, and the design of the genome commons. *Minnesota Journal of Law, Science, and Technology, 12*(1), 61–125.

Covin, J. G., & Miles, M. P. (1999). Corporate entrepreneurship and the pursuit of competitive advantage. *Entrepreneurship Theory and Practice, 23*(3), 47–63.

Cyert, R. M., & March, J. G. (1963). *Behavioral theory of the firm*. New Jersey: Prentice Hall.

Data USA. Retrieved from https://datausa.io.

Dess, G. G., Ireland, R. D., Zahra, S. A., Floyd, S. W., Janney, J. J., & Lane, P. J. (2003). Emerging issues in corporate entrepreneurship. *Journal of Management, 29*(3), 351–378.

Eisenmann, T., & Bower, J. (2000). The entrepreneurial M-Form: Strategic integration in global media firms. *Organization Science, 11,* 348–355.

Freeman, R. B. (2007). The. market for scientists and engineers. National Bureau of Economic Research, *Report Summary*. Retrieved from https://www.nber.org/reporter/2007number3/freeman.html.

Galvin, G. (2018). Fighting for breath in near-highway neighborhoods. *US News*.

Glaeser, E. L., & Hausman, N. (2019). *Spatial mismatch between innovation and joblessness*. (National Bureau of Economic Research Working Paper No. 25913).

Henderson, R., & Cockburn, I. (1996). Scale, scope, and spillovers: The determinants of research productivity in drug discovery. *RAND Journal of Economics, 27,* 32–59.

Kuratko, D. F., & Covin, D. G. (2015). Forms of corporate entrepreneurship. In C. L. Cooper (Ed.), *Wiley encyclopedia of management*. Chichester: Wiley. https://doi.org/10.1002/9781118785317.weom030016.

Leonard-Barton, D. (1992). Core capabilities and core rigidities: A paradox in managing new product development. *Strategic Management Journal, 13*, 111–125.

Mahoney, J. T., McGahan, A. M., & Petleis, C. N. (2009). Perspective- The interdependence of private and public interests. *Organization Science, 20*(6), 941–1076.

McGregor, A., & McConnarchie, M. (1995). Social exclusion, urban regeneration and economic reintegration. *Urban Studies, 32*(10), 1587–1600.

Niosi, J. (2000). Science-based industries: New Schumpeterian taxonomy. *Technology in Society, 22*, 429–444.

Organization for Economic Cooperation and Development (OECD). (2004). *Entrepreneurship: Catalyst for urban regeneration*. Paris: OECD.

Orr, J., & Topa, G. (2006). Challenges facing the New York Metropolitan area economy. *Current Issues in Economics and Finance, 12*(1). Retrieved from https://www.newyorkfed.org/medialibrary/media/research/current_issues/ci12-1.pdf.

Penrose, E. T. (1959). *The theory of the growth of a firm*. New York and Oxford: Blackwell.

Pisano, G. P. (1990). The R&D boundaries of the firm: An empirical analysis. *Administrative Science Quarterly, 35*, 153–176.

Pisano, G. P. (2006). *Science business: The promise, the reality, and the future of biotech*. Boston: Harvard Business School Press.

Roberts, P. (2000). The evolution, definition and purpose of urban regeneration. In P. Roberts & H. Sykes (Eds.), *Urban regeneration: A handbook* (pp. 9–36). New York: Sage.

Ryan, A., Freeman, J., & Hybels, R. (1995). Biotechnology firms. In G. R. Caroll & M. T. Hannan (Eds.), *Organizations in industry* (pp. 332–358). New York: Oxford University Press.

Saviotti, P. P. (1996). *Technological evolution, variety and the economy*. Cheltenham: Edward Elgar.

Sharma, P., & Chrisman, J. J. (1999). Toward a reconciliation of the definitional issues in the field of corporate entrepreneurship. *Entrepreneurship Theory and Practice, 23*(3), 11–27.

Shelton, B. (2005/2006). Journal Articles (Due to the de-identification of the case, the names of articles and the journal are removed).

Sutton, J. (1998). *Technology and market structure*. Cambridge: The MIT Press.

Wadhua, V., Rissing, B., Gereffi, G., Trumpbour, J., & Engardio, P. (2008). The globalization of innovation: Pharmaceuticals. Available at *SSRN* 1143472.

Wernerfelt, B. (2016). *Adaptation, specialization, and the theory of the firm: Foundations of the resource-based view*. Cambridge: Cambridge University Press.

Zahra, S. A., Neubaum, D. O., & Hayton, J. C. (2016). *Handbook of research on corporate entrepreneurship*. Cheltenham and Northampton: Edward Elgar.

CHAPTER 5

Emergence and Dynamism of New Material Sciences

1 Schumpeterian Mark II Category

This chapter pursues research sub-questions on what categories or attributes are appropriate for material environmental sciences; what organization forms facilitate their emergence and contribution to variety.

The former chapters extract two new attributes: mimic of nature and integration into systems design. A problem is to what extent they are valid in new material sciences.

Some material sciences start with a research of life science and biotechnology. The industrial science category of biotechnology falls into the Mark I that has attributes of low entry and exit barriers. However, new material science is not at all easy to enter. It necessitates a large-scale facility for both research and manufacturing. It is because nano-science scientists often have to overcome the existing limit of physics. Then, how do they mimic nature while integrating systems approach to attain sustainability?

Also, it is not always clear how environmental material technologies add variety to the economy. Some technological trajectories bases on biotechnology, others on Variation-Intensive technologies. They apparently alter the internal technological structure. A problem is what new services they add to the extent they add a net variety.

In basing on Saviotti and Metcalfe (1984), the processes of substitution, specialization, and emergence of new products can be the basic

© The Author(s), under exclusive license to
Springer Nature Switzerland AG 2021
E. Okada, *Management of Science-Intensive Organizations*,
https://doi.org/10.1007/978-3-030-64042-2_5

105

components of more complex processes in the real economies. Saviotti and Melcalfe (1984) define these processes in twofold characteristics: technological elements and services. According to them, these processes constitute of three types:

a. A new product defined in a new internal technological structure that supplies the almost same services as a previous one, but either at a lower price or providing higher levels of the same services.
b. A new product with a new internal technological structure and provides some similar services to a previous one and some new services.
c. A new product with a new internal technological structure and provides new services.

According to them, if a product with a new internal technological structure substitutes a previous product and provides the same service with it, the new product does not add variety to the economy.

Further, many established chemistry multinationals are in Schumpeterian Mark II category. Then, a problem is where the emergence comes from and what organization forms facilitate the emergence.

This chapter investigates R&D investment and technological trajectories of the entrepreneurs and established multinationals. The objective is to seek adequate organizational arrangements to increase a net variety. Then it will examine additional attributes for new material sciences to understand a basis of their R&D dynamism.

2   Variation and Capability Renewal

2.1   Variation

According to the literature of economic development, the growth in variety is a necessary requirement for long-term development (Saviotti, 1996. See, Pasinetti, 1981, 1990). At the same time, this occurrence has moderating factors.

According to Pasinetti (1990), the productivity growth due to technological change temporarily entails unemployment and underutilization of productive capacity, if a situation of demand deficiency simultaneously occurs in many vertically integrated sectors. Meanwhile, another effect of technical change is introducing new goods that add new demands to the system. The added needs counterbalance the tendency to underemployment. In Saviotti's words, growing variety offset underemployment and underutilization of capacity.

Therefore, the growth of variety is a necessary condition for the long-term continuation of economic growth.

The variety growth and productivity growth are complementary aspects of economic development (Saviotti, 1996). If a growing productivity in existing sectors can liberate the resources that are necessary to generate new commodities, this condition increases a variety in technology, products, and services. Therefore, the growth of productivity and that of variety are complementary to each other (Saviotti, 1996).[1]

This economic relationship holds to the science-intensive businesses in the Variation-Intensive category in which companies have developed diversified products, services, and submarkets. However, little is not known whether variation generating dynamism holds to science-intensive firms in the material environment field.

Regarding the variety generation mechanisms, Schumpeter (1983/1912) states that entrepreneurs increase temporal net variety through innovation that has the potential to substitute existing goods and technologies that routine activities produce. Under this condition, not all of the innovations are beneficial. According to Holling (1973), some innovations that generate variety are same as biological mutations in human cells. These mutations invoke uncontrollable cell death, that is, cancers. Similarly, though some innovations generate variety that benefits economy and society, some harms existing technological systems (Holling, 1973). The latter includes bias that categorically harms specific populations by undermining privacy.

Schumpeter (1983/1912) states that the net variety remains unchanged when an innovation replaces previous goods, artifact, and technology. At the same time, previous goods, artifact, and technologies also can specialize and provide a foundation of variety generation in the face of disturbance.

In either case of productivity growth or specialization, some mechanisms are necessary for the growth of net variety to benefit economy and society (see, Saviotti, 1996).

In IBM, it provides a foundation to generate numerous variety-intensive firms in the 1980s while moving to the dynamic increasing

---

[1] Saviotti (1996) also is drawing examples from a transportation sector by starting from a steam engine and the economy.

return (DIR) category by specializing in supercomputing and solution businesses. The focused domain is business-to-business transactions, such as designing a system to automatically measure and control extremely high temperature of heavy material industries.

However, it is unknown whether the introduction of environmental material sciences to Mark II chemicals leads them to relate to the Variety-Intensive category or specializing in specific services. Here is a need to specify what does "variety" means.

Based on Saviotti and Metcalfe (1984), the processes of substitution, specialization, and emergence of new products can be the basic essential components of more complex processes in the real economies. Saviotti and Melcalfe (1984) define these processes in twofold characteristics: technological elements and services. According to them, these processes constitute of three types as stated in the previous section.

2.2 Definition of Variety

It is then necessary to specify the definition of variety to investigate whether Mark II's environmental material sciences add variety. For this purpose, this study differentiates the concept of variety from that of complexity by following Saviotti (1996). In following Ashby (1956), Saviotti (1996) defines the concept of variety as follows.

> If an economic system is a set of elements, then the variety of this set will increase when the number of distinguishable elements of the set increases. ----- In information theory, the variety of a set is defined as the logarithm in base 2 of the number of distinguishable elements in the set. (---: inserted by the author)

$$V = \log_2 n$$

Where V = variety,

n = number of distinguishable elements in the set.

Given the function of the logarithm, this particular definition implies that the marginal contribution to the variety made by new and distinguishable products will decline with an increasing number of products present in the system. This relation is a behavior that is actually found in the model of technological evolution that relates to replicator dynamics (Saviotti, 1996).

2.2.1 Replicator Dynamics

There are two types of replicator dynamics model: a micro-level model and an aggregate representation of technological revolution. According to the micro model by Saviotti, the technology or its product models based on two sets of characteristics: the internal structure of technology, and the services performed for its users. These two sets of characteristics relate to each other through a pattern of correspondence (Saviotti, 1996).

Each technology is represented by a collection of models that have similar characteristic values. The models that have a given technological population then concentrate on a specific region of characteristics space. Meanwhile, it is possible that a technological population changes its position and density and fragment into two or more distinguishable technological populations, leading to specialization (Saviotti, 1991).

The changes in the density of the population indicate either a growing product differentiation or a growing density drove into the more severe competition. (1) The intense competition motivates members to reduce competition and establish themselves in a differentiated niche, increasing net variety (Saviotti, 1996). Variety also increases when niches lead to (2) the emergence of new technologies and their product models, creating new dimensions in characteristics space. The balance between intra-technology competition and inter-technology competition has significance in determining the emergence of a new technological population and net variety (Saviotti & Mani, 1995).

It is then necessary to investigate the conditions for a variety's growth, which depend on the relationship between variety and competition (Saviotti, 1996). The replicator dynamics model is critical to research the relationship between competition and variety (Saviotti, 1996).

In the micro model, replication occurs when the members of the technological population with unchanged characteristics increase (Saviotti, 1996). Strategy scholars call this phenomenon a part of learning whose types depend on their absorptive capacity (Cohen & Levinthal, 1991). The rate of replication increases with the increase of investment, the fitness of the technology, and consumers' or users' income. The tradeoff occurs between the rise of investment in the existing process technology and that in search activities (Nelson & Winter, 1982). Meanwhile, search activities can reduce unit costs and lead to a higher replication rate (Saviotti, 1996).

On the other hand, the aggregated models (the Loka Volterra equations) describe the rate of change of a population in the presence of competing species (Roughgarden, 1979; Saviotti, 1996). The exponential growth of the population is the carrying capacity of the environment

(Saviotti, 1996). In this space, the relationships between the intra-technology competition and inter-technology competition matter. The rate of change at the population-level must be the same as that in the above stated micro-level replication.

2.2.2 Differentiating Variety from Complexity

Whether the emergence of new technological sets is induced or the specialization of preexisting sets occurs depends on the nature of competition, as mentioned above (Saviotti, 1996).

Meanwhile, by referring to Nicolis (1986), Saviotti (1996) defines the complexity in two fold as follows. (a) Structural complexity increases with the number of interacting subunits. (b) On the functional level, complexity increases with the minimum length of the most compressed algorithm from which one can retrieve the full behavior of the system.

Given the previous definition, the structural complexity of a system can change by changing the interaction between subunits and their distribution function while maintaining the number of subunits, the variety of the system, constant. Therefore, variety is a component of complexity but not equivalent to it (see, Saviotti, 1996).

A system characterized by a variety of constituents is also a system that requires a more significant amount of information (see, Galbraith, 1973). Given that the growth of a variety of the economic system leads to positive welfare implications along with a continued process of economic growth, this process of economic growth will realize if information processing costs do not grow as rapidly as the growth of variety (Saviotti, 1996).

A greater variety of processes increase information processing costs to produce new goods and services. The organizations can reduce these costs that occur under the condition of variety growth through the following two measures.

a. The organizations can increase the efficiency with which the information in the system is stored and processed.
b. The organizations can change processes so that an organizational constituent stores and processes a smaller number of data sets to achieve the same output variety (Saviotti, 1996).[2]

---

[2] At a feature level, the former can be achieved through digital technologies, the latter through adopting an agile system that depends on the algorithm capacities.

2.3 Organization Forms that Manage a Given Outcome Variety

In other words, organizations can reduce the process variety in achieving a given output variety (Saviotti, 1996). The increase of this acquired output variety will increase economic growth.

Achieving this relationship requires the introduction of the concept of entropy (Saviotti, 1996). Entropy measures the randomnes s or uncertainty of a given set of elements (Gatlin, 1972). It is higher when the components are randomly placed each other and is lower when the elements are in an ordered configuration (Shannon & Weaver, 1949; Saviotti, 1988).

Then, organizations can reduce information processing costs by putting the elements in the configuration as ordered as possible. This action entails the optimization of categorization that is to better represent attributes of the group constituents. This point is how an AI-powered system works in deep learning. Saviotti (1996) frames this point by using the theory of variety as follows.

a. One way to achieve this optimization in the catastrophic condition is to store and process a smaller number of data sets by configuring the elements as ordered as possible (Saviotti, 1996).

It suggests the introduction of more divided organization units connected by efficient information processing and restoration system (Saviotti, 1996). The creation of sets will matter in this condition.

b. The other is the reconfiguration of routines (Saviotti, 1996. Also see, Caves, 2007/1982; Nelson & Winter, 1982; Feldman, 2000).

The variety will partly destroy or substitute once established routines (Nelson & Winter, 1982). The reconfiguration of renewed routines will necessitate placing new and heterogeneous elements in a manner they reduce randomness and thus entropy (Saviotti, 1996).

Routines emerge in an organization through a practiced process of organizational learning (Lewitt & March, 1988; Winter, 1994). The initial learning phase ends when satisfactory performance is achieved. After that, the improvement and renewal of routines become significant. The nature of the processes that end an initial learning phase would be of no significance if a timely renewal of improvement efforts were absent (Winter, 1994).

2.4 Capability Renewal of Mark II Multinationals

Thus, when Mark II firms are going to create a variety and strengthen science-intensive environmental products, the organizational reconfiguration or renewal is necessary to achieve a given level of outcome variety. This effort entails reducing the entropy of process variety.

Regarding part (A), Mark II firms have an option to alliance with dynamic increasing return computer science firms to have information processing more efficient. For example, BASF, Dow Chemical, and others announced to partner with IBM and Hewlett Packard Enterprise (HP). Mainly, IBM is a company that specialized in developing and providing solution services. Such behaviors of Mark II firms are to introduce the computing-intensive components of science and business operation into their process. Regarding the restoration and data access, the advancement of cloud technologies has generated more reasonable and efficient systems.

Adopting artificial intelligence-enabled methods also broadens the scope of experimentation by using data available in the lab and manufacturing plants. It will promote the application and development of complex modeling and simulation approaches (News Release) in the variety-added material science R&D.

Regarding part (B), reconfiguration of renewed routines, the technological variety requests the Mark II firms to divide their organizations into smaller subunits while reconfiguring newly emerged routines. Simultaneously, Mark II firms need more concentration on their R&D investment. These two requirements are contradictory to each other. Mark II firms are overcoming this conflict by introducing more data-intensive cloud and supercomputing while integrating distant sciences, technologies, and operations.

A problem is what kind of organizational design to adopt to divide the operations into small subunits.

Multinationals have used intermediate organizations to reconfigure smaller sets of subunits. Under this design, the intermediate institution bears a function of a node that supports the variety, as below stated.

2.4.1 *Intermediate Institution*

a. One is to adopt the organizational structure that has foreign and domestic area hub corporations. It is an extension of a multidivisional organization (hereafter, M-Form) that manages products and functional divisions in a specific scope of geographic areas. For example, BASF Corporation, headquartered in New Jersey, defines itself as the North American affiliate of BASF SE in Germany.[3]

b. Another structure is the use of a large-scale incubator. A large incubator can be an intermediate organization for global Mark II to increase the variety in their products and R&D (see Chapter 4).

Regarding part (a), multinational enterprises initially delegated several functional and product decision autonomy to the area corporation. It assures the requirement of responsiveness while taking advantage of global coordination (see, Bartlett & Ghoshal, 1989; Stopford & Wells, 1972). When resource redeployability (Sakhartov & Folta, 2014. See also, Montgomerry & Wernerfelt, 1980; Rumelt, 1982; Silvermann, 1991) is not assured among geographically distant organizational segments, the adoption of area corporations is reasonable. Similarly, a pure M-Form is more suitable than a corrupted M-Form to manage variety (Eisenmann & Bower, 2000. See also, Saviotti, 1996). On the other hand, when multinationals divide its value chain into several units in several countries in the region, they can assign roles to the organizational units and measure their performance regarding the contribution to the goals (Silvermann, 1991; Tang, 1981). This style has evolved due to the decreased inflictions of contract and data processing.

The increased information restoration and processing efficiency (since the 1980s) enabled the multinationals to gradually move to transnational corporations (Bartlett & Ghoshal, 1989). This form simultaneously fulfills the responsiveness to local needs and centralized coordination advantages. Thus, theoretically, transnationals can increase resource redeployment also with remote organizational units (see, Bartlett & Ghoshal, 1989; Sakhartov & Folta, 2014).

The current market environment further requires multinationals to move beyond the transnational solutions to be metanational (Doz, Santos, & Williamson, 2001). The current expectations include to sense

---

[3] http://www.basf.us. Last visited in August 2020.

area-specific unalienable resources, to mobilize resources of headquarter and other areas, develop and produce products and bring them to the foreign or global market (see Doz et al. 2001). The area-specific resources include not only cultural heritages (such as a beverage product, Red Bull) but also university research conducted with regional partners.

For example, the U.S. corporation of BASF launched the Advanced Research Initiative with a Cambridge (U.S.)-based university. They discovered a specific process that significantly increases the efficiency of current essential processing (below mentioned). Its success model built a partnership with several nearby universities to further integrate academic sciences. According to the BASF (U.S.), the Initiative significantly advanced the BASF (U.S.)'s research on biofilms.

Biofilms[4] have long been used as natural filters in industrial wastewater treatment systems. Therefore, scientists and industries have already tested and validated the robust and stable properties of the films. By paying attention to the stable and robust properties, one BASF science team has developed a viable reactor. This reactor pumps a chemical substrate over support coated with a biofilm. The biofilm then converts the substrate into a product (Jarvis, 2020). Due to biofilms' robust and stable properties, scientists plan to replace conventional fermentation processes with biofilm-based reactors. The traditional processes need to start over (or inoculate) a reactor every other day that waste times (Jarvis, 2020).

Thus, BASF expects to renew the organizational processes by adopting its new invention started as regional research. Also, BASF plans to move the biofilm experiment to the commercial-scale production of the biofilm-based reactors (Jarvis, 2020). This reactor can add a variety to the reactor market.

Regarding part (b), a large-scale incubator plays an intermediary role with a two-sided or multiple-sided market. A two-sided market is an intermediate space in which an intermediate organization coordinates buyers and sellers of goods by attracting both-side participants (see, Hagiu & Spulber, 2013). In the typical two-sided market, market participation depends on their expectations of participation conditions on the other side of the market (Hagiu & Spulber, 2013). The cross-market benefits of the participants derive from the product variety and scale effects, being

---

[4] As already stated in Chapter 3, biofilm is an assemblage of surface-associated microbial cells enclosed in an extracellular polymeric substance matrix (Donlan, 2002). Microbial cells include those of bacteria.

given of the market liquidity and connectivity of communication networks (Hagiu & Spulber, 2013; Spulber, 2010).

Similarly, the incubator can act as an intermediate with the cross-market benefits and scale effects. This movement has the potential to yield a positive spiral and spillovers to the participants and society.

2.4.2 Capability Renewal of Mark II Firms

When Mark II firms create a variety by strengthening science-intensive environmental products, the timely renewal is necessary to achieve a given level of outcome variety (Winter, 1994). Its precondition is the domain redefinition.

The domain redefinition entails redefining and deploying organizations' new competence in social exchange (Dess et al., 2003; Eisenmann & Bower, 2000). It has the potential to embed the self-renewal capability to the organization (Eisenmann & Bower, 2000).

At the same time, the variety has the potential to destroy once established routines (Caves, 2007/1982). It is necessary to reconfigure renewed routines so that new and heterogeneous elements reduce randomness (Table 1). This action will accelerate the economic and social change in a redefined domain. Then, such reconfiguration can lead to enhance the beneficiaries of environmental material sciences.

3   SUBSEQUENT COMPETITION IN THE URBAN CONTEXTS

3.1   *The Involvement of Other Industrial Science Categories*

As stated above, the competition types that follow the new sciences' emergence affect whether we gain net variety. Then, the next issue is the more factual investigation of the emergence associated with science categories.

3.1.1   Starting from Mark II Sciences to Recombine with Emerging Sciences

There is a pathway in which the Mark II science recombines with other new sciences in the Mark II science area. One is the recombination with neutron science.

A representative case is a metal-organic framework (MOF) material. A scientific team, led by the University of Manchester in the U.K. developed a MOF material, MFM-520. This material provides a selective, fully

Table 1 Organization forms to optimize a variety

Condition of variety	Methods to reduce process variety	Methods to reduce randomness, thus achieve optimization	Organization forms	Concrete organization forms to achieve output variety
A greater variety of the processes increase information processing costs to produce new goods and services	Increase efficiency with which the information in the system is stored and processed	Store and process a smaller number of data sets by configuring the elements as ordered as possible	a. The introduction of more divided organization units connected by efficient information processing and restoration system b. Reconfiguration of renewed routines so that new and heterogeneous elements reduce randomness (Reason: Variety will partly destroy or substitute once established routines)	a. Alliance with Dynamic Increasing Return supercomputing firms, including the adoption of Artificial Intelligence-enabled methods b. Use of intermediate organizations and data-intensive cloud computing. (Reason: Technological variety requests the Mark II firms to divide their organizations into smaller subunits, while Mark II firms need more concentration of their R&D investment. The adoption of this organization design can overcome this conflict)

Condition of variety	Methods to reduce process variety	Methods to reduce randomness, thus achieve optimization	Organization forms	Concrete organization forms to achieve output variety
	Change processes so that organizational constituents store and process a smaller number of data sets to achieve the same output variety	Adoption of an agile system that depends on the algorithm capacity		

118 E. OKADA

reversible, and repeatable capacity to capture nitrogen dioxide produced by combusting diesel and other fossil fuels. The function of the MFM-20 is that it converts the captured gas into nitric acid for other industrial uses, including fertilizer, rocket propellant, nylon, among others. Its mechanism consists of the use of water and air (Oak Ridge National Laboratory, 2019).

This invention comes from the Chemistry and Catalysis Initiative at Oak Ridge National Laboratory (ORNL)'s Directorate of Neutron Sciences. According to the director and a lead scientist,

> "—thanks to the penetrating power of neutrons, we tracked how the nitrogen dioxide molecules arranged and moved inside the pores of the material, and studied the effects they had on the entire MOF structure.
> What made these observations possible is the VISION vibrational spectrometer at ORNL's Spallation Neutron Source. This spectrometer has the highest sensitivity and resolution of its kind in the world."
> "The interaction between the nitrogen dioxide molecules and MOF causes extremely small changes in their vibrational behavior. Such changes can only be recognized when the computer model accurately predicts them."
> "Neutron vibrational spectroscopy is a unique tool to study adsorption and reaction mechanisms and guest-host interactions at the molecular level, especially when combined with computer simulation."

Thus, the involvement of supercomputer science in the DIR category indirectly supports this field's advancement.

The supporter of the neutron research is the U.S. Department of Energy (DOE)'s Office of Science. This research project also uses the Integrated Computer Environment Modeling and Analysis for Neutron data software program funded by the Laboratory Directed Research and Development program at the ORNL.

3.1.2 Starting from Chemical Mark II to Enhance to Other Categories

Recombination with Biotechnology

The observation suggests the chemical Mark II's potential to integrate other industrial science categories. The measures are the academic involvement and the use of large-scale incubators. Recent decades notably witnessed the recombination with biotechnology. Examples include bioinspired materials.

The bioinspired materials are synthetic materials whose structure, properties, and function imitate those of living matter. For example, light-harvesting photonic materials mimic photosynthesis, structural composites that imitate the structure of nacre, and metal actuators inspired by the movements of jellyfish.[5]

Several applications will invoke inter-technology competition in Mark II sciences. Among them, bioinspired materials have the potential to contribute to energy efficiency of building architectures (Imani, Donn & Balador, 2018). Donn and Balador conduct systematic literature analyses on bioinspired materials whose applications are in architecture, construction, and building sciences.[6] They reveal that the mimic of nature and integrating into the design process is an effective strategy that will contribute to designing innovative and sustainable buildings. The imitation of biological systems (functions, structures, and processes) leads to designing and developing bioinspired materials to increase energy efficiency of the buildings (Imani et al., 2018; Pacheco-Torgala & Labrinchab, 2013). The sources of imitation are animals/plants' or microorganisms' innovative biological systems regarding functions, structures, and processes (Imani et al., 2018).

Imani et al. (2018) also state that the existing application of bioinspired material is not necessarily broad. On the other hand, what is unique is its extension to encompass bioinspired construction materials. Some examples include

a. biotech concrete incorporating ureolytic bacteria,
b. self-cleaning materials inspired by lotus leaves,
c. tough materials such as spider silk and nacre shells, and
d. adhesives such as mussel byssus and barnacle cement (Donn & Baladar, website[7]; Pacheco-Torgala & Labrinchab, 2013).

These new and innovative materials serve different functions in buildings (Imani, et al., 2018).

---

[5] Retrieved from: https://www.nature.com/subjects/bioinspired-materials. Last visited in August 2020.

[6] Retrieved from: https://www.masicgroup.mit.edu/post/bioinspired-construction-materials. Last visited in August 2020.

[7] *Ibid.*

120   E. OKADA

For example, scientists expect that barnacle cement will contribute to the construction and repair of infrastructure. Barnacles can attach to a wide variety of surfaces by secreting proteinaceous cement, one of the strongest underwater adhesives on Earth (Crisp, Walker, Young, & Yule, 1985; Donn & Balador, website[8]). The goal of researching attachment mechanisms is to characterize it with the composition and properties' change during the curing process. Gaining such understanding will help to develop strong underwater adhesives, including concrete adhesives and marine adhesives. However, the components of attachment mechanisms are still unknown (Imani, et al., 2018; Kamino, 2013).

The general barrier to the integration of biology to building construction is the lack of a bio-architectural workflow. It assists scientists and designers in finding the relevant organisms in nature as the source of inspiring innovative design (Imani et al., 2018). The resolution of this barrier lies in the zoology discipline, as already mentioned.

Partnership with the DIR Supercomputing Sciences

This classification corresponds to the organizational efforts for reducing the process variety to facilitate the net outcome variety. Table 1 states this direction in terms of organizational forms. The example of neutron vibrational spectroscopy indirectly relates to this category.

3.1.3   Starting from Architectural Engineering Science

This field began to mimic living organisms along with computer science's advancement. Examples include engineered urban algae strands. Engineered algae variants are under development at a U.K.-based architecture company in collaboration with the Biochemical Engineering Department, University College London.[9]

Algae-based bioplastics produce photo-bioreactor modules made from the biomass. This invention is to contribute to building the circular material economy. According to the company, it has accumulated proprietary strands with optimized characteristics of resilience to urban conditions. Its priorities are in the resilience to thermal stress and the capacity to absorb and re-metabolize air pollutants.[10]

[8] *Ibid.*

[9] Retrieved from: www.photosynthetica.co.uk. Last visited in August 2020.

[10] *Ibid.*

This perspective corresponds to the reduction of PM2.5 that intensifies under urban conditions.

This organization already created a prototype of 3D printed facades. It demonstrates the potential to create material structures receptive to life. Scientists apply this material to generate thin skin that can be optimized for specific environments. The goal is to increase air pollution filtering performance.

Their product development strategy also includes the recombination with the artificial intelligence (hereafter, AI) algorithm. This technological recombination is blurring the interface among the architectural engineering science, Mark II, and Variant-Intensive categories.

Thus, the architectural engineering science is enhancing its field at the interface among science categories of Mark II, Variant-Intensive, and Mark I sciences by translating academic discoveries.

The involvement of architectural science in environmental engineering appears to be new. However, the participation of architectural engineering in clean technologies dates back to the 1980s. The early day efforts of screening pollutant traits fall in this category. The technological trajectory is the ion generation by electronics devices. The hazard of indoor air pollutants was already reported in the 1980s. At that time, the particles of metals were the focus.

In this submarket, the electronics and semiconductor companies in the Variant-Intensive category invented a variety of products. This variety invoked an inter-technology competition. The technological trajectories include ion generators, ozone generators, among others. They intend to clean air particles in buildings (see, Waring & Siegel, 2011; The U.S. Environment Protection Agency: EPA). Many trajectories coexist without substituting others.

After a while, the focus of the pollutant has shifted to PM 2.5. The indoor pollutant of PM2.5 is often more severe than the outdoor exposure (Harriman, Stephens, & Brennan, 2019).

Due to the above trajectory, the academic investigators of pollutant filtering in the Variant-Intensive category mainly come from civil and architectural engineering, focusing on environment.

3.2 Subsequent Competition in the Urban Context

Then, the next issue is nature of the subsequent competition. As already stated, the theory of technology and market structure (Sutton, 1998) presents two possible directions.

- a. When an organization intensifies R&D investment in a technological trajectory at a certain point of a fragmented submarket where other firms no more intensify R&D, the resultant new product will outperform existing ones in the market.
- b. When a new product enters a viable submarket, a marginal R&D spent on the technological trajectory will contribute to enhancing other technological trajectories or submarkets, thus the scope of market itself.

Based on the theory of variety, competition is one of possible interactions between organizations. The types of interactions range from

- competition,
- commensalism (collaboration), to
- predation (Saviotti, 1996).

In the competition, each organization has an inhibiting effect on the other. They are an analogy of interactions between pairs of species in biology (Saviotti, 1996; Maynard Smith, 1974).

In comparing the two theories, part (a) is equivalent to competition and predation of biological species, and part (b), to commensalism (collaboration). Thus, the theory of the market structure of technology reaches the same consequence as that of variation and evolution through a different logic.

The example of a biofilm-based reactor represents a case of a possible replacement. The inventing company will replace the current process with a biofilm-based process in a manner that will reduce the process variety. This renewal has the potential to strengthen the company's implementing ability of strategies. The company also intends to commercialize the biofilm-based reactor and sell it to other companies. This product will enhance the productivity also of other companies. Also, it will invoke the inter-technology competition. Competitors are immobilized cell reactor (covalent bond formation and entrapment) and membrane reactor (Qureshi, Annous, Ezeji, Karcher, & Maddox, 2005). The degree of the replicator dynamics will depend on the others' search activities and absorptive capacity.

Meanwhile, a couple of Mark II firms have provided their novel machines to intermediate organizations so that environmental entrepreneurs can test their prototypes with the devices. This relationship of corporate entrepreneurship falls into the category of commensalism (collaboration). It will follow the enhancement of the market itself to encompass more environmental products.

Thus, one organization can engage in all types of interaction simultaneously. And it is the net variety that contributes to economic growth. The source of resilience and transformation is the redundancy in resources converted to new resource services. Thus, the sciences with new attributes can provide sources of resilience by being integrated into organization mechanisms.

4   New Science-Intensive Category

This chapter analyzes how new material sciences are creating a new science-intensive category in combination with Mark I, Variant-Intensive, and dynamic increasing return (DIR) categories. The theoretical base is that of variety by Saviotti (1996). Also, it analyzes the organization forms that facilitate the net variety through the inductive–deductive analysis.

If an economic system is a set of elements, then the variety of this set will increase when the number of distinguishable elements of the set increases. The growth in variety is a necessary requirement for long-term development (Saviotti, 1996. See, Pasinetti, 1981, 1990). Suppose growing productivity in existing sectors can liberate the resources that are necessary to generate new commodities. This condition has the potential to increase further a variety of technology, products, and services.

At the same time, what should be noticed is that a system characterized by a variety of constituents is also a system that requires a more significant amount of information (see, Galbraith, 1973). Given that growth of a variety of the economic system leads to positive welfare implications along with a continued process of economic growth, the economic growth will realize if information processing costs do not grow as rapidly as the growth of a variety (Saviotti, 1996).

124   E. OKADA

The organizations can reduce the information processing costs that occur under a growing variety through the following two measures.

a. The organizations can increase the efficiency with which the information in the system is stored and processed.
b. The organizations can change processes so that an organizational constituent stores and processes a smaller number of data sets to achieve the same output variety (Saviotti, 1996).

In other words, organizations can reduce the process variety in achieving a given output variety. The increase of this acquired output variety will increase economic growth (Saviotti, 1996).

Achieving this relationship requires introducing the concept of entropy (Saviotti, 1996) that measures the randomness or uncertainty of a given set of elements (Gatlin, 1972). It is higher when the elements are randomly placed each other and is lower when the elements are in an ordered configuration (Shannon &Weaver, 1949; Saviotti, 1996).

Organizations can then reduce information processing costs by putting the elements into the configuration as ordered as possible. This action entails the optimization of categorization that is to represent attributes of the group constituents better.

One way to achieve this optimization in the catastrophic condition is to store and process a smaller number of data sets by configuring the elements as ordered as possible (Saviotti, 1996). The creation of sets will matter in this condition.

The other is the reconfiguration of routines (Saviotti, 1996. Also see, Caves, 2007/1982; Nelson & Winter, 1982; Feldman, 2000). The variety will partly destroy or substitute once established routines (Nelson & Winter, 1982). The reconfiguration of renewed routines will necessitate placing new and heterogeneous elements to reduce randomness and thus entropy (Saviotti, 1996). What is significant in the reconfiguration is a timely renewal. It is necessary to reconfigure renewed routines in a manner that new and heterogeneous elements reduce randomness (Table 1). The nature of the processes that end an initial learning phase would be of no significance if a timely renewal of improvement efforts were absent (Winter, 1994).

Related to variety, the emergence of new science and technologies follows either of the two: (a) a growing product differentiation or (b) an ever-growing density of the technological population where more severe competition occurs, either of intra-technology competition or inter-technology competition (Saviotti, 1996).

The next issue is the more factual investigation regarding what science categories of emerging sciences affect the variation and technological alteration of Mark II firms. For this purpose, this study starts with investigating the emergence that come from Mark II sciences, then those that come from civil engineering sciences.

First, there is a pathway that the Mark II science recombines with other new sciences in the Mark II science area. One is the recombination with neutron science. A representative case is a metal-organic framework (MOF) material.

What should be noticed is the involvement of supercomputing. The strengthened precision by neutron vibrational spectroscopy enables the observation of the interaction between the nitrogen dioxide molecules and MOF. This interaction causes exceptionally tiny changes in their vibrational behavior. Such changes can only be recognized when the computer model accurately predicts them.

Second is the recombination with biotechnology. Examples include bioinspired materials.

The bioinspired materials are synthetic materials whose structure, properties, and function imitate those of living matter. There are several applications of bioinspired materials, including architecture, construction, and building sciences (Donn & Balador, website[11]). Applying these materials, the mimic of nature and integrating into the design process is an effective strategy that will contribute to designing innovative and sustainable buildings. The imitation of biological systems (functions, structures, and processes) leads to the design of bioinspired materials to increase energy efficiency of the buildings (Donn & Balador, website; Pacheco-Torgala & Labrinchab, 2013). The sources of imitation are animals/plants' or microorganisms' innovative biological systems regarding functions, structures, and processes (Imani et al., 2018).

Imani et al. (2018) also state that the existing application of bioinspired material is not necessarily broad. On the other hand, what is unique of the

---

[11] Retrieved from: https://www.masicgroup.mit.edu/post/bioinspired-construction-materials.

bioinspired material is its extension to encompass bioinspired construction materials.

These new and innovative materials serve different functions in buildings. The general barrier to integrating biology to building construction is the lack of a bio-architectural workflow that assists scientists and designers in finding the relevant organisms in nature as the source of inspiring innovative design (Imani et al., 2018). The resolution of this barrier lies in the zoology discipline, in which academic KIOs should have a critical role.

The emergence also starts with the civil engineering sciences. Along with the advancement of computer sciences, this field began to mimic living organisms. Examples include engineered urban algae strands under development at a U.K.-based architecture company in collaboration with an academic KIO.

This invention is to contribute to building the circular material economy. According to the company, it has accumulated proprietary strands with optimized characteristics of resilience to urban conditions. Its priorities are in the resilience to thermal stress and the capacity to absorb and re-metabolize air pollutants.

This perspective corresponds to the reduction of PM2.5 that intensifies under urban conditions.

The study of Chapter 3 extracts attributes of "mimic of organism (environment)" and "integration into design systems (systems approach towards sustainability)" through the abstract inference. The review of emerging material sciences in his chapter suggests that they are useful attributes. These attributes will generate competition and entrepreneurship commensalism among science-intensive organizations, leading to resilience and transformation of urban areas.

References

Ashby, W. R. (1956). *Introduction to cybernetics*. New York: Wiley.

Bartlett, C. A., & Ghoshal, S. (1989). *Managing across borders: The transnational solution*. Cambridge: Harvard Business School Press.

Caves, R. E. (2007/1982). *Multinational enterprise and economic analysis* (3rd Ed.). New York: Cambridge University Press.

Cohen, W. M., & Levinthal, D. A. (1991). Absorptive capacity: A new perspective on learning and innovation. *Administrative Science Quarterly, 35*(1), 128–152.

5 EMERGENCE AND DYNAMISM OF NEW MATERIAL SCIENCES   127

Crisp, D. J., Walker, G., Young, G. A., & Yule, A. B. (1985). Adhesion and substrate choice in mussels and barnacles. *Journal of Colloid and Interface Science, 104*(1), 40–50.

Dess, G. G., Ireland, R. D., Zahra, S. A., Floyd, S. W., Janney, J. J., & Lane, P. J. (2003). Emerging issues in corporate entrepreneurship. *Journal of Management, 29*(3), 351–378.

Donlan, R. M. (2002). Biofilms: Microbial life on surfaces. *Emerging Infectious Diseases, 8*(9), 881–890.

Doz, Y., Santos, J., & Williamson, P. (2001). *From global to metanational.* Boston: Harvard Business School Press.

Eisenmann, T., & Bower, J. (2000). The entrepreneurial M-Form: Strategic integration in global media firms. *Organization Science, 11,* 348–355.

Feldman, M. S. (2000). Organizational routine as a source of continuous change. *Organization Science, 11*(6), 629–661.

Galbraith, J. R. (1973). *Designing complex organizations.* Reading: Addison-Wesley.

Gatlin, L. L. (1972). *Information theory and the living system.* New York: Columbia University Press.

Hagiu, A., & Spulber, D. (2013). First-party content and coordination in two-sided markets. *Management Science, 59*(4), 933–949.

Harriman, L., Stephens, B., & Brennan, T. (2019). Reduction of PM2.5: New guidance for residential air cleaners. *ASHRAE Journal, 2019,* 14–23.

Holling, C. S. (1973). Resilience and stability of ecological systems. *Annual Review of Ecology and Systematics, 4,* 1–23.

Imani, M., Donn, M., & Badalar, Z. (2018). Bio-inspired materials: Contribution of biology to energy efficiency of buildings. In L. Martinez, O. Kharissova (Eds.), *Handbook of ecomaterials* (pp. 2213–2236). Cham: Springer. https://doi.org/10.1007/2F978-3-319-68255-6_136.

Jarvis, L. M. (2020). Exploiting biofilms. *Chemical and Engineering News.* American Chemical Society. https://cen.acs.org/articles/86/i23/Exploiting-Biocilms.htnl.

Kamino, K. (2013). Mini-review: barnacle adhesives and adhesion. *Biofouling, 29*(6), 735–749.

Lewitt, B., & March, J. (1988). Organization learning. *Annual Review of Sociology, 14,* 319–338.

Maynard Smith, J. (1974). The theory of games and the evolution of animal conflicts. *Journal of Theoretical Biology, 47,* 209–221.

Montgomerry, C. A., & Wernerfelt, B. (1980). Diversification, Ricardian rents, and Tobin's 1. *RAND Journal of Economics, 19*(4), 623–632.

Nelson, R. R., & Winter, S. G. (1982). *An evolutionary theory of economic change.* Cambridge: Harvard University Press.

Nicolis, J. S. (1986). A study program of chaotic dynamics applied to information processing. In W. Ebeling, & H. Ulbricht (Eds.), *Selforganization by nonlinear irreversible processes*. Springer Series in Synergetics, 33. Springer, Berlin, Heidelberg. https://doi.org/10.1007/978-3-642-71004-9-23.

Niosi, J. (2000). Science-based industries: New Schumpeterian taxonomy. *Technology in Society, 22*, 429–444.

Pacheco-Torgala, F., & Labrinchab, J. A. (2013). Biotechnologies and bioinspired materials for the construction industry: an overview. *International Journal of Sustainable Engineering*. https://doi.org/10.1080/19397038.2013.844741.

Pasinetti, L. L. (1981). *Structural change and economic growth*. Cambridge: Cambridge University Press.

Pasinetti, L. L. (1990). Structural change and unemployment. *Structural Change and Economic Dynamics, 1*, 7–14.

Qureshi, N., Annous, B. A., Ezeji, T. C., Kracher, P., & Maddox, I. S. (2005). Biofilm reactors for industrial bioconversion processes: Employing potential of enhanced reaction rates, *Microbial Cell Factories, 24*(4). https://doi.org/10.1186/1475-2859-4-24.

Roughgarden, J. (1979). *Theory of population genetics and evolutionary ecology: An introduction*. New York: Macmillan.

Rugman, A. M. (1981). *Inside the multinationals: The economics of internal markets*. London: Croom Helm.

Rumelt, R. P. (1982). Diversification strategy and profitability. *Strategic Management Journal, 3*(4), 359–369.

Sakhartov, A. V., & Folta, T. B. (2014). Resource relatedness, redeployability, and firm value. *Strategic Management Journal, 35*, 1781–1789.

Saviotti, P. P. (1988). Information, variety and entropy in technoeconomic development. *Research Policy, 17*, 89–103.

Saviotti, P. P. (1991, May 27–28). Technological evolution, production characteristics, competition and variety. Presentation at the Colloquium Management of Technology, Paris. As cited in P. P. Saviotti. (1996). *Technological evolution, variety and the economy*. Cheltenham: Edward Elgar.

Saviotti, P. P. (1996). *Technological evolution, variety and the economy*. Cheltenham: Edward Elgar.

Saviottil, P. P. & Mani, G. S. (1995). Competition, variety and technological evolution: A replicator dynamics model. *Journal of Evolutionary Economics, 5*, 369–392.

Saviotti, P. P., & Metcalfe, J. S. (1984). A theoretical approach to the construction of technological output indicators. *Research Policy, 13*, 141–151.

Schumpeter, J. (1983/1912). *The theory of economic development*. Harvard Economic Studies, 46. Cambridge: Harvard University Press.

Shannon, C. E., & Weaver, W. (1949). *The mathematical theory of communication*. Champaign: University of Illinois Press.

Silvermann, B. S. (1991). Technological resources and the direction of corporate diversification: Toward an integration of the resource-based view and transaction cost economics. *Management Science, 45*(8), 1109–1124.

Spulber, D. F. (2010). Solving the circular conundrum: Communication and coordination in internet markets. *Northwestern University Law Review, 104*(2), 537–591.

Stopford, J. M., & Wells, L. T. (1972). *Managing the multinational enterprise: Organization of the firm and ownership of the subsidiary*. New York: Basic Books.

Sutton, J. (1998). *Technology and market structure*. Cambridge: The MIT Press.

Tang, R. (1981). *Multinational transfer pricing: Canadian and British perspective*. Tronto: Butterworths.

Waring, M. S., & Siegel, J. A. (2011). The effect of an ion generator on indoor air quality in a residential room. *Indoor Air, 21*(4), 267–276.

Winter, S. G. (1994). Organizing for continuous improvement: Evolutionary theory meets the quality improvement. In J. A. C. Baum & J. V. Singh (Eds.), *Evolutionary dynamics of organizations* (pp. 90–108). New York and Oxford: Oxford University Press.

CHAPTER 6

Artificial Intelligence to Broaden Beneficiaries

1 NEW AND ESTABLISHED SCIENCE CATEGORIES

This chapter pursues a research question on whether artificial intelligence technologies (AI) contribute to the broadening of beneficiaries of environmental sciences. AI is the discipline of creating algorithms that can learn and reason about tasks that would be considered intelligent if performed by a human or animal (King & Robert, 2018). It has the potential to increase the productivity of science, produce novel forms of discovery, and enhance reproducibility (King & Robert, 2018).

In the environmental sciences, some scientists apply AI to analyze chemical structural data to predict chemical hazard levels. Other scientists use satellite images of 2.5-micron Particulate Matter (PM $_{2.5}$) measurements from 6000 sites worldwide. It is to predict annual average PM $_{2.5}$ concentration across the globe (National Academies of Science, Engineering, and Medicine: NAS, 2019). They will contribute to the policymaking by more precisely identifying the geographic areas and levels of hazards.

The AI can contribute to broadening beneficiaries of sciences in its nondiscriminatory way. This potential comes from removing human prejudice in its functioning. The so-called big data is supposed to facilitate this function.

However, AI also has the potential to reinforce human prejudice. If the input variants do not adequately represent the set characteristics,

© The Author(s), under exclusive license to
Springer Nature Switzerland AG 2021
E. Okada, *Management of Science-Intensive Organizations*,
https://doi.org/10.1007/978-3-030-64042-2_6

131

outcomes of AI calculation are deviant. For example, when AI is applied to predict humans' biological profiles, it can systematically bias heterogeneous people's results. It is tough to adequately optimize data so that a dataset represents the set characteristics (see, King & Roberts, 2018, among others).

Regarding urban resilience, NAS is arranging a research program on environmental exposure. It addresses the influence of urban planning on human genetics and biomes (NAS, 2019). They began to introduce AI to the research stream of environmental exposure. The adoption of satellite imaging is one example.

At the same time, it is unknown what science categories such endeavors belong to, whether the attributes, "mimic of natrue" and "integration into systems design" hold to such scientific efforts. Also, a question arises of a better use of AI for science-intensive organizations regarding broadening beneficiaries of environmental sciences.

The organizational problem is the impact the AI will bring to organization processes and structures. Therefore, this chapter will analyze whether the AI use will broaden beneficiaries through the effects on science-intensive organizations.

This chapter at first reviews researches that use AI to environmental exposure. Then, it will analyze their relevance with broadening beneficiaries. Then, it will consider what impacts AI will bring to science-intensive organizations related to broadening beneficiaries.

2   New Vehicle of Tier-II Translation

2.1   New Image of Tier-II Translation

Practices of urban regeneration originally started in the field of urban engineering, planning, and design. Environmental aspects also are a part of the urban planning. On the other hand, recent urban resilience requires more integrated approach between several disciplines of basic sciences and practices. This condition necessitates the introduction of the translational science.

Translational science is a process to apply discoveries of a laboratory to a bench side and the broader public. It is an integrated process in which, by starting from basic science, all phases are expected to inform other ones with the involvement of beneficiary-driven (non-identifiable) data or beneficiaries themselves. Translational science itself is a process model.

It is not necessarily new (Rubio et al., 2010; Trochim et al., 2011). What is distinct of the recent model is the integration of mechanism bases of scientific understanding. It began to diffuse in the biomedical and its policy formulation. The ultimate goal is to make sciences more beneficiary-centered (Adams et al, 1991; Boon et al., 2002; Hamburg & Collins, 2010; Rubio et al., 2010; Trochim et al., 2011; Zenhouni, 2005).[1]

At the same time, as being a process model, it should apply to other science fields. The intention is to accelerate knowledge coproduction of basic scientists, applied scientists, regulatory scientists, and beneficiaries, particularly beneficiary-driven data and knowledge.

Historically, there are two types of translational sciences: Tier-I translation and Tier-II translation. Tier-I translation is to apply discoveries in basic science to a bench side. On the other hand, Tier-II translation is to apply discoveries or the results of Tier-I translation to the public. As the current processes of translational science are more integrated, the names of Tier-I and Tier-II have disappeared. However, this naming can be useful to stress the broadening of beneficiaries.

Recent efforts of broadening beneficiaries include a more precise identification of the affected population through the combination of environmental science, biology, and AI. The next section and Chapter 7 state the examples. The NAS also began to introduce the elimination of poverty in the outcome measures. As the NAS states, if cities cannot adequately address the rise of poverty, hunger, resource consumption, and biodiversity losses in their borders (NAS, 2016), the cities would not prosper in a sustainable manner.

In addressing the rise of poverty and environmental inequity, it is necessary to measure and simulate how the current dynamism of system and environmental exposure affects vulnerable populations. It is an AI-driven anticipation in the practice of Responsible Research and Innovation. For this purpose, AI algorithm integrates satellite data, image, and other beneficiary-driven datasets in measuring and predicting the variation of air quality.

---

[1] This phrase is a summary of the following: Okada (2019), pp. 27–28.

2.1.1 The Specific Property of AI-Driven Sciences

The specific property of sciences that adopt AI is the volume of input data. The generation of direct experimentation is replaced by the era of data collection. Rather than directly performing scientific experimentation, scientists design experiments to record and archive data at an unprecedented scale (Hey et al., 2009; King & Robert, 2018). AI-based processing and simulation take part in the application of the massive data. The effective current methods are machine learning and deep learning.

Machine learning is a method that focuses on developing systems that learn from data. Machine learning algorithm is to create solutions by learning from training datasets, rather than being explicitly told how to solve a problem (Kings & Robert, 2018). Deep learning, or deep neural networks, is a type of machine learning. In being common with other nonparametric methods, deep learning does not specify the functional form of solutions. Instead, it is flexible to handle complexity: It arbitrarily learns a mapping from input data (training datasets) to output data (King & Roberts, 2018). Deep learning transformed a way in which algorithms achieve human-level performances in specific areas (King & Roberts, 2018).

One of the motivations to introduce AI to science processes derives from the AI's systematic thinking: AI systems think differently from humans (King & Roberts, 2018). Humans' cognition involves bounded rationality (Simon, 1957). Humans observe events by reinforcing the past. Its inference encompasses cognitive biases (Kahneman & Sunstein, 2005; Kahneman &Tversky, 1979). Unrecognized biases involve even sciences related to how we approach problems (King & Roberts, 2018). Therefore, the expectation of adopting AI is to combine both human and AI thinking to gain more efficient and effective solutions (Kasparov, 2017; King & Roberts, 2018).

Thus, laboratory automation is now essential to most science and technology fields (King & Roberts, 2018). For example, Nielsen et al. (2016) apply the principles from electronic design automation (EDA) to enable increased circuit complexity and to simplify incorporating synthetic gene regulation into a genetic engineering project. EDA was initially developed to engineers in the design of semiconductor-based electronics.

On the other hand, scientists has not thoroughly examined whether the introduction of AI will broaden beneficiaries of sciences.

The translational science first diffused in life science and biomedical. The original motivation is to make each phase more patient-centered. The framework of the process spread to other experimental science fields, including environmental sciences. In other words, the original motivation is to make science more beneficiary-oriented.

Under this situation, there are two ways to achieve beneficiary-oriented outcomes. The first is to upgrade the quality of science. The dimensions of science quality encompass (a) the freedom from bias and errors, (b) reproducibility, as well as (c) the utility to beneficiaries. The early stage bias and irreproducibility are incredibly crucial to address, since these biases and irreproducibility widen in later stages and degrade the effectiveness of application (see, IOM, 2012).

In adopting AI-based automation, scientists have to optimize input datasets and AI algorithms to improve biases, errors, and the irreproducibility. The model validation and confirmation need to be done through a standardized procedure before scientists proceed with the model to the application stage (IOM, 2012). Also, they need to achieve the desired utility by integrating other functional data (IOM, 2012).

These activities have already occurred in several science-intensive organizations (King & Roberts, 2018). An upgraded quality through intensified research investment on a specific R&D trajectory will reward the organization (Sutton, 1998) in several ways.

The second is to enhance the scope and volume of beneficiaries. As Chapter 4 states, there remain problems in the environmental aspects of urban resilience regarding the range and volume of beneficiaries.

One possible resolution is to accelerate the translation of academic discoveries more directly to the benefit of public. This direction consists of the direct participation of potential beneficiaries in each phase of the sciences. The participation does not always mean the physical attendance. In the biomedical field, scientists pursue this direction by applying discoveries from patient-derived biological material to human studies.

In this field, patients donate unidentifiable (or in specific cases, identifiable) data and materials to biomedical scientists and organizations with informed consent. Under this situation, patients (beneficiaries) enter what Philips (2004) calls a cooperative scheme with academic knowledge-intensive organizations (KIOs) in performing experimental research of biomedical sciences (see, Okada, 2019). The use of patient-derived biological material and data is also one form of beneficiary involvement (Strom, Norman, & Margolis, 2000).

The other is to more precisely detect areas and populations that the degradation of environmental quality affects.

The latter is also performed in the field of biomedical science. For example, the so-called precision medicine initiative originates in serial analysis gene expression (SAGE) in the 1990s (Adams et al., 1991). SAGE is a methodology that allows the quantitative and simultaneous analysis of a large number of transcripts of which organisms present (Velculescu et al., 1995). This methodology emerges as recombination of algorithm-based computer science and biology. Recent phenomena include the integration of machine learning and deep learning algorithms. Through this integration, biomedical scientists expect the biomarkers based on genomics, proteomics, and metabolomics, etc., to distinguish health-related characteristics of humans more precisely than previous methodologies (Institute of Medicine, 2012).[2] One of the applications is that medical doctors are using the biological markers for the detection of the fit between humans' biological profiles and clinical interventions to minimize the adverse events.

The current precision medicine is not necessarily broadening the volume of beneficiaries due to economic issues. However, biomedical scientists believe that, when they apply genomics, proteomics, metabolomics to more common disease, they will accumulate more data to lead to more reasonable and accurate medical procedures for broader beneficiaries.

These characteristics of AI involvement apply to environmental aspects of urban resilience. For example, scientists are detecting the PM2.5 affected areas with more specifications through the combination of AI and satellite data. They also identify geographic regions by crossing the borders of jurisdictions. The involvement of beneficiaries also started in environmental science. It is because the public easily perceives the influence of PM2.5, that is, physical fatigue and the decline of in-door work productivity.

At the same time, data science also has the potential to alter the focus of urban resilience practices. As Barns (2020) states,

> "—much of our cities' basic utilities and infrastructures are becoming more shaped by their data infrastructures, constituted of information systems and protocols that determine how and where the services should be located.

---

[2] This description is based on Okada (2019), p. 22.

6 ARTIFICIAL INTELLIGENCE TO BROADEN BENEFICIARIES 137

> As a consequence, the protocols and conditions governing the design and management of data infrastructure now play an increasingly influential role in shaping the way our cities actually operate."

This tendency appears to be favorable and convenient for residents. However, it also can bring negative consequences to the population whose data availability is scarce.

The positive aspects of AI occur when datasets represent attributes of a group more adequately. However, his condition does not always occur for humans with heterogeneity. It is already established in ethics communities that a machine-learning-based diagnosis systematically produces a bias for minority populations. It occurs because the health-related data of minority populations are not always available in the system.

Therefore, we should be cautious about integrating AI in the environmental aspects of urban resilience practices. The section below stated discusses this direction.

2.2 Application to Urban Resilience Models and Practices

2.2.1 Challenges Passed on to the Twenty-First Century

In the late twentieth century, European urban economists summarized the challenges of a local economic resilience as follows.

- First, it failed to bring inward investment.
- Second, resilient practice needs to support and develop indigenous industries.
- Third, the resilience invites a shift away from a property-led approach to a direct investment in the production process (Roberts, 1989).

Firstly, according to the European Communities (EC: 1983), the scarcity of private investment projects and the freezing of public sector expansion pose difficulties to attract foreign firms from outside of a specific urban area. The motivation for attracting foreign firms is to introduce monetary investment and employment in the urban area.

However, foreign direct investment requires supportive industries in the area.

When complementary industries are absent in the location, foreign firms expect some public subsidies, such as tax incentives and direct employment subsidies (see, Gleaser and Hausman, 2019). If both complementing industries and supportive public sectors are scarce in the region, foreign firms cannot collect their investment in the long run.

Such concerns shifted the 1990-style urban regeneration toward more comprehensive and integrated forms of policy and practice. They are a partnership approach and the introduction of a broader concept of environmental sustainability (Roberts, 2000). The United Nation (1987)'s Brundtland Report introduced the concept of the long-term sustainability of the planet through the term, "sustainable development." In this Report, sustainability mainly depends on allowing ideas of economic development, environmental protection, and social equity to coalesce (Brinkmann, 2020).

Among these components, environmental sustainability is the idea that the environment can maintain its ability to support human life and maintain all existing ecological systems and life into the future despite resource depletion from human activities (Brinkmann, 2020). However, as stated in Chapter 4, the environmental ability varies by geography regarding supporting human life and maintaining existing ecological systems.

Such variation requires the emphasis on community (Roberts, 2000). Thus, the response to the first challenge is the community emphasis.

In the U.S., the Empowerment Zone Partnerships brought federal funds for ten years to six cities through a competition. The funds are for social services, employment credits, and tax-exempt facilities. The funds helped to establish several social enterprises in one of these cities that primarily care for vulnerable populations. Many of them were organizations that mainly provided essential items directly to such people.

In responding to the second challenge, private foundations began to support indigenous industries, such as arts and crafts. They strictly defined the scope of the grant application to the ends.

Private foundations also led the response to the third challenge. Some private foundations specialized in funding small businesses' endeavors to integrate digital technologies in their process.

Along with these responses, some enterprises began to concern elements that constructed ecological systems, such as water quality. They are mainly medium-sized social enterprises specialized in civil and environmental engineering (see, Chapter 7). Architectural companies stepped in by designing buildings that incorporate renewable energies.

However, the scale of the resilience practice was too small. It was as if these cities believed that doing things on a small scale is a better practice.

Further, local governments tended to isolate less-resourced cities within their boundaries. Such a tendency resulted in the condition that enterprises no longer provided the tax base to develop the necessary services to regenerate communities (Shutt, 2000). Thus, many of the social enterprises that concern vulnerable populations began to sink with them.

2.2.2   Adoption of AI in the Tier-II Translation

Such cities have to design a spiral of more bold resilience practices by using a full capacity of Tier-II translation. In other words, academic KIOs need to integrate more potential beneficiaries in their translation. The federal governments began to back up Tier-II translation efforts around the 2010s not only through funding but also through training programs of academics. The themes of training include the improvement of interaction and partnerships with beneficiaries.

The adoption of AI can enhance the scope of partnership and beneficiaries, since the AI can extend the search activities more efficiently when a set represents proper attributes. As AI's property complements cognitive limit of humans (King & Roberts, 2018), academics, and scientists can use new knowledge that the AI generates in the routines of research activities (King & Roberts, 2018).

Problems are (a) what skills humans should add to the AI and automated research systems regarding environmental aspects of urban resilience. (b) How to enhance the positive aspects of AI while overcoming its adverse effects in extending the scope of beneficiaries.

3   How Algorithms Affect Organizations

3.1   Shift of Desired Skills of Humans

Scientists and economists began to understand the significance of overcoming inequality as a prioritized issue for the sustainable future. For example, Frank et al., (2018) address AI and robotics that extend the social divide due to the changing demand of skillsets. They reveal that large cities present the increase of occupational and skill specialization due to the advancement of managerial and technical professions. As these professional skills are not easily replaceable by automation, they reduce the potential negative impacts of automation. On the other hand, small cities are undertaking more significant adjustments, such as job content substitutions (Frank et al., 2018).

Alabdulkareem et al. (2018) also demonstrate that skills exhibit a polarization into two clusters: One is a cluster of specific high social-cognitive skill s and sensory-physical skills. The other is that of low social-cognitive skills and sensory-physical skills that represent low-wage occupations.

Gaeser and Hausman (2019) pursue space mismatch between skillsets and geography. According to them, the U.S. technological creativity is geographically concentrated on distant areas from the country's most persistent needy regions. They conclude that geographically targeted entrepreneurship policies could potentially enhance employment in such areas without any special reallocation. Such policies include the elimination of barriers to creating a new business near universities and in distressed areas. They intend to absorb underused resources through innovation. However, scholars do not know the detailed contents of how such innovation occurs.

As Frank et al. (2018) state, urban areas are the most successful form of human agglomeration that provide a variety of employment opportunities. Therefore, the decline of urban systems is a significant issue for human prosperity.

At the same time, Frank et al. (2019) also state that there are barriers that inhibit scientists from measuring the impacts of AI and automation on the future of work. These barriers derive from an insufficient understanding of the human–machine complementarity and how cognitive technologies interact with broader economic dynamics and institutional mechanisms (Frank et al., 2019).

3.2   Human Tasks in Measuring Environmental Exposure

Under this condition, the U.S. National Academy of Science (NAS, 2016) examines that agglomeration of populations can compound both positive and negative aspects. Many modern urban areas are experiencing growing inequality, debility, and environmental degradation. The spread and continued growth of urban regions present several concerns for a sustainable future. It is an urgent issue for cities to address the rise of poverty, hunger, resource consumption, and a loss of biodiversity in their borders (NAS, 2016).

In responding to the alert, many cities and academic knowledge-intensive organizations (KIOs) began to measure causal relationships and recognizing patterns of the following issues.

a. How the environmental exposure negatively affects humans.
b. To what extent the exposure systematically influence more on specific business and residential areas.

Regarding the measurement of environmental exposure, data and tools of the earth science that NASA and several research agencies produce offer excellent, potential resources for air quality management (Jacob, Holloway, & Haynes, 2014). Further, the complex landscape of satellite instruments, model capabilities, monitor networks, and data synthesis methods provides opportunities for research development (Diao et al., 2019).

The satellite instruments require a vast and irreversible scientific investment. The trend of concentration of scientific investment will be reinforced if there were no interventions. This attribute corresponds to the Mark II sciences based on the science categorization by Niosi (2000). On the other hand, the main scientific actors in this category are governmental or public research agencies. They disclose generated data by posting them in specific databases in a public domain and make them available to the public. Thus, the disclosure and access to data are moderating the trend toward concentration.

What the AI adds to the scientific processes is the research automation cycle that consists of execution, collection, and synthesis (see. King & Roberts, 2018). Scientists in almost all of the scientific categories can have an opportunity to introduce the automation cycle to their science process.

What should be cautious is that there are inconsistencies among several publicly available datasets: For example, data on $PM_{2.5}$ estimation highlight uncertainties in the exposure datasets that are often overlooked in health effects analyses (Diao et al., 2019). There are three primary sources used to create $PM_{2.5}$ exposure data: (a) ground-based measurements (especially regulatory monitoring), (b) satellite retrievals (especially aerosol optical depth, AOD), and (c) atmospheric chemistry models. According to Diao et al. (2019), major differences among $PM_{2.5}$ estimates emerge from: (1) the choice of data source (ground-based, satellite-based) and/or model, (2) the spatiotemporal resolutions, and (3) the algorithms that are used to fuse data sources.

The above indicates the need for human intervention. Scientists should intervene in the choice of input data, analysis of results, and the update of

142   E. OKADA

the systems model (see, King & Roberts, 2018). In other words, humans' tasks are as follows.

- The choice of datasets that is to represent the attributes of the groups or geographic conditions,
- the analysis of the results, and
- the modification of the systems model (the optimization or rearrangement of the datasets based on the feedback loop).

3.3   *Impacts on Organizations*

The framework of King and Roberts (2018) also applies to industrial science and practice. Management scholars Raisch and Krakowski name these two dimensions as "automation (that AI and robotics take part)" and "augmentation (in which humans take part)." Unlike natural scientists, scholarly management is more concerned with the tensions related to organizations and societies, as well as possible resolutions. For example, the literature review of Raisch and Krakowski (2020) elucidates the augmentation that allows machine limitations to overcome. Humans' tasks in augmentation are choosing between options and contextualizing beyond the specific task at hand. These measures explore and exploit humans' more holistic and intuitive information processing (Brynjolfsson & McAfee, 2014).

The emphasis on contextualization is unique to scholarly management, compared with that of scientists, such as Diao et al. (2019) and Kings and Roberts (2018). As Shad and Bansal (2018) warn, narrowing organizational attention to just one dimension of tensions can trigger unintended consequences, as later stated (Raisch & Krakowski, 2020).

As Raisch and Krakowski stress, human responsibility retained in the managerial processes facilitates integration and transcendence of automation and augmentation.

The retaining of human responsibility is a notion that exists in medical law and practices. For example, hospitals can introduce a deep-learning-based device in which an algorithm optimizes several sources of information. Data sources range from patients' behavioral patterns, genomics and proteomics profiles, and others. The device is to suggest possible interventions. However, as humans' illness is so complex, the machine's suggestion can differ from physicians' judgment based on their experiences of physician–patient relationship. The legal regime that regulates such conditions is the tort law. Under the tort law, physicians owe the final responsibility for the judgment of the best interests of patients, that is, the practice that will benefit patients most.[3]

In the management domain, organizations can achieve better performance by automation by AI. However, too much focus on AI automation will eventually stagnate performance (Raisch & Krakowski, 2020; Daugherty & Wilson, 2018). Also, focusing on "either or" can lead to reinforcing cycles that harm long-term performance.

The benefit of differentiating two dimensions of automation and augmentation depends on allocating them in their organizational processes. For example, as Raisch and Krakowski (2020) state, automation could free up scarce resources for augmentation, which, in turn, could help identify the rules and models that regulate and enable automation. At the same time, it is essential to notice that the augmentation does not mean to intensify the interaction between machines and humans. Too much interaction may carry over human prejudice to the algorithm: Machines, then confirm humans' biased intuition. This cycle has the potential to reinforce humans' preconceptions further. A representative case is the adoption of AI in hiring software engineers that also degrades the current minor population in the field (Huang et al., 2012; see, Raisch & Krakowski, 2020).

Therefore, the independent analysis and subsequent integration are essential to reduce human biases by differentiating two dimensions (Raisch & Kralowski, 2020; see also, Hoc, 2001).

3.3.1   *Potential Impacts on Resilience Practices*

Though cities' sustainable future depends on their ways to address the vulnerability in their borders (see, NAS, 2016), cities do not necessarily identify more specific areas with vulnerability. When they do not specify the locations of vulnerability, they can fail to deliver the adequate intervention. As stated in previous chapters, cities and their constituents benefit from a variety. However, as series of empirical research shows, many constituents have lost opportunities through biased resource allocation that might otherwise bring benefits of economic growth.

---

[3] Cohen, I. G. February, 2019, in answering to the author's question.

Several funders are calling for economic development projects that are to ameliorate inequity. Funders and relevant actors can use AI-based tools in recruiting and accessing potential applicants. However, if they intensify the human–machine interaction, they will reinforce the prejudice in allocating resources.

On the other hand, cities and relevant actors can better manage their resilience practices by differentiating automation and augmentation.

Firstly, the current AI use presents benefits in diagnosing and simulating vulnerable areas more precisely. For example, cities are interested in detecting the most affected geographic areas and populations by the heat wave (see, Chapter 7). As the heat wave activates the toxicity of PM2.5, it is urgent to distinguish affected areas from others. This requirement necessitates the differentiation between automation and augmentation, followed by the integration of data from ground-based AI and other sources. As mentioned in Chapter 7, a particular city also dispatched university students to conduct a site visit and interviewing residents. The integration of case observation will further verify the results and detect a potential difference between general trends and individually identified events. Then, the integration of economic, social, and environmental dimensions will be able to produce a more effective service to affected populations.

Secondly, AI adoption in the partnership approach of resilience (Roberts, 2000) can further extend the scope of beneficiaries. There is a relevant example of a contractor of World Health Organization (WHO) that responded to the International Health Emergency of the first Ebola outbreak (declared in 2014). At the first outbreak, no single agencies had enough budget to develop effective medicine. A U.S. academic scientist already discovered the mechanism of how Ebola virus invades humans' physical bodies in the early twentieth century. However, no single agency had the financial capacity to conduct clinical trials (a presentation and communication at Medical Ethics Seminar, Division of Medical Ethics, Harvard Medical School, winter 2014).

Then, a WHO-designated contractor (hereafter, Contractor Z) designed a contract infrastructure to search project participants, coordinate the clinical development, and deliver to affected populations. Recruited participants include academic scientists, scientists at multinational and entrepreneurial pharmaceuticals, global, nonprofit funders, and local healthcare practitioners (a presentation of Contractor Z at a forum,

Harvard Global Health Institute, fall 2018). The project participants succeeded in translating the academic discovery to affected populations.

In this process, Contractor Z owes a responsibility for the alignment of incentives, management of workflows and intellectual property, and the fair distribution of developed medicine regardless of beneficiaries' socioeconomic status and physical comorbidity conditions.

The above represents a case of the combination of AI's automation and contractors' augmentation. AI automation enables a distant search that includes a variety of participants who might otherwise be screened out from the process. The augmentation of the contractor succeeded in aligning and coordinating a variety of interests and incentives that base on managerial and cognitive skills.

A failed case of adopting algorithm, in general, comes from a bias in grouping subsets. As already stated, recruitment of candidates through a search of social media disclosure systematically reinforces a bias in heterogeneous populations. An AI-based search systematically discriminates against a specific population. Such bias occurs because a particular population systematically lacks social media disclosure regarding a desired skill (Murciano-Goroff, 2018. Cf. Ameri, Rogers, Schur, & Kruse, 2020). In such case, the data grouping does not adequately represent the specific population regarding the desired skills.

In general, the adoption of algorithm makes it easier to identify potential participants of scientific projects by aggregating scientific papers and intellectual property. Also, the digital technology enables a variety in participants through reducing inflictions of remote communication and negotiation (the ex-ante contractual costs). The reduced infliction further makes it easier for humans to augment and adjust the rules of incentives and coordination of workflows.

Organizations can use the AI's automated, faceless mechanism in the full capacity in proper delivery of the outcome of the project. In the case of a pandemic, medical organizations can distribute drugs and vaccines without bias, regardless of patients' economic and social status.[46] As already stated, recruited participants include academic scientists, scientists at multinational and entrepreneurial pharmaceuticals, global, nonprofit funders, local healthcare practitioners. By focusing on each role, the

---

[4] There remained a specific population that could not be delivered medicine or denied the acceptance of medicine. Addressing this population is beyond the capacity of this study.

project participants succeeded in translating the academic discovery to affected populations.

This type of AI-powered infrastructure and human augmentation apply to resilience practices. If organizations differentiate two dimensions of AI, the resilience designers and practitioners can extent a variety of partnerships in urban resilience practices.

In the past, the increase of variety and the scale economy had a disproportionate relationship. However, the efficiency of automation will offset the negative aspects of variety that come from giving up the scale. Digital automation reduces inflictions related to a distant search, distant communication, and negotiation. Further, the efficiency spares time for humans to augment social and cognitive skills. Humans have more time identifying heterogeneous talents, aligning different incentives, and ruling better processes and monitoring. These skills are to deliver a higher quality of services. Thus, the AI has the potential to support both the variety and scale that used to conflict each other.

4   More Inclusive Organizations

This chapter pursues a research sub-question on whether artificial intelligence technologies (AI) contribute to the broadening of beneficiaries of environmental sciences.

The AI's potential to contribute to the broadening of beneficiaries is its nondiscriminatory way. It has the potential to remove human prejudice in its functioning.

However, if the input variants do not adequately represent the set characteristics, AI calculation outcomes are deviant (Cohen, 2019). Also, while organizations should differentiate two dimensions of AI automation and augmentation (see, King & Roberts, 2018; Raisch & Krakowski, 2020), too much interaction between them will introduce human prejudice into AI. Such a human–machine interface reinforces human bias (Huang et al., 2012; Raisch & Krakowski, 2020).

Also, the retaining of human responsibility is crucial. This insight comes from the tort law in which physicians owe the final responsibility for the judgment of patients' best interests (Cohen, 2019 in responding to the author's question).

When we turn eyes to urban resilience, policymakers acknowledge the cities' responsibility to address the rise of poverty, hunger, resource consumption, and a loss of biodiversity (NAS, 2016). Ameliorating these components is a prerequisite for the cities to prosper in a sustainable manner. The first step is the anticipation in an inclusive manner. They should anticipate how the current system dynamism and environmental exposure affect the vulnerability in a geographic area and population. The AI-based algorithm has the potential to make the anticipation easier. For example, the AI algorithm integrates satellite data, ground-based data, and other datasets to measure and predict the variation of air quality.

The research tools for environmental science necessitate concentrated and irreversible R&D investment. Thus, the institutions in this field belong to the Mark II category of sciences. Meanwhile, as actors in emerging stage sciences are academic and government research agencies, these scientists post the input and output data at open depositories. Therefore, their open data policy is potentially moderate the trends toward concentration.

Also, automation's efficiency will offset the negative aspects of variety that might otherwise lead to giving up the scale. Instead, the digital technology reduces the infliction of communication and negotiation in remote areas that will reduce the ex-ante/ex-post contract costs. Further, the efficiency spares humans' time to intervene in the process: They can augment social, cognitive skills to rule the better quality of services to diversified people.

Then, the AI will support both the variety and scale in urban resilience used to conflict with each other. Thus, the adequate adoption of AI will broaden beneficiaries of sciences in urban transformation in the future.

References

Adams, M. D., Kelley, J. M., Govayne, J. D., Dubnick, M., Polymeropoulos, M. H., Xiao, H., & Venter, C. (1991). Complementary DNA sequencing: Expressed sequence tags and human genome project. *Science, 252*(5123), 1651–1656.

Alabdulkareem, A., Frank, M. R., Sun, L., AlShebli, B., Hidalgo, C., & Rahwan, I. (2018). Unpacking the polarization of workplace skills, *Science Advances, 4*(7), https://doi.org/10.1126/sciadv.aao6030.

Ameri, M., Rogers, S. E., Schur, L., & Kruse, D. (2020). No room at the inn? Disability access in the new sharing economy. *Academy of Management Discoveries, 6*(2). https://doi.org/10.5465/amd.2018.0054.

Barns, S. (2016). Mine your data: Open data, digital strategies and entrepreneurial governance by code. *Urban Geography, 37*(4), 554–571.

Barns, S. (2020). *Platform urbanism: Negotiating platform ecosystems in connected cities.* New York: Palgrave Macmillan.

Boon, K., Osorio, E. C., Greenhut, S. F., Schaefer, C. F., Shoemaker, J., Polyak, K., & Riggins, G. J. (2002). An anatomy of normal and malignant gene expression. *Proceeding of the National Academy of Sciences, 99*(17), 11287–11292.

Brinkmann, R. (2020). *Environmental sustainability in a time of change*. New York: Palgrave Macmillan.

Brynjolfsson, E., & McAfee, A. (2014). *The second machine age: Work, progress, and prosperity in a time of brilliant technologies*. New York: W. W. Norton & Co.

Cohen, I. G. (2019, February, 8). Black-box medicine. Legal and ethical issues. *A Health Policy and Bioethics Consortium*, held at Petrie-Flom Center for Health Law Policy, Harvard Law School.

Daugherty, P. R., & Wilson, H. J. (2018). *Human + machine: Reimaging work in the age of AI*. Boston: Harvard Business Press.

Diao, M., Holloway, T., Choi, S., O'Neill, S. M., Al-Hamdan, M., & Donkelaar, A. V., & Vaidyanathan, A. (2019). Methods, availability, and applications of $PM_{2.5}$ exposure estimates derived from ground measurements, satellite, and atmospheric models. *Journal of the Air and Waste Management Association, 69*(12). https://doi.org/10.1080/10962247.2019.1668498.

Frank, M. R., Autor, D., Bessen, J. E., Brynjolfsson, E., Cebrian, M., Deming, D. J., & Youn, H. et al. (2019). Toward understanding the impact of artificial intelligence on labor. *Proceedings of the National Academy of Sciences of the United States of America, 116*(14), 6531–6539.

Frank, M. R., Sun, L., Cebrian, M., Youn, H., & Rahwan, I. (2018). Small cities face greater impact from automation. *Journal of Royal Society of Interface, 15*, 20170946. https://doi.org/10.1098/rsif.2017.0946.

Glaeser, E. L., & Hausman, N. (2019). Spatial mismatch between innovation and joblessness. *National Bureau of Economic Research Working Paper* No. 25913.

Hamburg, M., & Collins, F. S. (2010). The path to personalized medicine. *The New England Journal of Medicine, 363*, 301–304.

Hey, T., Tansley, S., & Tolle, K. (2009). *The forth paradigm: Data-intensive scientific discovery*. Redmond: Microsoft Research.

Hoc, J.-M. (2001). Towards a cogniive approach to human-machine cooperation in dynamic situations. *International Journal of Human-Compuer Studies, 54*, 509–540.

Huang, H.-H., Hsu, J. S.-C., & Ku, C.-Y. (2012). Understanding the role of computer-mediated counter-argument in countering confirmation bias. *Decision Support Systems, 53*, 438–447.

Institute of Medicine. (2012). *Evolution of translational omics. Lessons learned and the path forward*. Washington, DC: National Academies Press.

Jacob, D. J., Holloway, T., & Haynes, J. D. (2014, February 7–8). The NASA air quality applied science team (AQAST). *Environmental Managers.*

Kahneman, D., & Sunstein, C. R. (2005). Indignity: Psychology, politics, law. In J. P. Changeux, A. R. Damasio, W. Singer, & C. Yves (Eds.), *Neurobiology of human values* (pp. 91–106). Berlin, Heidelberg: Springer.

Kahneman, D., & Tversky, A. (1979). Prospect theory: An analysis of decision under risk. *Econometrica, 47*(2), 263–292.

Kasparov, G. (2017). *Deep thinking: Where machine intelligence ends and human creativity begins.* New York: PublicAffairs.

King, R. D., & Roberts, S. (2018). Artificial intelligence and machine learning in science. In OECD. *Science, technology and innovation outlook 2018: Adapting to technological and societal disruption.* Paris: OECD Publishing. Retrieved from https://doi.org/10.1787/sti_in-outlook-2018-10-en.

Murciano-Goroff, R. (2018). *Missing women in tech: The labor market for highly skilled software engineers.* Retrieved from http://stanford.edu/~ravimg/pap ers/JMP.pdf.

National Academies of Science, Engineering, and Medicine (NAS). (2016). *Pathways to urban sustainability: Challenges and opportunities for the United States.* Washington, DC: National Academies Press. https://doi.org/10.17226/23551.

National Academies of Science, Engineering, and Medicine (NAS). (2019). *Building and measuring community resilience: Actions for communities and the Gulf Research Program.* Washington, DC: National Academies Press. https://doi.org/10.17226/25383.

National Institute of Health. *Translational science spectrum.* Retrieved from https://ncats.nih.gov/translation/spectrum. Last visited at August, 27, 2020.

Nielsen, A. A. K., Der, B. S., Shin, J., Vaidyanathan, P., Paralanov, V., Strychalski, E. A., & Voigt, C. A. (2016). Genetic circuit design automation. *Science, 352*(6281). https://doi.org/10.1126/science.aac7341.

Okada, E. (2019). *Management of knowledge-intensive organizations: Governance models for transformative discovery.* New York: Palgrave Macmillan.

Philips, R. (2003). *Stakeholder theory and organizational ethics.* San Francisco: Barrett-Koehler.

Raisch, S., & Krakowski, S. (2020). Artificial intelligence and management: The automation-augmentation paradox. *Academy of Management Review.* https://doi.org/10.5465/2018.0072.

Roberts, P. (2000). The evolution, definition and purpose of urban regeneration. In P. Roberts & H. Sykes (Eds.), *Urban regeneration: A handbook* (pp. 9–36). New York: Sage.

Rubio, D. M., Schoenbaum, E. E., Lee, L. S., Schteingart, D. E., Marantz, P. R., Anderson, K. E., & Esposito, K. (2010). Defining translational research. *Academic Medicine, 85*(3), 470–475.

Shad, J., & Bansal, P. (2018). Seeing the forest and trees: How a systems perspective informs paradox research. *Journal of Management Studies, 55*(8), 1490–1506.

Shutt, J. (2000). 12 Lessons from America in the 1990s. In P. Roberts & H. Sykes (Eds.). *Urban regeneration: A handbook* (pp. 257–279). New York: SAGE Publications.

Simon, H. A. (1957). *Models of man, social and rational.* New York: Wiley.

Strom, B. L., Norman, S., & Margolis, D. J. (2000). Patient-oriented research: Definitions and new paradigms. *American Journal of Medicine, 109,* 164–165.

Sutton, J. (1998). *Technology and market structure.* Cambridge: The MIT Press.

Trochim, W., Kane, C., Graham, M. J., & Pincus, H. A. (2011). Evaluating translational research: A process marker model. *Clinical Translational Science, 4*(3), 153–162.

United Nations Brundtland Commission. (1987). *Our common future.* Oxford and New York: Oxford University Press.

Velculescu, V. E., Zhang, L., Vogelstein, B., & Kinzler, K. W. (1995). Serial analysis of gene expression. *Science, 270*(5235), 484–487.

Zenhouni, E. A. (2005). Translational and clinical science—Time for a new vision. *The New England Journal of Medicine, 353,* 1621–1623.

PART III

Revolution of Beneficiaries

CHAPTER 7

Scale-up of Social Enterprises

1 Significance of Scale-up

Part III argues proper organization designs to broaden beneficiaries. This part pays particular attention to mobilizing beneficiaries to scale-up the resilience model.

This Chapter addresses a research sub-question on appropriate organization designs for academic institutions and established and entrepreneur social enterprises in replicating and scaling up their resilience model.

Several academic programs and entrepreneur firms (that include social enterprises) are concerned about urban environmental problems. Their practices implicitly embrace ecological equity that will lead to sustainable and transformative resilience. However, only a few scale-up to claim economies of scale (Organization for Economic Cooperation and Development: OECD, 2004) and scope.

It is partly because their performance criteria are different from industry organizations. Several of them are introducing ontological reasoning that does not converge with efficiency. Also, these objectives embed ethics to more plural stakeholders. Even so, scale-up is vital to broadening beneficiaries. It is possible since these organizations have less human factors associated with know-how (Teece, 1980; Wernerfelt, 2016, among others) than established industry firms. Therefore, academic and social enterprises and entrepreneur firms have the potential to design a unique organization to diffuse successful models.

© The Author(s), under exclusive license to
Springer Nature Switzerland AG 2021
E. Okada, *Management of Science-Intensive Organizations,*
https://doi.org/10.1007/978-3-030-64042-2_7

Examples include X Programs of an academic knowledge-intensive organization (KIO) and Y social entrepreneur firm. They are directly translating climate and environmental sciences to their activities in addressing end beneficiaries. Though their immediate objectives are different each other, the ultimate goals are the same. It is to mitigate the impacts of climate change by reversing or inhibiting contributing mechanisms.

In this space, the previous management literature has not thoroughly explained the organization forms environmental scientists use. Further, it is not clear what and how multilateral organizations are involving in facilitating the process (such as the World Bank coastal resilience project). One of the involvements consists of providing norms and conscience in politically salient issues (see, Justo-Hanani & Dayan, 2014) that bind governments' negotiation with potentially related groups and organizations. However, little is known how they are facilitating the scale-up of socially desirable activities in the practice of resilience.

This chapter addresses the question mentioned above through a case-based inductive–deductive methodology. The theoretical starting point is the adaptation cost theory by Wernerfelt (2016). After the review of Wernerfelt (2016), this study will modify the framework by analyzing science-intensive organizations that are diffusing resilience models. The unit of analysis is the specific programs of these organizations.

2 REPLICATION TO OTHER SETTINGS

2.1 *Adaptation Costs to Firms*

Firms are generally based on the assumption that the organizational forms they adopt are most appropriate for their activities (Wernerfelt, 2016). Enterprises that address environmental aspects of urban resilience may base on the same assumption. Academic institutions are creating a research and educational program designated for their purposes; Social enterprises and entrepreneurs have adopted a business model that fits their strategies. Also, scientists have begun to adopt a variety of forms to fulfill their objectives. However, it is not autonomous what factors determine their choice in the first place (Wernerfelt, 2016).

Previous management literature has not always explained a variety of the forms that environment-related scientists use. This chapter examines the organization forms that environmental scientists adopt. The theoretical starting point is Wernerfelt (2016).

Wernerfelt (2016) builds the adaptation cost theory by questioning why people commonly use the forms of firms, markets, and contracts. Wernerfelt (2016) is transforming Coase (1937), which examines why organizations emerge. Coase (1937)'s framework has evolved to develop the concept of bargaining costs (Coase, 1960; Williamson, 1981). The bargaining costs is, in general, too subtle to be introduced in economic theories. However, Wernerfelt (2016) pays attention to its sub-additive nature.

Wernerfelt (2016) starts with a simple model in which a worker provides a particular service for an entrepreneur whose needs have changed (Wernerfelt, 2016). Either the change of a service or the employment will require adaptation costs for the worker. In such a case, the adaptation costs for workers encompass the bargaining of labor prices and the lowering of productivity due to the change.

Wernerfelt (2016)'s analysis of workers and entrepreneurial firms will be applied to scientists and science organizations in later sections. Therefore, this section reviews the Wernerfelt model that uses simplified cases of workers and employers.

In a simple model of employment, the adaptation costs determine a form of employment. The option of forms encompasses the following three:

a. Hires a worker through a once-and-for-all wage contract in return for performing any of the sequences of services.
b. Uses a workforce through a market mechanism, or
c. Uses a workforce through sequential contracting.

In the Wernerfelt model (2016), actors do better if they adapt to a broader range of sequences of services and do so more frequently. In other words, the value creation depends on parameters of the diverse adaptation and frequent adaptation.

Governance costs play a critical role in the adaptation cost framework. The direct governance costs consist of two folds:

1. Communication and bargaining costs (Williamson, 1979) that are necessary to adapt to a change, and
2. Costs to resolve incentive conflicts (Grossman & Hart, 1986; Hart, 1989; Hart & Moore, 1988). Adaptation invokes incentive conflicts (Wernerfelt, 2016).

The indirect costs of governance consist of those of imperfect adaptation (Wernerfelt, 2016). Apart from the imperfect adaptation, the direct governance costs are critical for determining action sequences in his model.

Suppose it is more frequent that an employer asks a worker to change a sequence of work. Since the adaptation is more valuable and cheaper than other alternatives, the parties will adopt an employment relationship. When it is more frequent that parties negotiate a new contract for a new sequence of services when negotiation costs are smaller, parties will adopt sequential contracting mechanisms. When a price list is longer, when it is more important and cheaper to negotiate, parties will adopt price list mechanisms. In comparing these mechanisms, Wernerfelt (2016) suggests that, in the simplified form, the adaptation cost is lower in the employment than in the sequential contracting and the price list mechanisms when the frequency and types of change are larger. Thus, adaptation is more frequent and diverse in the employment relationship. In other words, when there is a need for more frequent and varied adaptation, the employment mechanism moderately dominates other means (Wernerfelt, 2016).

The adaptation cost model can be enhanced to include production costs by introducing three factors: They are (1) a price determination, (2) a change in a service provided, and (3) an alteration in a business served.

These factors necessitate the concept of specialization (Wernerfelt, 2016).

In this framework, parameters interact are

a. a worker's advantage of specialization in a particular service,
b. the benefit of specialization in providing services for a specific entrepreneur, and
c. the frequency of which their needs change (Wernerfelt, 2016).

Wernerfelt (2016) starts by analyzing trades in which an entrepreneur may need a wide variety of services but does not know his/her need in advance.

The above parameters can apply to a relationship between a scientist and a science-intensive organization. The parables are as follows:

a. a scientist's advantage of specialization in a particular scientific practice,
b. a scientist's advantage of specialization in providing science practices for one specific science organization, and
c. the frequency of which their needs change.

A setting is that a scientific KIO and a scientist trade a sequence of science practices.

In this framework, a scientist must choose whether specialization in a single service is more efficient, or remaining in a bilateral relationship or an employment is better. It depends on the comparative advantage of a market, organization, and a contract (see, Wernerfelt, 2016).

The first essential component of this model is a gain from the two kinds of specialization: service specialization in the market and business specialization in a bilateral trade. The second essential component is mutually incomplete information in a bilateral relationship (Wernerfelt, 2016).

In such a case, search costs (Nelson & Winter, 1982) occur for players in learning (a) how the employer evaluates their opponents in a single period and (b) the types of opponents (Wernerfelt, 2016).

Firstly, an assumption of the market mechanism is a single price: players can find a single price in the market. Market payoffs only differ by a worker's switching cost between entrepreneurs. If a trade is very infrequent, it is cheaper for the entrepreneur to pay the switching cost instead of employing the worker (Wernerfelt, 2016).

This mechanism can apply to a scientific KIO seeking a very specialized solution in a research project. For example, recent years have witnessed intermediate firms that connect scientific and academic KIOs and independent scientists regarding a highly complex and complicated problem. Compensations are almost predetermined when the intermediate organization seeks scientists. The intermediate entities use information technology to call for problems to solve and search scientists globally. They

158   E. OKADA

use a mechanism of the two-sided market through the connectivity of information technology.

Secondly, in a sequential contract mechanism, an entrepreneur and a worker pair up on a once-and-for-all basis and negotiate a new contract whenever the entrepreneur's needs change. The worker, in this case, cannot specialize in a single service. Thus, a production cost can be higher while economizing a switching cost. Further, due to the loss of market mechanism, players must engage in a bargaining over each potential, subsequent trade. They desire to know each other's reservation value for specific services that the entrepreneur needs (Wernerfelt, 2016).

Scientific KIOs frequently use this mechanism to hire a science workforce in their research projects. They hire academic scientists in internal and external KIOs on a three-to-five-year basis to conduct grant-funded research. They renegotiate the contract upon the change of conditions or a renewal of the grant. As science processes in the biochemicals and biotechnology fields are more specified and standardized, the production cost will be lower relative to non-science organizations.

In the employment mechanism, the two players agree once and for all on a single per-period contract that applies to all future trades.

In determining the hiring mode, the size effect also matters (Wernerfelt, 2016). For example, several conditions are different between independent laboratories and large-scale KIOs. Also, assumptions are necessary regarding a player's evaluation format, private information to collect, and variables that measure a fit between the player and the service (Wernerfelt, 2016).

The adaptation costs theory has strength in its consistency with a resource-based view. From the resource-based perspective, a significant determinant of firms' strategy and behavior is heterogeneity in their resource and experience (Barney, 1991; Wernerfelt, 1984, 2003).

Based on the resource-based view, a small difference emerges in firms' resource and experience even if firms are ex-ante identical, and the slight difference has the potential to evolve into a massive difference between firms' strategy and behavior (Wernerfelt, 2003, 2016). Such a framework has theoretical consistency with the evolutionary view of urban resilience.

2.2   Productive Assets

The adaptation cost theory (Wenerfelt, 2016) applies to the scope economies by defining resource as a productive asset. This framework assumes that a productive asset is economically inalienable from a firm if it causes inefficiency for other firms that use any part of it (Wernerfelt, 1984, 1997, 2016). This conceptualization holds to a condition in which a worker's service has too little demand and a sub-additive bargaining cost is too expensive for the worker to possess two employment simultaneously. Under this condition, the worker can use his/her extra time to perform a specialized service for another business operated by the same entrepreneur (or otherwise find out a different entrepreneur through a market) (Wernerfelt, 2016). In this model, the redundant resource (excess capacity of inalienable, productive assets: Penrose, 1959; Wernertelt, 1986) as well as resource redeployability (Sakhartov & Folta, 2014a, 2014b)[1] play a critical function in the organizational expansion.

In the Wernerfelt (2016) model, the scope economy presents a situation in which an entrepreneur is active in multiple businesses and is responsible for allocating resources to the businesses. In this setting, the employer compares a marginal bargaining cost that incurs from assigning the worker to a specific unit with a lower or higher adaptation cost that incurs in the bargaining free market (Wernerfelt, 2016).

The above conditions of workers apply to scientists that provide scientific knowledge to science organizations.

When the environmental change is incremental, a science-intensive organization can create a new organizational division by moving scientists and other resources within the existing segment. It will incur a lower marginal bargaining cost and thus, an adaptation cost than other forms. When the environmental change is disruptive, the science-intensive organization will create a new organizational unit by shifting scientists and other resources of the existing organizational segments to the new unit. It will incur more extensive bargaining and thus, an adaptation cost relative to the former method. In the latter, the comparison of bargaining and adaptation costs with the market mechanism will depend on the redundancy of organizational capacity and scientists' properties.

The former is consistent with the technical integration of general organizations, whereas the latter, the strategic integration (See, Burgerman & Doz (1997); Eisenmann & Bower, 2005). Thus, the adaptation cost

---

[1] According to Sakhartov and Folta (2014a, 2014b), the concept of resource reployability embeds two attributes: better use of resources and switching to better applications. Thus, it is beyond the concept of economies of scope and better fits the evolutionary model of resilience.

160   E. OKADA

reasoning leads to a consistent result with the resource allocation process model of strategy.

The next step is to consider whether, how, and what types of external knowledge science-intensive organizations should introduce to capture opportunities in the environmental turbulence. It will incur a larger adaptation cost while broadening beneficiaries.

2.3   Case Observations

2.3.1   The Case of an Academic Knowledge-Intensive Organization

This section observes cases that succeed in introducing external knowledge and scaling up.

The case selection criteria are as follows:

a. Organizations whose major input factors and output factors are scientific knowledge or practices
b. Organizations that are contributing to the environmental aspects of urban resilience
c. Organizations that succeeded in the scale-up of their program

Data sources are those posted at the public domain (organizations' website description, newspapers' and journals' articles, among others), organization members' presentation, and complementary interview.

The first case is a program of X University that applies frameworks of urban planning and environmental science to inner-city areas. The areas of focus are (a) sustainability and climate change, (b) environmental issues, and (c) public health and safety. They examine problems that public and private organizations raise, conduct field research, and provide a report to the sponsors with recommendations. This Program has succeeded in the scale-up from resolving regional issues to global areas.

The essence of the Program consists of contract research requested by sponsoring organizations. The Program not only is to resolve practical needs of sponsors, but meets the theoretical models for education.

Project types include (a) that to resolve problems of a city government in the state. For example, there is a city that suffers from extreme heat that negatively affects the vulnerable residents. This city asked the KIO to form a project. The purpose of the project is two folds: One is to identify populations and geographic areas that the extreme heat provides the worst impact. The other is to suggest recommendations to the city to mitigate the effects. This Program of academic KIO has several experiences in this type of project. For example, they developed guidance materials for another city government to increase the preparedness to the cyanobacterial harmful algal blooms in the fresh water system.

Other types include (b) that to solve problems of non-government institutions. One example is a project to assess program effectiveness for a nonregulatory agency regarding climate change resiliency and chemical safety. This agency has a program to train manufacturing companies related to the "preparedness for resilience" and "chemical safety." For the purpose of training, it conducts a site visit of companies and assesses them related to the criteria they develop. They are continuously exploring the operational criteria on what it means by "prepared for resiliency" and what it means by "harmful to others." At the same time, they also notice the need to evaluate themselves on the program effectiveness adequately. The project they asked the academic KIO is to help them to explore the evaluation criteria of the program's effectiveness. For the purpose of the project, students of the KIO conducted a structured interview with trainees. They suggested recommendations based on their interviews.[2]

The geographical scope of the KIO's Program was, at first, limited to the region that it located. Many of the project themes are those for state-level institutions that are responsible for urban resilience. This tendency reflects the decentralization policy of nations on the area resilience.

For example, the first-year projects include building resilience strategies for the coastal area of a specific city. A problem to address is the rising sea level. The rise of the sea level occurs due to the thermal expansion of water caused by greenhouse gases, along with the increased severity of storms. The faculties of the project submitted a strategic recommendation to build a resilient urban complex mix.

On the other hand, the scope of climate change is global. Also, local governments and institutions are suffering from unprecedented, infrequent, and overwhelming issues. As Roberts (2000) states, there is a limit to allocate responsibilities to such institutions.

Under such conditions, it is often more efficient to transfer knowledge mutually between regions that are already exposed to hazards or have the

---

[2] The description of the projects is based on the information disclosed at the website of the university and related regulatory and nonregulatory agencies.

potential to be exposed to similar threats. The scale-up of the Program of academic KIO follows this logic. The Program extended its geographic scope to be global. The organization mechanisms that enable the scale-up will be discussed in the next section. This section first describes the process and educational effects of the worldwide scale-up of the academic Program.

Scale-up of the Program

The Global Program is a scale-up version of the Program. It already dispatched students to 53 locations in 35 countries (updated in 2019).

The Program description of the KIO's website and the related articles suggests that the Program encourages students to adopt the abductive approach. The abduction is a discovery-oriented approach to generate a plausible, conjecturable explanation. In this space, roles of theory are to provide assumptions to frame anomalies or plausible post hoc explanations for observations. Roles of data are to diagnose phenomena and narrow a range of possible explanations. The type of reasoning is a contrastive reasoning. It is to identify patterns indicative of alternative processes, mechanisms, or means-end linkages (Banberger, 2018).

One good example is an Albanian project to improve a disaster planning related to a storm water conveyance system that is outside the main channel. A newspaper article by Pappano (2019) featured this project. According to Pappano (2019), a student team visited residents who have lived with the moldy doors and water-stained walls since the 2010 flood. Though the local community had conceptual and abstract planning, it lacked detail on what people should do under what circumstances. The students developed a recommendation that consists of concrete solutions for the emergency move related to the storm water conveyance system outside of the main canal.

Thus, students who learn theoretical assumptions at a classroom teaching must explore a more plausible linkage between ends and means by using data. They earn credits by enrolling in a project.

Beginning with the Class of 2022, all of the first-year undergraduate students have an obligation to complete a global project by receiving up to $5000 grant from the Program. The contents of the projects are more interdisciplinary in the Global Program than in the former Program.

Thus, the first driver of the student to engage in the Global Program is the credits. The next step is to consider the educational impacts of this Program on students. Interdisciplinary projects require more social skills (coordination and communication skills) that are essential to the evolving workplace environments. A problem is whether there is any positive effect of the Program that presents in students' learning attitudes.

Positive Educational Effects of the Program

According to Boudreau and Marx (2019), there is a theoretical debate regarding the work requirements in higher education. Work requirements disrupt students from regular academic studies on the one hand. However, the simultaneous development of theoretical and practical knowledge can be complementary to the other. The early exposure also familiarizes the youth to work contexts and professional norms. It is also beneficial to expose young people to a professional network and mentors while earning an income (.Boudreau & Marx, 2019).

The possible tradeoffs associated with the transition from theory to practice can present, particularly, to Engineering and Applied Sciences (Boudreau & Marx, 2019). It is partly because many high school students choose to enter the Engineering Department without knowledge that the Department requires them to complete a highly theoretical and mathematical program (Brophy et al., 2008; Felder and Silverman, 1998; Felder, 1982; Felder et al., 2000). Under this condition, the early exposure can benefit them by developing "connective tissue" between theoretical academic training and expected careers (Seely, 1999) that they have to choose under a considerable uncertainty (Froyed et al., 2012; Manski, 1993; Bleemer & Zafar, 2018).[3] Also, they have opportunities to build receptors for distant knowledge that will be necessary for broader contexts.

Boudreau and Marx (2019) do not necessarily provide a reason regarding the systematically higher impact on children from a low-income background. A possible explanation is that children with a low-income background have less opportunity to be exposed to professional networks, mentors, and workplace culture (see, Boudreau & Marx, 2019). If

---

[3] According to Boudreau and Marx (2019), some employers, university administrators, and education policymakers before the 1990s had perceptions that the increasingly abstract, conceptual, and mathematical content of programs left junior Engineers ill-prepared to enter the full-time workforce (Seely, 1999; Jørgensen et al., 2007). As a consequence, since the 1990s, many American Universities began to incorporate varying degrees of practical training and experience into the curriculum. Among several programs with practical experience, the X academic KIO mainly receives a favorable reputation among sponsoring organizations.

the early exposure positively affects students' academic performance, it will affect relative more to students who might otherwise have little opportunity of the exposure.

It is then an empirical question of what factors determine a favorable effect that presents relatively more on low-income students.

The favorable effects of the Program are considered to be two folds:

a. The problem raised by sponsor institutions is, in many cases, ill structured.

According to Pappano (2019), the Global Project relies on sponsors regarding the framing the problems. They are often not clearly stated. Students have to solve ambiguous problems independently. This point can be confirmed by the Program description of the academic KIO. The project begins with a series of sponsor presentation meetings to discuss and narrow the problems.

The cultural difference poses additional challenges. In different cultures, what is essential is often different from what they are accustomed to. Thinking patterns that they are used to are not always applicable to other cultural systems and conditions (see Adler with Gundersen, 2007). Although theories and scientific assumptions are common all over the world, regional, cultural contexts affect technological development and its application (Gottweis et al., 2009).

These challenges, on the other hand, must have a positive educational effect on students. First, students have to construct ill-structured problems by themselves. Ill-structured problem solving is an essential component of scientific innovation (Simonton, 2004).

Second, students need to contrast theoretical assumptions, prior knowledge, and data from the fieldwork to seek synergetic solutions. It is a process to seek a new linkage between ends and means (Banberger, 2018). Thus, they have an opportunity to make some contribution to their scientific discipline.

b. Students with low-income background benefit relatively more.

The President of the academic KIO evaluates the Program to have a positive educational effect on overall students. Further, the positive impact is relatively more on students with a low-income background

(Pappano, 2019). This evaluation is consistent with the empirical studies in higher education economics.

On the other hand, the evaluation of the university President is partly inconsistent with Boudreau and Marx (2019). According to the President, the Program positively impacts more on students who entered the university with low SAT scores relative to those with high SAT scores related to the academic performance (Pappano, 2019). However, according to Boudreau and Marx (2019), the work-requirement programs, in general, lower academic performance of students with low SAT scores. The reason is unknown. A possible explanation is that the early workplace experience deepens the struggle of low-score students, making their academic score worse (Boudreau, 2020, in answering the author's question).

If Boudreau and Marx (2019) provide the average statistical results while the President's evaluation bases on more in-depth individual cases, this inconsistency is not contradictory to each other. First, it is possible that, in Program X, projects are more tailored to individual students, as they limit the number of team members to three or four. Second, the project advisor and other team members can help to resolve several barriers to the low-score students. Third, students who are weak at the standardized exam have the potential to perform better at resolving more ill-structured problems. Some students struggle to integrate too much consideration into problem-solving that makes them to choose inappropriate answers. Such individuals can overcome their potential struggles with the tailored, useful guidance of an advisor.

There are several empirical evidence regarding co-relations between the income divide and the children's later-year performance. For example, the U.S. children in high-income classes of the upper one percent are more consistent in engaging science jobs and productive with innovative works than children in low-income classes. The measurement is by their patent application in later years (Mitnik & Grusky, 2015).

The interpretation of this result should be careful. This result does not imply that the resource allocation to children with a high-income background is more profitable to nations. There is a series of empirical evidence that there is a limit (for countries or the public) to benefit from allocating more resources to the highest performance ones while sacrificing others.

This line of research questions the current resource allocation for education that undermines specific populations that might otherwise be innovative and contribute to economic growth. What it implies is that it would be more profitable for nations to allocate a certain amount of resources to upgrade the currently undermined populations while retaining that for the top one percent talents.

The above empirical research streams also suggest that early exposure of students in an innovative environment will help develop skills to tackle ill-structured problem solving. Ill-structured problem-solving is one of the essential components to generate creativity in science (see, Simonton, 2004). Low-score students also have the potential to be innovative in ill-structured problem settings. Some of them could have struggled to adapt to well-structured standardized problem-solving.

Thus, the Program is exposing students to innovation-facilitating workplace contexts that have the potential to moderate bias in the educational resource allocation due to the social divide.

2.3.2 The Case of Social Entrepreneurial Firm

The Y social entrepreneur firm began its operation by translating theories of an academic scientist to practice. The expertise of the academic scientist is in the field of international environmental policy, physical chemistry, and environmental sciences. His current focuses include addressing the climate change through soils. It is to compliment emission reductions of carbon dioxide by land use changes. The academic is also active in helping to formulate international, intergovernmental environmental policies. The founders of Y are also involved in translating the policy frameworks into practices.

Despite the enthusiasm, the founders (and the academic scientist) do not come out to the surface. This attitude may have contributed to mobilizing collective forces.

The starting point of their activity is to reverse the advancement of dessert by remedying dry land. They successfully changed the withered land in Arizona State and regenerated the green field. They further are replicating the practice to other U.S. states and an African tribal area. The ultimate goal is to discontinue the vicious cycle of land withering and reduce the impacts of climate change.

The causal pathways between soil remediation and the reversion of climate change are complex and not thoroughly, empirically established (see, European Environment Agency: EEA, 2009). The grounding theory is further complex and requires integrating several science disciplines (see, Moomaw, 2002; Susskind, Moomaw, & Galagher, 2002). It is beyond this article to explain and evaluate the ground theory. However, according to several earth scientists, it is a foundation to recover specific mechanisms of absorbing toxic substances that is contributing to the abnormality of ecological cycles (see, Hristov et al., 2013). Also, based on the Climate Hubs at the U.S. Department of Agriculture (hereafter, USDA),

> "—grazing and proper land management contribute to climate resilience."[4]

European Environment Agency (EEA) also states:

> "—soil is a major factor in our response to tackling climate change as it is the second-largest carbon pool after the oceans."

According to EEA and other studies, the estimated recovery amount of carbon due to proper land management is approximately the same as the reduced amount of industrial CO_2 emissions during 1990–2006 (EEA, 2009). It is feasible and reasonable, as below mentioned.

Therefore, soil remediation is vital not only for removing toxic chemical contaminants that have the potential to negatively affect humans' bodily functions but also for the climate resilience.

Soil carbon losses are due to changes in land use, land management, and the climate. They lead to soil degradation and the loss of soil organic matter (EEA, 2009). In the case of Arizona State, the soil degradation started in the mid-twentieth century, whose immediate cause was the discontinued strolling of buffalo. It occurred because a crowd of buffalo damaged nearby crop fields.[5] Based on the environmental economics, a question to be asked is to what extent the landowners of crops have a claim right to reduce the amount of buffalo or create a fence (see Arrow, 1951). However, some collective forces likely decided the drastic removal of buffalo.

Under this background, the social entrepreneurs adopted the logic of grazing system (see, Allen et al., 2011) to recover the withered land. The grazing method is multi-paddock grazing. The grazing system is a defined, integrated combination of soil, plant, animal, social

---

[4] Retrieved from http://www.climatehubs.usda.gov. Last visited on April 1, 2020.

[5] The founder of Y, answering to the unstructured interview in 2015.

168   E. OKADA

and economic measures, stocking methods, and management objectives designed to achieve specific results or goals (Allen et al., 2011). The grazing method is a defined procedure or technique to manipulate animals in space and time to achieve a specific objective (Allen et al., 2011. Also see, Sollenberger, Agouridis, Avanzant, Fronzluebbers, & Owens[6]).

According to Teague, Dowhower, Baker, Haile, DeLaune, and Conover (2011; Also see, USDA[7]), adaptive management that uses multi-paddock grazing is more effective than the light-continuous or heavy continuous grazing regarding conservation and restoration of resources. Multi-paddock grazing, also known as rotational grazing, is a measure that utilizes recurring periods of grazing and rest among paddocks in a grazing management unit (see, Sollenberger et al., 2012). In addition to several agricultural performances, the fungal and bacterial ratio was the highest in the multi-paddock method. This high ratio indicates the superior water-holding capacity, nutrient availability, and retention (Teague et al., 2011).

As the U.S. and E.U. agencies acknowledge, soil carbon sequestration cannot be alone the solution to climate change due to the magnitude of its effect and potential reversibility. However, it can be an effective, short-term measure that plays a significant role in increasing climate resilience combined with other measures (EEA, 2009; USDA[8]).

Scale-up Mechanism

The organization forms that support scale-up are discussed in the next section. This subsection is to understand the mobilization of collective forces that underpin the scale-up of Y.

The common aspect of the Y with the academic Program X is the framework of organizing and mobilizing intellectual workers. Problems they are tackling are broader and abnormal conditions that challenge ecological cycles. Under this uncommon condition, the methodology is outside of market mechanism, sequential contract, or employment in Wernerfelt (2016)'s model.

---

[6] Retrieved from https://www.nrcs.usda.gov/Internet/FSE_DOCUMENTS/stelprdb1 080495.pdf.

[7] Retrieved from: https://www.nrcs.usda.gov/wps/portal/nrcs/detailfull/?cid=nrcs14 2p2_053865.

[8] *Ibid.*

On the other hand, what distinguishes Y entrepreneurial organization from X academic KIO is the scale-up mechanism.

The scale-up mechanism of Y relies on the mobilization of a variety of societal constituents, including academics, scientists, other professionals, concerned citizen scientists, and university students. The method is to stimulate their conscience, intellectual capacity, and anticipation. As stated in Chapter 1, the "anticipation" is a phase in which urban resilience evolves from the adaptation toward transformation. It is also one of the dimensions of Responsible Research and Innovation (hereafter, RRI. Stigloe et al., 2013).[9] It is a dimension that envisions and understands how the current dynamics affect or help to design the future (Stigloe, Owen, & Macnaghten, 2013. See, Barben, Fischer, Selin, & Guston, 2008).

RRI is one of the governance modalities[10] that do not work in an isolated manner. RRI does not necessarily rely on laws with enforceable mechanisms and instead depends on internal and societal norms. On the other hand, the grazing system is not necessarily embedded in societal norms, particularly in urban areas. The location that the entrepreneurial organization Y was founded is the U.S. urban area. A problem is how to stimulate peoples' conscience under the absence of societal norms regarding the grazing system.

A possible approach in this context is to stimulate people's moral responsibility to activate collective forces. The concrete method the founders adopt is to spread the theory and practices by creating small inner circles (see, Krogh, Ichijo, & Nonaka, 2000). When the procedure results in a success of greenfield regeneration, it becomes a part of scientific evidence that strengthens their commitment. The circles include those of citizen scientists, students' clubs in several universities, as well as an advisory committee that consists of scientists and professionals. These constituents at least share the internal norms that drive the anticipation.

---

[9] RRI is an approach that anticipates and assesses potential implications and societal expectations with regard to research and innovation, with the aim to foster the design of inclusive and sustainable research and innovation (European Union, 2020). It takes care of the future through collective stewardship of science and innovation in the present (Stigloe et al., 2013).

[10] According to Lessig (1999), governance modalities consist of laws, codes of conduct, (internal and societal) norms, and choice architecture.

3 Governance to Support Scale-up

3.1 Modification of Framework

3.1.1 The educational Program of Academic KIOs

The case of the academic KIO and relevant empirical studies suggests the following implications to the management sciences:

Firstly, an issue of the adaptation theory lies in the comparison between gains from service specialization in the market and gains from business specialization in bilateral trade. The students' enrollment in a specific project does not occur based on the market mechanism. The exchange between the academic KIO and students regarding a particular project does not frequently happen nor in a recurring manner. There is no single price determined through the market forces. The negotiation between the academic KIO and sponsor organizations also is, in principle, infrequent. Though some institutions are coming back to sponsor a project, it is not so frequently as to determine a single price.

On the other hand, the Program of the academic KIO is specialized in its activities, i.e., research, education, and social contribution through them. The Program started from the civil and environmental engineering discipline and extended to a global, interdisciplinary program. It also has the character of social contribution, as students write a recommendation report for a set of social and environmental problems. The occurrence of the educational project is recurring every year, while the types of knowledge and skills required in leading projects can change depending on sponsors' framing of problems.

Therefore, it is more beneficial for the academic KIO to employ a faculty specialized in the field. The employment will enhance the flexibility to adapt a variety of outside requirements toward the Program. Also, the employment mode will accumulate the know-how, such as the teaming-up of students and the work assignment to them. These advantages will lower bargaining costs on the side of the academic KIO.

The above logic will also support the global scale-up of the Program. First, the essential theory that underlies a problem does not change depending on countries. The experiences of projects accumulate around the routines that are partially transferrable to other foreign centers. Therefore, such accumulation will lower the adaptation costs to other geographic areas.

However, practices that come from civil and environmental problems vary depending on the regional and local contexts. For example, the past projects in Lyon include a field study related to the impacts of migrants and entrepreneurship on the city. Those in Bucharest include the development of educational resources on historical heritages. These problems are also significant in the cities in the home country. However, these problems do not always come to the surface in the home country.

Such variety requires the employment of faculties with the expertise of the area studies. At the same time, the KIO needs to build a partnership in foreign countries in the sequential contract mode that depends on the frequency of the event.

The case observation supports the above model. The academic KIO, in this case, has global centers in 39 countries (in the early 2020) outside of the U.S. Thus, the academic KIO uses the mode of employment for faculties with specialized academic knowledge at Global Centers. It also partners with core sponsors in a sequential contract mode. The core sponsors include a museum in the UNESCO-designated historic heritage site in a particular country.

Research, education, and administrative activities to connect students and sponsoring organizations are specialized, recurring activities for faculties. On the other hand, for students, involvement in a specific project is an infrequent activity. It is also infrequent for many sponsoring organizations to ask for help from the KIO.

In the Wernerfelt model, if the trade is infrequent, it is cheaper for entrepreneur employers to pay switching costs related to workers than employment, that is, the use of specialized services on the market mechanism (Wernerfelt, 2016). However, this mode is also different from the market mechanism in which a single price exists for a specialized service. There is no market force for projects to determine a price since they also have educational attributes. The sponsoring organization also involves in the educational aspects of a project by framing problems and interacting with students.

Here needs a mechanism that is different from either the market, sequential contract, or employment.

Secondly, two-sided incompleteness of information exists in bilateral relationships between students and sponsoring organizations. According to the Wernerfelt model (2016), the mode of bilateral sequential contract would be appropriate for such cases due to the increased search costs. One of the search costs derives from workers' learning on the evaluation of employers regarding their competitors. However, being different from the relationship between entrepreneur employers and workers, the search costs are unlikely to occur related to the learning of the evaluation of opponents and their types on the side of students. Assessment of an individual student does not affect that of other students related to whether they are adopted by projects. Instead, search costs would occur pertaining to students' learning about the contents of projects, their geographic locations, and sponsors' types in selecting a project. On the side of sponsoring organizations, search costs could occur related to learning on a fit of their problems to students' preferences, capacities, educational implications, and alternatives to resolve issues. They can also search for academic KIO's evaluation over competing options regarding the educational effects.

Here is a mechanism that enables for sponsoring organizations and students to "pair up a once- for -all basis" with some form of flexibility.

In the focal Program of the academic KIO, a faculty advisor provides guidance in connecting sponsoring organizations and a student team. The faculty advisor discusses the problem with potential sponsoring organizations before paring up with students. After the paring up, students and the sponsoring organization have meetings for seven months. During this preparation period, students acquire background knowledge related to the problem specific to the sponsoring organization. They start the fieldwork only after they complete the preparatory period. The faculty advisor(s) indirectly involve the process through the guidance of students.

This mode incurs less cost for a sponsoring organization than paying a higher production (service) cost to specialized agencies in a sequential contract mode. Though students are not specialized in the conduct of the project, faculty advisor(s) have academic, theoretical, and specialized knowledge in the field. During the abductive reasoning of students, the essential knowledge will be transferred to students that lead to more comprehensive and novel resolutions combined with their fieldwork.

A factor that motivates students is, at first, to obtain the credit that is necessary to get a degree. At the same time, students' commitment to a specific project likely to grow during the fieldwork since, without the growing commitment, it would not occur that low SAT-score students benefit relatively more regarding subsequent academic performance. This motivation can be greater than the average work-requirement credits. In the average work-requirement program, students provide services to sponsoring organizations in exchange of a credit. In this context, the students with a "low-income" background benefit relatively more by the early exposure to professional knowledge, network, and workplace culture. However, it does not occur to "low-score" students.

One of tendencies for poor performance students is the inability to exchange credits by taking expected actions. On the other hand, Program X has benefited "low-score" students relatively more while also upgrading academic performance of high score students. This fact suggests that the Program succeeded in inspiring more commitment and a sense of responsibility in a diversified talent than the average work-experience program.

Thus, the performance of Program should include the upgrade of academic score of students by exposing them to innovation-facilitating workplace contexts. It has the potential to moderate bias in the educational resource allocation that derives from the social divide.

3.2 Social Entrepreneurial Organizations

In the case of Y social entrepreneurial organization, it is unconsciously practicing the Responsible Research and Innovation (RRI). As stated earlier, RRI is an approach in which a variety of actors take care of the future through collective stewardship of science and innovation in the present (Stigloe et al., 2013). The aim is to foster the design of inclusive and sustainable research and innovation (European Union, 2020).

In the process of RRI, societal players (including researchers, citizens, policymakers, businesses, third-sector organizations, etc.) work together to better align the research process and outcomes with the societal values, needs, and expectations (EU, 2020). The intention is to realize the "Science with and for Society's objective." Actions on the thematic elements include public engagement, open access, and science education (EU, 2020).

The activities of the entrepreneurial firm Y unconsciously cover these attributes.

One of the distinguishing attributes is the activation of citizen sciences. Citizen sciences are defined as sciences conducted by citizens who have no background of formal scientific education and training. Then, a question arises why and how the founders could activate the nonscientists. The founders are not citizen scientists. They have a formal education in science.

A possible explanation is that they are good at enhancing people's awareness and moral responsibility regarding science.

Moral responsibility and self-regulation are often confused. However, these two concepts differ in the sources. A source of moral responsibility is a moral ownership of people, whereas that of self-regulation, a self-identification. Moral ownership derives from conscious or unconscious possession of natural rights (see, Hannah, Avolio, & May, 2011) rooted in the natural law. The natural law is a precept of collaboration (Finnis, 1980). Therefore, the stimulation of moral responsibility leads to the activation of a collective force that includes a variety of people. This variety develops to a collective stewardship of science and innovation that care about the present and future of climate resilience.

The organization mechanism that connects diversified people is the creation of multi-sided space. The logic of multi-sided space is similar to that of multiple-sided market. What is different is that the constituents' motivation is not necessarily economic benefits. The academics and scientists are producing conceptual and empirical knowledge; professionals are developing more specialized and practical knowledge; students and citizen scientists are willing to understand and participate in authentic conducts. Being different from internet-based business models, founders (employers) travel to potential participants to explain the intentions and missions. They translate the academics' theoretical bases, stimulate awareness, and invoke citizens' anticipation and commitment. Transactions occur not between material things (such as money, credit, status, etc.), but primarily between moral ownership and conscientiousness.

This transaction does not mean the allowance of unprofessional practices. According to empirical research, the precision of citizen scientists in measuring environmental contaminants is robust enough to use in the study of academic and professional scientists (See, Carvlin et al., 2019; Kaufman et al., 2017).

Then, this study modifies the organization model of Wernerfelt (2016) as follows.

First, the employer needs fewer full employment employees relative to a massive variation of environmental, economic, and societal circumstances.

Second, some advisory committee members (academics, scientists, and professionals) may be on a sequential contract basis. However, the contents of the contract may be limited to essential items. It is to leave flexibility to cope with a variation of circumstances.

Third, the transactions between students and citizen scientists can be more infrequent. Also, what is distinct is that the objects of transactions are different from the market-based transaction. The objects are primarily moral ownership and conscientiousness. Anticipation motivates them to strengthen their commitment.

All the constituents commonly participate in the organizational activities through their moral responsibility that derives from moral ownership. Thus, the internal norms will govern their conduct beyond the law and external codes.

As stated above, the anticipation is a transitioning mode from the adaptive model to the evolutionary model of urban resilience (see, Coafee & Lee, 2016). The case of the entrepreneur organization Y supports this theory. The entrepreneurs of Y started from the adaptive resilience model to cope with the land withering. The vision is to transform the present human behaviors to taking care of future climate resilience.

Thus, the activation of a variety of moral responsibilities is the critical component not only of the scale-up model but also of the organizational model that corresponds to the evolutionary urban resilience.

4   NEW CATEGORIZATION

This chapter addresses a research question on appropriate organization designs for academic institutions and social entrepreneurial organizations in replicating and scaling up their resilience model. Their practices implicitly encompass ecological equity that will lead to sustainable and transformative urban resilience. However, there are only a few cases that have scaled up to expand the scope of beneficiaries.

The theoretical starting point is the adaptation cost theory that Wernerfelt (2016) explored. Wernerfelt (2016) is building a theory of adaptation cost by questioning the reason why people commonly use the forms of firms, markets, and contracts.

In the Wernerfelt model (2016), players do better if they adopt a more comprehensive sequences of services and do so more frequently. In other words, the value creation depends on parameters of the "diverse adaptation" and "frequent adaptation."

In this model, governance costs play a critical role. The direct governance costs consist of two folds: (1) communication and bargaining costs (Williamson, 1979) that are necessary to adapt to the condition and (2) costs to resolve incentive conflicts (Grossman & Hart, 1986; Hart, 1989; Hart & Moore, 1988). If an employer asks a worker more frequently to change a sequence of work, and when the adaptation is more valuable and cheaper than other alternatives, the parties will adopt the employment relationship. When parties more frequently negotiate a new contract for a new sequence of services, the parties will adopt the sequential contracting mechanism when the negotiation costs are smaller. When a price list is long and more important and cheaper than negotiating, the parties will adopt a price list mechanism. This model can be extended to include the production costs. In such extension, the choice is between the specialization in a single service or remaining in a bilateral relationship (Wernerfelt, 2016).

The above model needs a further extension since the representative cases in this chapter are outside the framework. They are the work-experience educational Program of the academic KIO and the social entrepreneurial organization.

In the work-experience educational Program, two-sided incompleteness of information exists in bilateral relationships between students and sponsoring organizations. The extension need for the Wernerfelt model (2016) lies in the search costs related to the bilateral sequential contract. In the Wernerfelt model, one of the search costs is workers' learning on the employer's evaluation regarding their competitors. However, being different from the relationship between entrepreneur employers and workers, search costs do not likely occur in the educational program related to the learning of the evaluation of opponents on the side of students. Instead, the search costs occur related to students' examining the contents of projects, their geographic locations, and sponsors' types in selecting a project. On the side of sponsoring organizations, search costs can occur related to learning a fit of their problems to students' preference, capacities, educational implications, and alternatives to resolve issues. They can also search for academic KIO's evaluation over competing options regarding the educational effects.

Such a program has mechanisms that enable parties to "pair up a once-for-all-basis" with some form of flexibility. In the focal Program of the academic KIO, a faculty advisor provides guidance in connecting sponsoring organizations and a student team. After the paring up, the due process is that students and the sponsoring organization have meetings during the preparation period. This period allows students to acquire background knowledge related to problems specific to the sponsoring organization. The faculty advisor(s) who are specialized in the academic field indirectly involve the process by guiding students. Therefore, the specialization occurs in the space where the Program works as the intermediate organization between students and sponsors. This mode incurs less cost for a sponsoring organization than paying a higher production (service) cost to specialized agencies in a sequential contract mode.

The object of the transaction also is different from the firms' transaction. An initial factor that motivates students is material: it is to obtain a credit that is essential to the degree. However, another intangible motivation grows more extensive in the course of the project. The indirect evidence is that low SAT-score students benefit relatively more regarding subsequent academic performance while upgrading the performance of high score students. It suggests that students' commitment to the specific project grows in the course of the fieldwork. Therefore, the object of exchange is fun of learning, scientific knowledge, and specialized resolutions. This point makes the tailored, work-requirement educational Program different from the average work-requirement programs.

On the side of the academic KIO, the stimulation of commitment and a sense of responsibility play a significant role in using diversified talents. The former is a critical factor for project formation (Bower, 1970; Bower & Gilbert, 2006). The latter is crucial in mobilizing diversified people in nonmonetary exchange for social issues (Hannah et al., 2011). At the same time, inclusion is critical to resolving ill-structured problems. Ill-structured problem solving is one of factors of fostering creativity in scientific innovation (Simonton, 2004). Thus, the Program is exposing students to innovation-facilitating workplace contexts. This effect can moderate bias in the educational resource allocation due to the social divide (see, Boudreau & Marx, 2019).

In the social entrepreneurial organization, an employer needs a few core employees. It is to correspond to the variation that occur environmental, economic, and societal circumstances. Some advisory committee members (academics, scientists, and professionals) can be on a bilateral, sequential contract basis to cope with the variation.

At the same time, what is distinct is the transactions between students and citizen scientists. They can be more infrequent. Further, the objects of transactions are different from the market-based transaction. The objects are primarily moral ownership and, or, conscientiousness. According to empirical research, the precision level of measurement in citizen science is equivalent to the professional level.

In any mode, they are commonly participating in the organization activities through their moral responsibility. The internal norms are governing their conducts beyond the enforceable laws and external codes. Anticipation motivates them to strengthen their commitment.

Anticipation is a transitioning mode from the adaptive model to the evolutionary model in the evolutionary model of urban resilience (see,

Coafee & Lee, 2016). The representative case of the entrepreneurial firm supports this theory. The entry mode of the focal entrepreneur organization is the adaptive resilience model. The short-term motivation is to cope with the land withering. Its long-term vision is to transform the present human behaviors by taking care of future climate resilience.

The activation of a variety of moral responsibilities is the critical component of the scale-up of the organizational model of social entrepreneurs that corresponds to the evolutionary urban resilience.

References

Adler, N. J., with Gundersen, A. (2007). *International dimensions of organizational behavior*. Mason: Thomson South-Western.

Allen, C. R., Fontaine, J. J., Pope, K. L., & Garmestani, A. S. (2011). Adaptive management for a turbulent future. *Journal of Environmental Management, 92*, 1339–1345.

Arrow, K. J. (1951). *Social choice and individual values*. New York: Wiley.

Banberger, P. (2018, November). Addressing the "too much theory" problem in management research. *Academy of Management Paper Development Workshop*.

Barben, D., Fischer, E., Selin, C., & Guston, D. H. (2008). Anticipatory governance of nanotechnology: Foresight, engagement, and integration. In E. J. Hackett, O. Amsterdamska, M. Lynch, & J. Wajcman (Eds.), *The handbook of science and technology studies* (3rd ed., pp. 979–1000). Cambridge: MIT Press.

Barney, J. B. (1991). Firm resources and sustained competitive advantage. *Journal of Management, 17*, 99–120.

Bleemer, Z., & Zafar, B. (2018). Intended college attendance: Evidence from an experiment on college returns and costs. *Journal of Public Economics, 157*, 184–211.

Boudreau, K. J. & Marx, M. (2019). *From theory to practice: Field experimental evidence on early exposure of engineering majors to professional work* (National Bureau of Economic Research Working Paper No. 20163).

Bower, J. L. (1970). *Managing the resource allocation process*. Boston: Division of Research, Graduate School of Business Administration, Harvard University.

Bower, J. L., & Gilberet, C. K. (Eds.). (2006). *From resource allocation to strategy*. Oxford: Oxford University Press.

Brophy, S., Klein, S., Portsmore, M., & Rogers, C. (2008). Advancing engineering education in P-12 classrooms. *Journal of Engineering Education, 97*(3), 369–387.

Burgerman, B. A., & Doz, Y. (1997). *Complex strategic integration in the lean multibusiness corporation* (*INSEAD Working Paper*, 97/03/SM), as cited by Eisemnann, T. R., & Bower, L. J. (2005).

Carvlin, G. N., Lugo, H., Olmedo, L., Bejarano, E., Wilkie, A., Meltzer, D., ..., Seto, E. (2019). Temporal modeling of particulate matter near the US/Mexico Border, *Atmosphere, 10*, 495. https://doi.org/10.3390/atmos1 0090495.

Coafee, J., & Lee, P. (2016). *Urban resilience: Planning risk, crisis and uncertainty.* London: Palgrave.

Coase, R. H. (1937). The nature of the firm. *Economica, 4*(16), 386–405.

Coase, R. H. (1960). The problem of social cost. *Journal of Law and Economics, 3*, 1–44.

Eisenmann, T., & Bower, J. L. (2005). The entrepreneurial M-Form: A case study of strategic integration in a global media company. In J. L. Bower & C. K. Gilbert (Eds.), *From resource allocation to strategy* (pp. 307–329). New York: Oxford University Press.

European Environmental Agency. (2009). *Soil and climate change.* Copenhagen: European Environmental Agency.

European Union. (2020). *Horizon 2020.* Geneva, EU.

Felder, R. M. (1982). *Does engineering education have anything to do with either one? Toward a systems approach to training engineers.* School of Engineering, North Carolina State University at Raleigh.

Felder, R. M., Woods, D. R., Stice, J. E., & Rugarcia, A. (2000). The future of engineering education II. Teaching methods that work. *Chemical Engineering Education, 34*(1), 26–39.

Felder, R. M., & Silverman, L. K. (1998). *Learning and Teaching Styles in Engineering Education, 78*(7), 674–681.

Finnis, J. (1980). *Natural law and natural rights.* Oxford: Oxford University Press.

Froyed, J., Hurtado, D., Lagoudas, M., Nite, S., Hobson, M., Hodge, J., & Monroe, J. (2012). Increasing access to engineering. Frontiers in Education Conference Proceedings, as cited in Boudreau, K. J., & Marx, M. (2019). *Op.cite.*

Gottweis, H., Salter, B., & Waldby, C. (2009). *The global politics of human embryonic stem cell science: Regenerative medicine in transition.* New Hampshire and New York: Palgrave Macmillan.

Grossman, S. J., & Hart, O. D. (1986). The costs and benefits of ownership: A theory of vertical and lateral integration. *Journal of Political Economy, 94*(4), 691–714.

Hannah, S. T., Avolio, B. J., & May, D. R. (2011). Moral maturation and moral conation: A capacity approach to explaining moral thought and action. *Academy of Management Review, 36*(4), 663–685.

180   E. OKADA

Hart, O. (1989). An economist's perspective on the theory of the firm. *Columbia Law Review, 89*(7), 1757–1774.

Hart, O., & Moore, J. (1988). Incomplete contracts and renegotiation. *Economica, 56*(4), 755–785.

Hristov, A. N., Oh, J., Lee, C., Meinen, R., Montes, F., Ott, T., Adesogan, A. et al. (2013). Migration of greenhouse gas emissions in livestock production-review of technical options for non-CO_2 emissions. In P. J. Gerber, B. Henderson, & H. P. S. Akkar (Eds.), *FAO animal production and health paper* No. 177. Retrieved from http://www.fao.org/3/i3288e/i3288e.pdf.

Jørgensen, H., Kristensen, J. B., & Felby, C. (2007). Enzymatic conversion of ignocellulose into fermentable sugars: challenges and opportunities. *Biofpr, 1*(2), 119–134.

Justo-Hanani, R., & Dayan, T. (2014). The role of the state in regulatory policy for nanomaterials risk: Analyzing the expansion of sate-centric rulemaking in EU and US chemicals policies. *Research Policy, 43*(1), 169–178.

Kaufman, A., Williams, R., Barzyk, T., Greenberg, M., O'Shea, M., Sheridan, P., Garvey, S., et al. (2017). A citizen science and government collaboration: Developing tools to facilitate community air monitoring. *Environmental Justice, 10*(2), 1–11.

Krogh, G., Ichijo, K., & Nonaka, I. (2000). *Enabling knowledge creation: How to unlock the mystery of tacit knowledge and release the power of innovation.* Oxford: Oxford University Press.

Lessig, L. (1999). *Code and other laws of cyberspace.* New York: Basic Books.

Mitnik, P. A., & Grusky, D. B. (2015). *Economic mobility in the United States.* Philadelphia: PEW Charitable Trusts and Russell Sage Foundation.

Manski, C. F. (1993). Identification of endogenous social effects: The reflection problem. *The Review of Economic Studies., 60*(3), 531–542.

Moomaw, W. (2002). Energy, industry, and nitrogen: Strategies for decreasing reactive nitrogen emissions. *AMBIO: A Journal of the Human Environment, 31*(2), 184–189.

Nelson, R. R., & Winter, S. G. (1982). *An evolutionary theory of economic change.* Cambridge (U.S.): Harvard University Press.

Organization for Economic Cooperation and Development: OECD. (2004). *Entrepreneurship: Catalyst for urban regeneration.* Paris: OECD.

Penrose, E. T. (1959). *The theory of the growth of a firm.* New York and Oxford: Blackwell.

Roberts, P. (2000). The evolution, definition and purpose of urban regeneration. In P. Roberts & H. Sykes (Eds.), *Urban regeneration: A handbook* (pp. 9–36). New York: SAGE Publication.

Sakhartov, A. V., & Folta, T. B. (2014a). Resource relatedness, redeployability, and firm value. *Strategic Management Journal, 35*, 1781–1789.

Sakhartov, A. V., & Folta, T. B. (2014b). Getting beyond relatedness as a driver of corporate value. *Strategic Management Journal, 36,* 1939–1959.

Seely, B. (1999). The other re-engineering of engineering education: 1960–1965. *Journal of Engineering Education, 88*(3), 285–294.

Simonton, D. K. (2004). *Creativity in science: Chance, logic, genius, and zeitgeist.* Cambridge: Cambridge University Press.

Sollenberger, L. E., Agouridis, C. T., Avanzani, E. S., Fronzluebbers, A. J., & Owens, L. B. (2012). Prescribed grazing on pastureland. In C. J. Nelson (Ed.), *Conservation outcomes from pastureland and hayland practices: Assessment, recommendations, and knowledge gaps* (pp. 111–204). Washington, DC: U.S. Department of Agriculture Natural Resource Conservation Service. Retrieved from https://uknowledge.uky.edu/cgi/viewcontent.cgi?art icle=1039&context=bae_facpub.

Stigloe, J., Owen, R., & Macnaghten, P. (2013). Developing a framework for responsible innovation. *Research Policy, 42*(9), 1568–1580.

Susskind, L., Moomaw, W., & Galagher, K. (2002). *Transboundary environmental negotiation: New approaches to global cooperation.* New Jersey: Jossey-Bass.

Teague, W. R., Dowhower, S. L., Baker, S. A., Haile, N., DeLaune, P. B., & Conover, D. M. (2011). Grazing management impacts on vegetation soil biota and chemical physical and hydrological properties in tall grass prairie. *Agriculture Ecosyems and Environment, 141*(3–4), 310–322.

Teece, D. J. (1980). Economies of scope and the scope of the enterprise. *Journal of Economic Behavior & Organization, 1*(3), 223–247.

Wernerfelt, B. (1984). A resource-based view of the firm. *Strategic Management Journal, 5*(2), 171–180.

Wernerfelt, B. (1997). On the nature and scope of the firm: An adjustment-cost theory. *Journal of Business, 70*(4), 489–514.

Wernerfelt, B. (2003). Resources, adjustments, and diversification: Evidence from production functions. *MIT Sloan Working Paper,* 4277-03.

Wernerfelt, B. (2016). *Adaptation, specialization, and the theory of the firm.* Cambridge: Cambridge University Press.

Williamson, O. E. (1979). Transaction-cost economics: The governance of contractual relations. *Journal of Law and Economics, 22*(2), 233–261.

Williamson, O. E. (1981). The economics of organization. The transaction cost approach. *American Journal of Sociology, 87*(3), 548–577.

CHAPTER 8

Strategy and Governance

1 Issues Present

This chapter summarizes the arguments of this study under a vision of a variety of heterogeneous knowledge. This book addresses research questions on what mechanisms enable science-intensive organizations to contribute to broadening beneficiaries of science by science in urban resilience settings.

This study focuses on managerial aspects of science-intensive organizations that engage in environmental sciences, particularly in environmental material sciences. It defines science-intensive organizations as those whose major driving force of the product and service development is science.

The theoretical starting point is the market structure of technologies (Sutton, 1998) of Mark II industrial sciences categorized by Niosi (2000. See also, Arthur, 1994; Kaldor, 1972). This study starts with investigating the R&D behavioral traits of organizations in concentrated market (Sutton, 1998). The reason is that it focuses on the organizational arrangements of anchor corporations that will contribute to the urban environmental resilience. The typical anchors that engage in the material sciences are in the chemical industry whose science is categorized as Mark II. The Mark II industrial science is characterized as the concentrated R&D both in the initial condition and the subsequent trends (Niosi, 2000). In such industrial sciences, only companies that have the ability to tolerate the intensified R&D can play in the market (Sutton, 1998).

© The Author(s), under exclusive license to
Springer Nature Switzerland AG 2021
E. Okada, *Management of Science-Intensive Organizations*,
https://doi.org/10.1007/978-3-030-64042-2_8

The problem is that in what organizational arrangements firms can introduce emerging environmental sciences into their R&D. Also, as anchor corporations are experienced firms by definition, their organization form is, typically, in M-Form (Bower, 1970; Bower & Gilbert, 2005; Burgelman, 1983; Burgelman & Doz, 1997; Eisenmann & Bower, 2000). M-forms encounter difficulties in redefining their economic and technological elements of projects since once established patterns of resource allocation processes persist (Bower, 2017; Bower & Gilbert, 2005).

The background is the urgent need for the environmental resilience in urban regions. Toxic nanoparticles, PM $_{2.5}$, linked to heat temperature penetrate inside of buildings, and affect human normal physical functioning, thus in-door workers' productivity (Chang, Zivin, Gross, & Neidell, 2016). The level of PM $_{2.5}$ is exceptionally high in specific locations than others (Chang et al., 2016). Then, the individuals who live or work in such places are more exposed to the toxicity that lead to a gradual loss of physical functioning. If this condition is combined with resource disparity (such as fewer resources to fight against the toxicity), it has the potential to invoke a vicious cycle of economic and societal loss.

The biological proposition tells us that diversity is a species' wisdom for survival. It does not imply that specific groups may live with burdens of environmental inequity. All people have a right to benefit from nature. However, the level of $PM_{2.5}$ is just one of the scientifically established examples of toxic substances that impact human physical functioning.

This study examines the research question by investigating representative cases. The case selection criteria are the following four:

a. The presence of anchor corporations that involve in environmental sciences,
b. cities that experience environmental inequity,
c. the existence of organizations that are engaging in environmental resilience through science, and
d. the resilience program is scaling up.

Based on the criteria, this study selects representative cases as follows.

a. Two foreign multinationals in the Mark II category that invest in the clean technology incubator in a U.S. urban area,

b. An educational program of an academic KIO in an inner city of the U.S. East Coast state: The justification is that, in this Program, students help to develop climate resilience plans of outside organizations: The Program is scaling up to include 39 countries to dispatch student teams.
c. A social entrepreneurial firm that translates the environmental theory into resilience practices. The justification is that it succeeded in reversing the land withering in the Arizona state, and is replicating the success to other regions, globally.

In explaining the potential of Mark II organizations, this study describes one of the U.S. largest energy companies that developed new soil remediation materials from an internal discovery.

The common attributes of the cases are the entrepreneurship and sustainability orientation. However, such organizational efforts do not occur automatically in established corporations and entrepreneurial firms. Also, not all of innovations necessarily broaden beneficiaries. There need some organizational and institutional arrangements for resilience practices to occur.

2 Voice of Silence

2.1 Urban Resilience Through Entrepreneurship

2.1.1 Definition of Urban Resilience

This study highlights a subject where the role of science is confused. It then investigates managerial aspects of science-intensive organizations to contribute to broadening beneficiaries of science in urban resilience settings. More specifically, it examines R&D behaviors and organizational arrangements of the M-Forms to enter specific submarkets of emerging sciences (Bower, 1970; Bower & Gilbert, 2005; Sutton, 1998). In other words, it seeks factors that motivate and distract M-Forms that are to take anchor roles in the environmental aspects of urban resilience.

By following Meerow, Newell, and Stults (2016), this book comprehensively defines urban resilience as

> the ability of the urban *system*-and its constituting socio-economic, ecological, and technological *networks* to recover desired functions in the face of a disturbance, adapt to change and to transform systems that limit current

186   E. OKADA

or future adaptive capacity quickly. (Meerow, Newell, & Stults, 2016. See, Coafee & Lee, 2016; Yamagata & Maruyama, 2016)

Thus, the concept of resilience embraces not only bouncing to the former, stable condition but more positively and discontinuously creating new dynamic conditions of transformation (Coafee & Lee, 2016).

2.1.2   Remaining Problems in a Resilience Setting

The driving forces of urban resilience in the 1990s are breakthroughs in the Variation-Intensive sciences (information communication technology) and Mark I sciences (life sciences and biotechnology). They turned redundant resources into productive service resources (Penrose, 1959) contributing to diversifying the product mixes in the economy (Penrose, 1959). This process integrated underused populations into the mainstream economy and the dynamism of resilience (Coafee & Lee, 2016).

On the other hand, specific populations of inner-city residents remained outside of the resilience (Organization for Economic Cooperation and Development: OECD, 2004; Orr & Topa, 2006, among others). The socioeconomic inequity correlates with environmental inequity that reinforces the vicious cycle of inequity. Specifically, certain populations are more exposed to environmental contaminants in their residential areas and workplaces that affect their physical functioning (the U.S. Environment Protection Agency: EPA).[1]

Previous literature on urban resilience has approached the issues through frameworks of urban planning, economics, sociology, psychology, civil and environment engineering, and public health (see, Yamagata & Maruyama, 2016). Subject matters are mainly related to disaster resilience. Some urban design literature addresses the roles of entrepreneurial firms in absorbing redundant resources in resilience. It is due to the insight that breakthrough sciences contributed to the U.S. and E.U. urban resilience by reversing the trend of the intergenerational inheritance of poverty (Giloth, 2004; Jargowski, 2003. See, OECD, 2004). Environmental aspects of urban resilience also began to enter the scope (Roberts, 2000).

---

[1] Retrieved from: https://www.epa.gov/sites/production/files/2015-02/documents/team-ej-lexicon.pdf. Last visited on November 2020.

The next step is to address the remaining populations of the inner-city residents while transforming the whole area.

2.1.3 Management and Organizational Roles in the Resilience

The roles of corporations have long been outside of the investigation in the resilience setting. It is Orr and Topa (2006) that shed the light on anchor corporations.

Orr and Topa (2006) investigate the resilience of the New York Metropolitan Area in the 2000s. In this examination, Orr and Topa (2006) define anchor organizations as those that offer product lines before the new technology revolution and produce new products based on new technologies. Anchor institutions are, by their definition, usually established firms including multinational enterprises.

Before Orr and Topa (2006), pieces of literature assume academic institutions and large-scale social enterprises (such as hospitals) as anchors in a cluster. They focus on cluster building, in which academic and social enterprises generate new knowledge, funding opportunities, and employment. However, as Orr and Topa state, while the presence of academic organizations is a necessary condition, that of established corporations is a sufficient condition of economic resilience.

This book's study follows Orr and Topa (2006) regarding the definition of anchor institutions and modifies it as below stated.

> Anchor organizations are established organizations that play an essential role in the area resilience or cluster building by assisting the emergence of new knowledge and technologies and providing product lines before the new technology revolution.

2.1.4 Two Conflicting Theories from Scholarly Management Viewpoints

Organization for Economic Cooperation and Development (OECD) (2004) and Orr and Topa (2006) do not based on theories of management. From scholarly management viewpoints, they are describing the phenomena of organizations in the economic resilience. However, the closer review reveals that they present conflicting theories regarding entrepreneur firms.

OECD (2004)'s insight is as follows: Entrepreneurial firms that commercialized breakthroughs were a driving force of urban economic resilience.

188 E. OKADA

From managerial economic viewpoints, OECD (2004) implicitly bases the escalation formula by Sutton (1998). Sutton (1998)'s escalation formula demonstrates how new entrants outperform established firms by intensifying R&D at a specific condition of the technology market. The assumptions are that,

a. when a market grows larger and matured, established firms discontinue intensifying R&D to the extent that the differentiation of one-firm concentration ratio becomes closer to zero.
b. This point of the condition provides new entrants with an opportunity to intensify R&D in a new technological trajectory relates to the quality upgrade of products.
c. Consumers' willingness to pay rewards the upgraded quality reflected in the high R&D elasticity.
d. The R&D in one technological trajectory strengthens a link to other submarkets that bring scope economies (Sutton, 1998).

On the other hand, Orr and Topa (2006) describe a phenomenon in which established firms offer production lines before the technological revolution to new firms that help them to convert their discoveries into products. This phenomenon implicitly bases on a contractual schema of transaction cost economics by Williamson (1979, 1991, 2005).

From the transaction-cost economics viewpoint, two sources of transaction costs affect the established firms' choice between in-house and external R&D when the locus of expertise shifts from established firms to new entrants. They are

a. small-number-bargaining-hazard and
b. expropriation concerns (Pisano, 1990).

The former cost occurs when discovery firms specialized in a specific scientific field limit the ability of established firms to switch partners. The latter derives from an inability for investment firms to specify or enforce intellectual property rights. It is possible for discovery firms to work for different sponsors that compete in the same product market (Pisano, 1990). Due to these transaction costs, established firms choose to internalize R&D projects initiated by new entrants.

From resilience viewpoints, both theories can coexist.

New entrants that outperform established firms further escalate the performance by absorbing and converting redundant resources into productive service resources. This process is that of the entrepreneurs' scale-up.

Based on the transaction-cost-based governance, it is less likely that new entrants outperform established firms in a specific area. Instead, discoveries move to subsequent commercialization phases in established firms. This process is that of corporate entrepreneurship. It will generate a variety of technology and products that lead to economic growth and resilience.

Orr and Topa (2006) investigate the New York Metropolitan area, where the pharmaceutical industry is representative. The exception of Sutton (1998)'s escalation formula is the pharmaceutical industry. It is due to the pharmaceutical specific features (Sutton, 1998). Therefore, these two theories are not necessarily contradicting in the resilience setting.

A problem is whether either of the above patterns applies to chemical and material sciences. The industrial sciences of chemicals and materials belong to the Mark II category. The Mark II industrial science is characterized as the concentrated R&D, both in the initial condition and the subsequent trends (Niosi, 2000). Previous literature has not necessarily investigated whether or how Mark II firms introduce dispersed sources of emerging sciences into their organizations.

2.1.5   *Corporate Entrepreneurship and Anchor Organizations*
Facilitators
This study first examines the corporate entrepreneurship of established corporations that motivate them to take anchor roles.[2]

The process of corporate entrepreneurship requires the change of the resource allocation process. Therefore, it is necessary first to understand facilitators and barriers to change the resource allocation process.

The primary force of the change is the external structural contexts (Bower, 1970; Bower & Gilbert, 2005; Eisenmann & Bower, 2000) that urge established companies to redefine technological and economic elements of their product development projects. Disruptive technological change is a representative example. The redefinition of their R&D

---

[2] As partnering with firms within the border has the potential to invoke a complication of rivalry (Caves, 2007/1982), foreign multinationals are good candidates of anchors.

190   E. OKADA

and technological domain often requires established firms to introduce discoveries of emerging technologies outside of their organizations (see, Eisenmann & Bower, 2000).

In general, product development and distribution that requires a huge, risky investment tend to prefer a vertical structure in the global market (Eisenmann, 2002; Sutton, 1998). Under this structure, firms are to spread fixed (R&D and production) costs, when only a small share of products and services are commercially successful (Eisenmann & Bower, 2005). Thus, companies with intensified, irreversible investments want to secure global distribution to spread the sunk costs (Eisenmann & Bower, 2005).

On the other hand, the environmental discoveries of Mark II industrial sciences do not necessarily have a large market from the beginning. Examples include bioinspired materials. It is also difficult to predict which emerging sciences will become a significant technological trajectory in a given submarket.

Therefore, these companies are motivated to invest in dispersed sources of emerging sciences to spread the risk of uncertainty.

Also, the recombination with industrial sciences of Mark I and Variation-Intensive categories has the potential to be sources of the future integration. However, these sciences have different attributes from the Mark II industrial sciences.

Such strategic considerations have the potential to motivate Mark II firms to take anchor roles through several organizational arrangements. Due to the potential complication of rivalry (Caves, 2007/1982) as above stated, the arrangements with foreign counterparts are vital options.

Constraints

On the other hand, there are a couple of internal factors that constrain the anchor roles.

As the organization form, the redefinition often accompanies with the strategic integration in established M-Forms (Eisenmann, 2002; Burgelman & Doz, 1997). Strategic integration involves the combination of resources from different organizational segments to create a new business and operational unit. It differs from operational integration that consists of putting resources together from routinely interdependent activities, such as joint procurement (See, Burgelman & Doz 1997; Eisenmann and Bower 2005).

However, despite its necessity, the existing coordination patterns differentiate the ways of adaptation and degree of persistence of organizations (Eisenmann & Bower 2000; Caves, 2007/1982; see, Feldman, 2000; Nelson & Winter, 1982). Once established patterns tend to persist in established M-Forms, even when they are confronted with a disruptive disturbance (Bower, 2017; Eisenmann, 2002). This tendency makes established firms to allocate resources to project alternatives that will facilitate to take anchor roles.

The strategic integration requires a strong CEO leadership (Eisenmann & Bower, 2000). It is because the corporate planning office, in general, is reluctant to support risky plans that require strategic integration. Though division managers are often aware of the threat from market competition, they are not to be involved in designing nonroutine works since their role is to develop standard operation processes (Eisenmann & Bower, 2000). Further, division managers may not monitor remote markets where strategic integration opportunities emerge, especially when such opportunities come from an emerging field (Eisenmann & Bower, 2005; Hamel & Prahalad, 1993).

However, strong leadership is not always available at M-Forms due to the internal process and structure (see Chandler, 1962).

These internal contexts moderate drivers to facilitate corporate entrepreneurship.

Drivers that Do Not Include Remaining Populations

Entrepreneurial firms grow by integrating redundant resources. However, when they grow enough to enter the Dynamic Increasing Return category, they begin to follow the patterns of M-Forms. Such behaviors are due to the high intensity of research and development (R&D) and specialized marketing activities (Niosi, 2000; Scherer, 1984; Sutton, 1998).

Phenomena show that many of Variation-Intensive entrepreneurial firms that later became multinationals began to seek sources of employees in the U.S. trained scientists who returned to less-developed home countries (Glaeser & Hausman, 2019). This trend may expand the market of U.S. and EU products by increasing the income level of less-developed countries. On the other hand, it at least constrains the hiring of specific populations that remain outside of the resilience (Glaeser & Hausman, 2019).

192   E. OKADA

2.1.6   Academic Knowledge-Intensive Organizations as the Necessary Condition

Then, a question arises whether new advanced material sciences further reinforce the market concentration. The literature of industrial science categorization even has not positioned them in their categorization.

A general driver to advance the scientific understanding is the basic research at academic knowledge-intensive organizations (KIOs). The academic KIOs have an expectation to produce basic science and epistemological knowledge performed without practical ends (Bush, 1945). It results in generalizable knowledge and an understanding of nature and its laws (Bush, 1945, p. 13; Radder, 2010; Rubio, et al., 2010). However, the public institutional reforms in Australia later became global trends (Christensen, 2011). Then, the public and their representing governments began to expect academic KIOs to produce knowledge that is more applicable to practical ends (Gibbons, 1999).

As Orr and Topa (2006) point out, the presence of academic KIOs is the necessary condition of urban resilience, while that of anchor institutions is the sufficient condition. In general, the commercialization of academic sciences has enhanced academics' scope to include applications while maintaining the ability of basic sciences (Schut, von Paassen, Leeuwis, & Klerlx, 2014; Thursby & Thursby, 2011) with some exception (Czamitzki, Glänzel, & Hussinger, 2008; Mowery & Ziedonis, 2002).

On the other hand, an investigation of emerging material sciences (Chapters 3, 5) reveals that critical knowledge lacks in translating environmental material sciences to application. Such knowledge is generated in zoology (Imani, Donn, & Badalar, 2018). Several academic KIOs closed a zoology discipline program in their restructuring around late 2000 to early 2010.

Since the significant academic KIOs discarded the critical discipline from their research and educational programs, it may take a time for material sciences to move to vital applications, particularly those related to biologically inspired construction material sciences.

2.2   Necessary Component to Add to New Industrial Sciences

2.2.1   Attributes of Sustainability

Though there is the above setback of the necessary discipline in the construction science, the new material sciences have advanced by integrating sustainability elements (Chapter 5). Many of them start with the

Mark II chemicals. The sources of integration include emerging science in the Mark II category (neutron sciences), Mark I biotechnology (bioinspired material), Variation-Intensive information technologies (simulation of architecture), and dynamic increasing return supercomputing (research design with artificial intelligence, a large-scale processing, data storage, and crowd computing). They are translated into corporate entrepreneurship that is to redefine their technological and economic elements.

At the same time, some sources do not belong to the existing categorization. They are architectural sciences. They are initiated at academic spin-offs and academic institutions. It is difficult to discern at the present moment that the entrepreneurial firms outperform incumbents in a specific product area. However, at least their technological trajectories are generating the scope economy in which a research investment in one trajectory strengthens a link with other trajectories in other submarkets. It is a constituent of Sutton (1998)'s escalation formula.

The common attributes of the above sources are a mimicking of nature and the systems approach.

This notion leads to adding a component of sustainability to the categorization of industrial sciences. The attributes consist of the mimic of nature (environment) and the integration into the design process (systems approach of sustainability).

2.2.2 Organizational Arrangements to Add Variety

The above two attributes also will contribute to increasing a variety in the economy and technology.

The institutional intention to increase variety has manifested in the cluster building by leveraging academic patents and entrepreneur firms. Particular attention in the 1990s was in the fields of biomedical (Mark I) and computer sciences (Variation-Intensive category). The common component that intends to stimulate their behavioral traits is the reduction of entry barriers. The barriers include institutional barriers and organizational barriers. The organizations can contribute to the decrease by changing their structure and process.

In following Saviotti (1996), this study defines the variety as follows.

If an economic system is a set of elements, then the variety of this set will increase when the number of distinguishable elements of the set increases.

194 E. OKADA

> Information theory defines the variety of a set as the logarithm in base 2 of the number of distinguishable elements in the set (Saviotti, 1996).

According to economic development literature, the growth in variety is a necessary requirement for long-term development (Saviotti, 1996. See, Rubio et al., 2010).

At the same time, the occurrence of variation and economic growth has moderating factors as below mentioned.

According to Pasinetti (1990), the productivity growth due to a technological change temporarily entails unemployment and underutilization of productive capacity if a demand deficiency simultaneously occurs in many vertically integrated sectors. However, another effect of technical change introduces new goods that add new demands. In Saviotti's words, growing variety offset underemployment and underutilization of capacity. Thus, the growth of variety and productivity growth are complementary aspects of economic development (Saviotti, 1996).

It depends on the nature of competition, whether to induce the emergence of new technological sets or to specialize in preexisting ones (Saviotti, 1996). Also, what should be noticed is the information processing capacity. A system that is characterized by a variety of constituents is also a system that requires a more significant amount of information (see, Galbraith, 1973).

What organizations can do under excessive information is to reduce the information burden through the following two measures. (a) The organizations can increase the efficiency with which the information in the system is stored and processed. (b) The organizations can change processes so that organizational constituent stores and processes a smaller number of data sets to achieve the same output variety (Saviotti, 1996). This action requires them to put the elements in the configuration as ordered as possible. It leads to reduce the randomness or uncertainty of a given set of elements measured by entropy (Gatlin, 1972; Shannon & Waver, 1949; Saviotti, 1988, 1996).

In other words, organizations can reduce the process variety in achieving the given output variety. The increase of thus acquired output variety will increase economic growth (Saviotti, 1996).

The concrete methods that fit Mark II firms are as below mentioned.

> a. One way to achieve the given output variety in the catastrophic condition is to store and process a smaller number of data sets by configuring the elements as ordered as possible (Saviotti, 1996).

It suggests the introduction of a more efficient information processing and restoration system. The organizational arrangement of Mark II firms to achieve this way is to partner with dynamic increasing return supercomputer science companies.

For example, several Mark II chemical multinationals are announcing to partner with the dynamic increasing return supercomputing multinationals. It is to reduce the process variety while strengthening the output variety of their technological trajectories and products. They are also adopting artificial intelligence (AI) methods to broaden the experimentation by using data available in their laboratories and manufacturing plants.

> b. The other is the reconfiguration of routines (Saviotti, 1996. See, Caves, 2007/1982; Nelson & Winter, 1982; Feldman, 2000).

The variety will partly destroy or substitute once established routines. Then, the reconfiguration of routines will require placing new and heterogeneous elements in a manner they reduce randomness, and thus, entropy.

This way requires Mark II firms to fulfill two contradicting elements.

In reconfiguring organizational units, the technological variety requires the Mark II firms to divide their organizations into smaller subunits. At the same time, Mark II firms need to intensify their R&D investment in a competitive market.

One way to overcome this conflict is to introduce more data-intensive cloud and supercomputing, as mentioned above. The other is to adopt a large-scale intermediate institution, typically, an incubator.

Multinationals have used intermediate organizations to reconfigure smaller sets of subunits. The use of a regional corporation is a traditional design. A recent trend is the use of independent incubator. Under the adoption of an intermediate organizations, the intermediate institution bears a function of what Saviotti (1996) calls a "node" that supports the variety.

196   E. OKADA

For example, a U.S. corporation of a German multinational launched the Advanced Research Initiative with a U.S.-based university (Chapter 5). The joint research discovered a specific process that significantly reduces the current essential process with the involvement of biofilm. In paying attention to the stable and robust property of biofilm, a scientist team of the company has developed a viable reactor that pumps a chemical substrate over the support coated with a biofilm. The biofilm, then, converts the substrate into a product (Javis, 2020).

Scientists of the company further plan to replace a conventional fermentation process with the biofilm-based reactor. This reactor is a product innovation that will increase the variety of the product market.

The other way is to use an independent incubator that intermediates the relations among multiple complementing actors.

The examples of the independent incubator include one in which the large-scale incubator (in Chapter 4) acts as a multi-sided market that coordinates relations among actors. Actors are entrepreneurs, anchor multinationals, social enterprises, local government agencies (that provide subsidies), and local manufacturers (that produce prototypes for entrepreneur companies). In this multi-sided market, the Mark II multinationals are taking the anchor role. They provide their first-class machinery to the global incubator so that entrepreneur firms test their prototypes with the Mark II machines. The expectation of the multinationals is to improve their process through the use and feedback of entrepreneurs.

This type of incubator has the potential to enhance the scope of end beneficiaries since the new environmental materials have the function to increase environmental resilience that embeds two new attributes of sustainability.

2.2.3   *From the Efficiency of the Transaction to Transformation*

The development of clean technologies necessitates more capital-intensive investment than that of other new industrial sciences. However, they usually have to research in less-resourced settings. Also, though they need a manufacturing function to produce prototypes, it is impossible for less-resourced startups to invest in manufacturing facilities.

Established firms in the chemical and construction industries are aware of the need to redefine the technological capabilities. They have production lines before the scientific revolution. These lines may be redundant resources from the efficiency viewpoints. However, such manufacturing lines are stable enough to produce prototypes of startups' discoveries.

Redundant resources are a driver to the resilience of the resource-based management theories. Therefore, established firms also have a motivation to find out entrepreneurial discoveries.

The moderating variable in this context is the way of protection of intellectual property. Traditionally, chemical and construction companies relied on the process and routines for their competitive advantage that accumulate tacit knowledge around them. Companies protected their inventions mainly through know-how. Under this protection, it is challenging to detect infringement that can be enforceable. Therefore, the related parties have to bear more inflictions than other categories of new industrial sciences to partner with each other.

When there is a problem of proprietability of inventions (see, Pisano, 1990), parties are more likely to choose internalization as an organizational form. However, the market size of emerging clean technologies is too small for the current Mark II multinationals to internalize the discoveries. Here is a mutual need for intermediate organizations to create a multi-sided market that helps to exchange resources and knowledge.

The next step is to transform the redundant resources beyond the efficiency of transactions. It depends on the two new attributes of sustainability that emerging technologies embrace, that is, a mimic of nature (environment) and the integration into the design process (systems approach of sustainability).

3   GOVERNANCE FOR BROADENING BENEFICIARIES

3.1   *Urban Planning Viewpoints*

3.1.1   *Stages to Broaden Beneficiaries*
This study seeks overlaps of management theories with urban planning theories regarding resilience. The overlapping problem is what factors enable the transition from adaptation to transformation; what is a promising modality of governance, particularly for the environmental resilience.

It is Roberts (2000)'s framework that positions environmental issues as an input factor of designing urban regeneration. The expectation is to determine the environmental actions to take during the resilience process. Critical variables in the planning are the internal and external drivers of change. The former includes preferences of residents, and the latter, transnational and national policies and strategies of competing cities.

Inter-city competition is a significant factor in recent years. It is because federal and national governments delegated responsibilities of urban resilience to local governments around the year of 2000 (Coafee & Lee, 2016). The underlying assumption is that cities compete with each other to increase the economic, social, and environmental welfare of residents and organizations through resilience (see, Roberts, 2000). However, not all the cities have both the necessary and sufficient conditions for economic and environmental resilience. Typically, the presence of anchor organizations tends to lack in many cities. If there are no potential anchors in their borders, cities have an option to attract anchor candidates that meet preferences of residents.

Potential anchors have a motivation to redefining their technological and economic elements by introducing academic and entrepreneurial discoveries. A problem is how to design a transformation by having anchors.

For example, a European-based multinational is one of the founding sponsors of a global center of an incubator (Chapter 4). Its industrial field is ceramics. It can enhance the technological trajectories to encompass ceramics that absorb nano-scale environmental contaminants.

A European-based chemical multinational is another founding sponsor (Chapter 4). It played a critical role in the launch of the Global Center by providing a wet lab to startups. The lab is to develop innovations for unmet needs in the water, materials, and green chemistry fields.[3]

As discussed in Chapter 5, water, materials, and green chemistry has unique attributes that are tough to classify in the existing industrial science categories. Under this condition, these two labs will help to define the technological and economic elements of entrepreneurs' projects that will ultimately transform the current system toward the environmental aspects of sustainable systems.

3.1.2 Organization Forms that Will Further Enhance Beneficiaries

The next step is to enhance the beneficiaries further. It requires the involvement of academic KIOs and social enterprises in the resilience process. Though the presence of academic KIOs is a necessary condition

---

[3] PRNewswire, 2018.

for urban resilience, not all of them have related to the resilience in the full capacity.

The KIOs need to choose adequate organization arrangements to involve in the resilience process while retaining their unique organizational identities. Also, it is necessary for firms to select proper organization forms in relation to KIOs.

Organization forms and structures determine what should be governed internally and what should be externally governed (Riordan & Williamson, 1985). Therefore, the choice of organization forms is synonymous with that of governance structure (Caves, 2007/1982). Organizational forms also determine adaptation costs from the resource-based viewpoint (Wernerfelt, 2016). What is different between the adaptation cost theory and that of governance economies is to what extent they allow resource redundancy.

Resource redundancy is a source of resilience and transformation in the theory of urban resilience (Coafee & Lee, 2016). The adaptation cost theory is based on the resource-based view (Wernerfelt, 2016) that regards resource redundancy as a source of growth and diversification (Penrose, 1959). Diversification provides a variety of organizations and the economy. Due to the overlap, this study bases it on a framework of adaptation cost and modifies it to explore suitable forms for new science-intensive organizations in a resilience setting. The methodology is case-based inductive–deductive reasoning.

Chapter 7 addresses a research question regarding appropriate organization designs for academic institutions and social entrepreneur firms to replicate and scale up their resilience model. Academic and social entrepreneur firms can have a unique organizational design to diffuse their successful models since they have less know-how than industrial organizations that entail human factors. The theoretical starting point is Wernerfelt (2016) that is building a theory of adaptation cost. In the Wernerfelt model (2016), players do better if they adapt to a broader range of sequences of services and do so more frequently. In other words, the value creation depends on parameters of the diverse adaptation and frequent adaptation.

Governance costs play a critical role in this framework. The direct governance costs consist of two folds: (1) communication and bargaining costs (Williamson, 1979) that are necessary to adapt and (2) costs to resolve incentive conflicts (Grossman & Hart, 1986; Hart, 1989; Hart & Moore, 1988).

The Wernerfelt (2016)'s model needs a further extension to include science-intensive organizations. This study investigated the representative cases that are outside of the Wernerfelt (2016) model. They are work-experience educational programs of academic KIOs and social entrepreneurial organizations.

The common attribute of these organizations is the mobilization of beneficiaries to replicate and scale-up the resilience model.

In the work-experience educational program of academic KIOs, two-sided incompleteness of information exists in bilateral relationships between students who will provide field research for sponsoring organizations and sponsoring organizations that are confronting with specific problems. This condition does not fit Wernerfelt (2016)'s bilateral sequential contract regarding search costs. Unlike private firms, search costs less likely to occur on the side of students to learn about the employer's evaluations of their competitors. On the side of sponsoring organizations, search costs can occur related to learning about a fit of their problems to students' preference, capacities, educational implications, and alternatives to resolve issues. Also, they are interested in searching academic KIO's evaluation over competing options regarding the educational effects.

In the educational program, a possible solution to reduce search costs is a mechanism in which sponsors and students "pair up a once-for-all-basis" with some form of flexibility. In the focal Program, a faculty advisor guides in connecting sponsoring organizations and a student team. The faculty advisor(s) is specialized in the academic field and indirectly involved in the process through the guidance of students. This mode incurs less cost for a sponsoring organization than paying a higher production (service) cost to specialized agencies in a sequential contract mode.

Regarding performance metrics, academic programs should include the benefits to students. The benefits include the impacts on academic performance and the fostering of connective tissue between theoretical academic training and expected careers (Bleemer & Zafar, 2018; Boudreau & Marx, 2019; Froyed et al., 2012).

In the focal Program, students with a low-income background and with low SAT-score benefit relatively more regarding subsequent academic performances.

In the social entrepreneurial organization, what is distinct is the objects of transactions. The objects of the transaction are primarily moral ownership and conscientiousness. These objects are outside of the production factors of traditional firms, thus outside of Wernerfelt (2016)'s model. The participants range from academics, professional scientists, students to citizen scientists. All of the participants are commonly involving in the activities through their moral responsibility derived from moral ownership. Although they are under the governance of the federal and state laws and codes of conducts, the internal (and some societal) norms play a more significant role in the governance modalities. Anticipation motivates them to maintain and strengthen their commitment.

Here is an overlap with the urban planning theory. According to the evolutionary view of urban resilience, the anticipation is a transitioning mode from the adaptive model to the evolutionary model (see, Coafee & Lee, 2016).

The empirical evidence of the focal entrepreneurial firm has coherence with this theory. The initial focus of the focal entrepreneur organization is the adaptive resilience model. The short-term motivation is to cope with the withering of land and bounce to the original condition. On the other hand, their long-term vision is to mitigate the pathway that is affecting the earth's magnetic poles.[4]

For the long-term vision to occur, the participants need to transform the present humans' and organizations' behaviors to taking care of the future. It is a process of the responsible research and innovation in which the anticipation of heterogeneous actors plays a critical role (Stigloe, Owen, & Macnaghten, 2013).

Thus, the activation of a variety of moral responsibilities is the critical component of the organizational model of social entrepreneurs. It also corresponds to that of the evolutionary urban resilience.

In the evolutionary model, the public good organizations likely provide global norms and conscientiousness to the rulings and activities. The representative case shows that the founders are translating environment theory that underpins the Principle Guidance of the international organization. The academic that impacted the founders is the lead author

---

[4] The theories of the academic that influenced the founders contain insights about the earth's magnetic poles. Based on an unstructured interview with one of the founders conducted in the summer of 2015. Regarding the influence of the earth magnetic poles, see, Worrall (2018).

of a series of the Principle Guidance at the Intergovernmental Panel. This case implies that the public goods play an implicit role in providing conscientiousness of global actions (Cf. Buse & Walt, 2002; Reich, 2002).

4   Vision of Heterogeneous Knowledge Variation

Thus, both established multinationals, academic KIOs, and a social entrepreneurial firm are developing proper organizational and governance structures to allocate resources to areas that will broaden beneficiaries. These efforts will lead to a vision of a variety of heterogeneous knowledge.

Also, observation of the emerging material sciences reveals that, though the sources of emergence are different, they commonly incorporate the following two attributes in their research strategy: that is, "mimic of organism (environment)" and "integration into design systems (systems approach towards sustainability)." Examples include bioinspired construction materials (see, Imani et al., 2018) and architectural materials. Suppose science-intensive organizations incorporate these two attributes in a systems model. In that case, it will be faster for them to detect and resolve environmental inequity and enhance the scope of beneficiaries. The added beneficiaries, in turn, will become a driver of urban resilience and transformation.

Thus, regarding the emerging sciences, it is necessary to add the attributes of "mimic of organism (environment)" and "integration into design systems (systems approach towards sustainability)" in new categories of industrial sciences.

References

Arthur, W. B. (1994). *Increasing returns and path dependency in the economy.* Ann Arbor: University of Michigan Press.

Bleemer, Z., & Zafar, B. (2018). Intended college attendance: Evidence from an experiment on college returns and costs. *Journal of Public Economics, 157,* 184–211.

Bower, J. L. (1970). *Managing the resource allocation process.* Boston: Division of Research, Graduate School of Business Administration, Harvard University.

Bower, J. L. (2017). Managing resource allocation: Personal reflections from a managerial perspective. *Journal of Management, 43*(8). https://doi.org/10.1177/0149206316675929.

Bowee, J. L., & Gilbert, C. G. (2005). *From resource allocation to strategy.* New York and Oxford: Oxford University Press.

8 STRATEGY AND GOVERNANCE 203

Boudreau, K. J. & Marx, M. (2019). *From theory to practice: Field experimental evidence on early exposure of engineering majors to professional work* (National Bureau of Economic Research Working Paper No. 20163).

Burgelman, R. (1983). A model of the interaction of strategic behavior, corporate context, and the concept of strategy. *Academy of Management Review, 3*(1), 61–69.

Burgelman, B. A., & Doz, Y. (1997). *Complex strategic integration in the lean multibusiness corporation* (INSEAD Working Paper, 97/03/SM), as cited by Eisemnann, T. R., & Bower, L. J. (2005). *op.cit.*

Buse, K., & Walt, G. (2002). The World Health Organization and global public-private health partnerships: In search of 'good' global health governance. In M. R. Reich (Ed.), *Public-private partnerships for public health* (pp. 169–195). Cambridge: Harvard Center for Population and Development Studies.

Bush, V. (1945). *Science, the endless frontier*. A report to the President by Director of Office of Scientific Research and Development. Washington, DC: U.S. Government Printing Office.

Caves, R. E. (2007/1982). *Multinational enterprise and economic analysis* (3rd Ed.). Cambridge: Cambridge University Press.

Chandler, A. D. (1962). *Strategy and structure: Chapters in the history of the American industrial enterprise*. Cambridge: MIT Press.

Chang, T., Zivin, J., Gross, T., & Neidell, M. (2016). Particulate pollution and the productivity of pear packers. *American Economic Journal: Economic Policy, 8*(3), 141–169.

Christensen, T. (2011). University governance reforms: Potential problems of more autonomy? *Higher Education, 62*, 503–517.

Coafee, J., & Lee, P. (2016). *Urban resilience: Planning risk, crisis and uncertainty*. London: Palgrave.

Czamitzki, D., Glänzel, W., & Hussinger, K. (2008). Heterogeneity of patenting activity and its implications for scientific research. *Research Policy, 38*(1), 26–34.

Eisenmann, T. R. (2002). The effects of CEO equity ownership and firm diversification on risk taking. *Strategic Management Journal, 23*(6), 513–534.

Eisenmann, T., & Bower, J. L. (2000). The entrepreneurial M-Form: Strategic integration in global media firms. *Organization Science, 11*, 348–355.

Eisenmann, T. R., & Bower, J. L. (2005). The entrepreneurial M-Form: A Case study of strategic integration in a global media company. In J. L. Bower & C. G. Gilbert (Eds.), *From resource allocation to strategy* (pp. 307–329). Oxford: Oxford University Press.

Feldman, M. S. (2000). Organizational routine as a source of continuous change. *Organization Science, 11*(6), 661–629.

Froyed, J., Hurtado, D., Lagoudas, M., Nite, S., Hobson, M., Hodge, J., & Monroe, J. (2012). Increasing access to engineering. Frontiers in Education

Conference Proceedings, as cited in Boudreau, K. J., & Marx, M. (2019). *Op.cite.* et al., 2012.

Galbraith, J. R. (1973). *Designing complex organizations.* Reading: Addison-Wesley.

Gatlin, L. L. (1972). *Information theory and the living system.* New York: Columbia University Press.

Gibbons, M. (1999). Science's new social contract with society. *Nature, 402,* C81–C84, 1993.

Giloth, R. (2004). Social enterprise and urban rebuilding in the United States. *Entrepreneurship: A catalyst for urban regeneration* (pp. 135–157). Paris: OECD.

Glaeser, E. L., & Hausman, N. (2019). *Spatial mismatch between innovation and joblessness* (National Bureau of Economic Research Working Paper No. 25913).

Grossman, S. J., & Hart, O. D. (1986). The costs and benefits of ownership: A theory of vertical and lateral integration. *Journal of Political Economy, 94*(4), 691–714.

Hamel, G., & Prahalad, C. (1993). Strategy as stretch and leverace. *Harvard Business Review, 71*(2), 75–84.

Hart, O. (1989). An economist's perspective on the theory of the firm. *Columbia Law Review, 89*(7), 1757–1774.

Hart, O., & Moore, J. (1988). Incomplete contracts and renegotiation. *Economica, 56*(4), 755–785.

Imani, M., Donn, M., & Badalar, Z. (2018). Bio-inspired materials: Contribution of biology to energy efficiency of buildings. In L. Martinez & O. Kharissova (Eds.), *Handbook of ecomaterials* (pp. 2213–2236). Cham: Springer.https://doi.org/10.1007/2F978-3-319-68255-6_136.

Jargowski, P. A. (2003, May 1). *Stunning progress, hidden problems: The dramatic decline of urban poverty in the 1990s.* Washington, DC: Brookings Institution Center on Urban and Metropolitan Policy Report.

Javis, L. M. (2020). Exploiting biofilms. Chemical and Engineering News. *American Chemical Society.* https://cen.acs.org/articles/86/i23/Exploiting-Biocilms.htnl.2020.

Kaldor, N. (1972). The irrelevance of equilibrium economics. *Economic Journal, 82,* 1237–1255.

Meerow, S., Newell, J. P., & Stults, M. (2016). Defining urban resilience: A review. *Landscape and Urban Planning, 147,* 38–49.

Mowery, D. C., & Ziedonis, A. A. (2002). Academic patent quality and quantity before and after the Bayh-Dole Act in the United States. *Research Policy, 31*(3), 399–418.

Nelson, R. R., & Winter, S. G. (1982). *An evolutionary theory of economic change.* Cambridge: Harvard University Press.

Niosi, J. (2000). Science-based industries: New Schumpeterian taxonomy. *Technology in Society, 22*, 429–444.

Organization for Economic Cooperation and Development (OECD). (2004). *Entrepreneurship: A catalyst for urban regeneration*. Paris: OECD.

Orr, J., & Topa, G. (2006). Challenges facing the New York Metropolitan area economy. *Current Issues in Economics and Finance, 12*(1). Retrieved from https://www.newyorkfed.org/medialibrary/media/research/current_issues/ci12-1.pdf.

Pasinetti, L. L. (1990). Structural change and unemployment. *Structural Change and Economic Dynamics, 1*, 7–14.

Penrose, E. T. (1959). *The theory of the growth of a firm*. New York and Oxford: Blackwell.

Pisano, G. P. (1990). The R&D boundaries of the firm: An empirical analysis. *Administrative Science Quarterly, 35*, 153–176.

Radder, H. (Ed.). (2010). *The commodification of academic research: Science and the modern university*. Pittsburgh: Pittsburgh University Press.

Reich, M. R. (2002). Introduction: Public-private partnership for public health. In M. R. Reich (Ed.), *Public-private partnerships for public health* (pp. 169–195). Cambridge: Harvard Center for Population and Development Studies.

Riordan, M. H., & Williamson, O. E. (1985). Asset specificity and economic organization. *International Journal of Industrial Organization, 3*(4), 365–378.

Roberts, P. (2000). The evolution, definition and purpose of urban regeneration. In P. Roberts & H. Sykes (Eds.), *Urban regeneration: A handbook* (pp. 9–36). New York: Sage.

Rubio, D. M., Schoenbaum, E. E., Lee, L. S., Schteingart, D. E., Marantz, P. R., Anderson, K. E., … Esposito, K. (2010). Defining translational research. *Academic Medicine, 85*(3), 470–475.

Saviotti, P. P. (1988). Information, variety and entropy in technoeconomic devlopment. *Research Policy, 17*, 89–103.

Saviotti, P. P. (1996). *Technological evolution, variety and the economy*. Cheltenham: Edward Elgar.

Scherer, F. (1984). *Innovation and growth. Schumpeterian perspectives*. Cambridge: MIT Press.

Schut, M., von Paassen, A., Leeuwis, C., & Klerlx, L. (2014). Towards dynamic research configurations: A framework for reflection on the contribution of research to policy and innovation processes. *Science and Public Policy, 41*(2), 207–218.

Shannon, C. E., & Weaver, W. (1949). *The mathematical theory of communication*. Champaign: University of Illinois Press.

Stigloe, J., Owen, R., & Macnaghten, P. (2013). Developing a framework for responsible innovation. *Research Policy, 42*, 1568–1580.

Sutton, J. (1998). *Technology and market structure*. Cambridge: The MIT Press.

Thursby, J. G., & Thursby, M. C. (2011). Has the Bayh-Dole act compromised basic research? *Research Policy, 40*(8), 1077–1083.

Wernerfelt, B. (2016) *Adaptation, specialization, and the theory of the firm: Foundations of the resource-based view*. Cambridge: Cambridge University Press.

Williamson, O. (1979). Transaction cost economics: The governance of contractual relations. *Journal of Law and Economics, 22*(2), 233–261.

Williamson, O. (1991). Comparative economic organization: The analysis of discrete structural alternatives. *Administrative Science Quarterly, 36*(2), 269–296.

Williamson, O. E. (2005). Why law, economics, and organization? *Annual Review of Law and Social Science, 1*, 369–396.

Worrall, S. (2018). *Earth's poles will eventually flip, so what then?* Retrieved from https://www.nationalgeographic.com/news/2018/02/earth-magnetic-field-flip-poles-spinning-magnet-alanna-mitchell/.

Yamagata, Y., & Maruyama, H. (Eds.) (2016). *Urban resilience: Transformative approach*. Switzerland: Springer International & Maruyama.

INDEX

A

Absorptive capacity, 109

Academic institution, 6

Academic knowledge-intensive organizations, 7

Adaptation, 4, 7, 8, 10, 19, 22, 175, 191, 197, 199

Adaptation cost (theory), 155, 156, 158–160, 170, 175, 199

Adaptive resilience model, 175, 201

Agglomeration, 140

AI algorithm, 133, 134

Anchor organization (firms; institution), 14, 16, 41, 75, 93, 183, 187, 190, 191, 196, 198

Anticipation, 22, 23, 29, 133, 146, 169, 174, 177, 201

Artificial intelligence (AI), 195

Augmentation, 28, 142–144, 146, 147

Automation, 28, 142–144, 146, 147

B

Bargaining costs, 155, 159, 170, 175, 199

Beneficiaries' preferences, relationship with, 74

Beneficiaries, broadening, 28, 132, 133, 183

Beneficiary-oriented, 135

Bilateral relationships, 200

Bounded rationality, 10

C

Characteristics space, 109

Citizen sciences (scientist), 7, 23, 173, 177

Communication costs, 175, 199

Competition, 109, 110

Complexity, 108, 110, 134

Configuration, 28, 111, 124

Conscientiousness, 201

Corporate entrepreneurship, 14, 44, 189, 193

© The Editor(s) (if applicable) and The Author(s), under exclusive licence to Springer Nature Switzerland AG, part of Springer Nature 2021
E. Okada, *Management of Science-Intensive Organizations*,
https://doi.org/10.1007/978-3-030-64042-2

208 INDEX

D
Data, 147
Deep learning, 134
Density, 109
Dynamic increasing return (industrial science category), 24, 26, 40, 47, 65, 83, 91, 108, 112, 123, 191, 193, 195

E
Emerging sciences, 189, 190
Empirical economic studies, 65
Entrepreneurship, 126, 140
Entropy, 111, 124
Environmental exposure, 132, 147
Environmental inequity, 5, 22, 27, 83, 84, 87, 96, 133, 184, 186, 202
Environmental material science, 3, 184
Environmental resilience, 183, 197
Escalation (formula; model), 17, 41, 46, 61, 188, 189, 193
Evolutionary approach (model; viewpoint), 8–10, 15, 22, 201
Evolutionary development, 71
Evolutionary economics, 71
Evolutionary innovation process, 15
Evolutionary model, 175
Evolutionary urban resilience, 175, 201
External fragmentation, 52
External structural contexts, 67

F
Frequency, 157

G
Governance, 3, 9, 11, 17, 23, 46, 47, 49–52, 61, 169, 189, 197, 199, 201, 202

Governance costs, 155, 175, 199

H
Heterogeneity, 158
Human–machine complementarity, 140
Humans' tasks, 142

I
Ill-structured (problem), 164, 166, 177
Incentive conflicts, 175, 199
Incentives, 16
Inclusive research, 173
Incubator, 195
Industrial science category (categorization), 16, 26
Industrial sciences, 202
Information processing, 142, 194, 195
costs, 110, 111, 123, 124
Innovation, 140
Integration into the design process (systems) (sustainability), 27, 61, 76, 96, 119, 125, 126, 132, 144, 193, 197, 202
Intermediate entities, 157
Intermediate firms, 157
Intermediate institution, 112, 195
Intermediate organization, 67, 95, 112–114, 176, 195, 197
Internal structural contexts, 27, 49, 50, 67
Internal technological structure, alteration of, 69
Inter-technology competition, 109
Intra-technology competition, 109

L
Loosely coupled, 8, 27, 51, 52
Loosely recoupling, 12

M

Machine learning, 134
Market-based solutions, 74
Market failure area, 74
Mark I (industrial science category), 64, 190
Mark II (industrial science category), 71, 183, 189, 190, 196
M-forms, 72, 113, 184, 185, 190, 191
Micro-level replication, 110
Mimic of living organism, 8, 120, 126
Mimic of nature (environment), 10, 26, 27, 61, 76, 96, 119, 125, 132, 193, 197, 202
Moral ownership, 174, 175, 201
Moral responsibility, 9, 29, 175, 178, 201
Multiple-sided market, 114, 174
Multi-sided space, 29, 67, 174

N

New attributes of industrial sciences, seeking, 96
New products, emergence of, 108
New technological sets, emergence of, 110

O

Optimization, 28, 111, 124
Organizational forms, 154, 155
Output variety, 111, 124, 194

P

PM2.5 (2.5-micron Particulate Matter), 126
Process model, 133
Process variety, 111, 112, 124, 194, 195
Product differentiation, 109

Production (service) cost, 176, 200
Productive asset, 158, 159
Productive capacity, 106, 194
Productive service, 11, 17, 186, 189
Productivity, 107

R

Randomness, 28, 111, 124, 195
Reconfiguration, 28, 111, 112, 124, 195
Redefinition, 12, 13, 73, 184, 189, 190, 198
Regeneration, 6, 7, 44, 169
Renewal, 13, 14, 73, 112, 114, 115, 124
Replication, 109
Replicator dynamics, 108, 109
Resilience, 4, 7–9, 126, 154, 197–199
    climate resilience, 175
    urban resilience, 3, 61, 132, 154, 175, 202
Resource allocation process model, 160, 184
Resource redeployability, 159
(Resource) redundancy, 10, 17, 159, 199
Responsibilization, 9, 22, 23, 28, 145, 201
Routines, 15, 28, 71, 111, 124, 195

S

Scale-up, 28, 29, 146, 147, 160, 162, 169, 175, 189, 200
Science-intensive organization, 3–6, 15, 16, 25, 28, 51, 107, 132, 154, 159, 160, 183, 185, 199, 200, 202
Scope economy, 159, 193
Search, 71, 72, 109, 144, 145, 157, 172
Search costs, 94, 171, 172, 176, 200

210 INDEX

Sequential contract, 158, 171, 172, 175, 176, 200
Skills, 140, 147
Specialization, 29, 107–110, 139, 156, 157, 159, 170–172, 176, 188, 194, 200
Stability, robustness, and reliability properties of, 72
Strategic contexts, 27, 49
Strategic integration, 48, 159, 190, 191
Structural complexity, 110
Structural contexts, 189
Substitution, 108
Sustainability, 5, 7, 146, 193
Sustainable research, 173
Systems approach, 72, 193

T
Technical integration, 159
Technological change, 62
Technological trajectories, 193
Training datasets, 134
Transaction cost economies (governance), 61

Transformation, 7, 10, 17, 197, 202
Translational science, 132, 133, 135
Two-sided incompleteness, 176, 200
Two-sided market, 158

U
Uncertainty, 111, 124
Urban regeneration, 65, 66, 68, 84, 132, 138, 197. *See also* Regeneration
Urban resilience. *See* Resilience

V
Variation, 12, 15, 16, 194
Variation-Intensive category (industrial sciences; technologies), 39, 73, 107, 190, 193
Variety, 10, 15, 17, 19, 27–29, 62, 69, 72, 83, 90, 91, 106–115, 123, 124, 145–147, 183, 189, 193–196, 199, 201, 202

W
Wernerfelt model (2016), 159

Printed in the United States
By Bookmasters